AMERICAN AFTERLIVES

AMERICAN AFTERLIVES

REINVENTING DEATH IN THE
TWENTY-FIRST CENTURY

SHANNON LEE DAWDY

WITH IMAGES BY
DANIEL ZOX

PRINCETON UNIVERSITY PRESS

PRINCETON & OXFORD

Published by Princeton University Press
41 William Street, Princeton, New Jersey 08540
99 Banbury Road, Oxford OX2 6JX

press.princeton.edu

First paperback printing, 2023
Paper ISBN 978-0-691-25470-8

All Rights Reserved

The Library of Congress has cataloged the cloth edition as follows:

Names: Dawdy, Shannon Lee, 1967– author.
Title: American afterlives : reinventing death in the twenty-first century / Shannon Lee Dawdy ; with images by Daniel Zox.
Description: Princeton, New Jersey : Princeton University Press, 2021. | Includes bibliographical references and index.
Identifiers: LCCN 2021008929 (print) | LCCN 2021008930 (ebook) | ISBN 9780691210643 (hardback) | ISBN 9780691228457 (ebook)
Subjects: LCSH: Funeral rites and ceremonies—United States. | Death—Economic aspects—United States. | Death—Social aspects—United States.
Classification: LCC GT3150 .D36 2021 (print) | LCC GT3150 (ebook) | DDC 393—dc23
LC record available at https://lccn.loc.gov/2021008929
LC ebook record available at https://lccn.loc.gov/2021008930

British Library Cataloging-in-Publication Data is available

Editorial: Fred Appel and James Collier
Production Editorial: Sara Lerner
Text and Jacket/Cover Design: Karl Spurzem
Production: Erin Suydam
Publicity: Maria Whelan and Kathryn Stevens
Copyeditor: Amy K. Hughes

Jacket/Cover art by Karl Spurzem

This book has been composed in Arno

For all the future ghosts out there, and for Anne.

CONTENTS

IMAGES

PREFACE

Each book I write seems to get a little odder than the last one. This is not on purpose. Perhaps it reflects a process of gradually letting go—of conventions, of anxieties, of expectations. Of being at peace with who I am as a writer and a thinker and trusting that someone out there will get it. This book has brought a lot of peace. It has been an unintended existential journey. I can comfortably say now that I am okay with dying. Don't worry, I'm not planning on it. But then, almost no one does. When I fly, I often think to myself: if I die today, it will be fine. I've had a pretty good run. Death is the natural ending of every life. It is strange how hard we humans fight that fact. We cause ourselves a lot of needless anxiety and suffering. I am not sure what the experience of reading this odd little book will be for the reader, especially in the aftermath of a devastating pandemic, but my wish is that some of this peace will rub off on you.

In fact, it is okay to laugh, to smile, to take comfort here. Gallows humor is easy. It's the nervous laugh of the uninitiated. But I mean something more deep-bellied and Buddha-like. It is hard to work on death and not have people assume you are a goth princess, or dispositionally morose. Or that your work is going to bring them down. I have come to believe that embracing the realities of death can make our hearts lighter, not heavier. As Esmerelda, one of my interviewees said, "it's all a point of view."

This book is odd for a couple different reasons, so let me prepare you just a little. First, although I have a doctorate and am cross-trained in anthropology, archaeology, and history, this is not meant to be an academic book for a specialist audience. I have written a few articles out of this material for my scholarly peers, and I have a few more ideas to throw at them in these pages, but the material here, and my journey with it, was too rich not to share more broadly. I can't help an anthropological curiosity about what makes people tick, but I have tried to translate terms and invite the reader in. It did not feel right to write an impersonal account about death. That's not how this project started for me, and that's not how it has ended for any of us. So the reader will find that I am present in these pages as a private, feeling person. This is an experiment—can a book be both anthropological and accessible, both personal and intellectual?

A second oddity. The writing emerged out of a five-year process of making a documentary film. I met my talented codirector and cinematographer Daniel Zox by happenstance. We were squeezed into a minibus with others on a tour of rural Oaxaca in early 2015. I was teaching in a study abroad program. He was on vacation with his family. Over lunch, we discovered that we both lived in Chicago, so we stayed in touch. At that time, I had an idea that I wanted to do an archaeological ethnography of contemporary American death practices. One day, after talking to Daniel about his filmmaking, I realized that this topic could make an interesting film. I was pretty sure it would involve some interesting people and visuals of deathscapes and artifacts were already running through my head. I pitched it to him over a Mexican brunch in my Chicago neighborhood. He said yes, and we were off running.

Our time, our budget, and our ideas about the project ebbed and flowed over this five-year period. We had no script. Most documentarians have some idea about the story they want to tell before they get started. I had no clue what was going on in American death practices other than that they were rapidly changing. I wanted to learn more. For me, filming was like collecting found objects until they start to assemble themselves into coherent patterns. We eventually collected over two hundred hours of footage. This magpie approach is not the easiest or most cost-effective way to make a film. Perhaps you can't take the archaeologist out of the filmmaker. Daniel was patient with my steep learning curve and this exploratory method, which was new for him too. It often felt like we were undertaking an old-fashioned expedition into unknown territory. Filmmaking was all new to me, and I loved (most of) it. It is physical and creative at the same time, with a necessarily intense camaraderie among the crew. That combination parallels the joyful labor of an archaeological dig.

It was in the film-editing process that the writing started to happen. At that point, I accepted that we had far too much material—and too many story lines—to fit into a single film. Films allow you to stretch and explore a topic, but they also need a tight focus to get ideas across. It is a more subtle medium than text. So what appears in this book is in part the cutting-room floor—all those themes, characters, dialogues, and subplots that we couldn't fit into the twenty-one-minute documentary we eventually produced. The film, *I Like Dirt.*, zeros in on contemporary California and the ways in which death care there reflects a particular regional culture. The scope of this book is larger and more cluttered, ranging across the American landscape and digging down into its historical roots.

The quality of the research presented here is inseparable from its origins in the filmmaking process. I would be telling a lie if I pretended that this book emerged from a standard ethnographic inquiry. The writing at times probably has a cinematographic quality. A behind-the-scenes narrative makes it clear that many of the people I was speaking to were being filmed. Whenever I say "we" in the text, I usually mean Daniel and myself, but about half of the time, there was a third or even a fourth person there recording sound or assisting (listed gratefully in the Acknowledgments). I often simplify the point of view to "I" in the text because I am trying to get across what was going on inside my head when I was talking to someone, or to convey the particular dynamic between interviewer (me) and interviewee. But Daniel was always there, watching behind the camera, adding his own questions for people, and stirring the pot of ideas—often as we talked over a well-earned meal. And he is here in this book. To complete this transmission of a documentary collage of material to book form, he has created twenty black-and-white still images from our footage, which are distributed throughout the chapters. I had a few requests, but most of the images you will find in the book tell their own stories and reflect his approach to image and point of view. They transcend being mere illustrations of things discussed in the text. Meditative and open-ended, they invite the reader to write their own captions.

I have already alluded to how my specialist training as an archaeologist affected the creative process, but it was my generalist training as an anthropologist that attuned me to ethical concerns. All the direct quotes in the book are transcribed either from audiovisual files made in the process of filming or from my written notes of one-on-one interviews conducted before or after filming, or independent of it. In terms of transcription editing, I cleaned up oral speech by eliminating "ums," false starts, and awkward repetitions, and for the sake of textual flow, I eliminated ellipses but never scrambled the order of statements. The principles I applied in editing quotes were: be true to the speaker and be easy on the reader. The project as a whole was conducted under an approved Institutional Review Board protocol from the University of Chicago (IRB15–1236 Exempt). Everyone I interviewed was informed about the purpose of the research, and all interviewees gave their consent. I am immensely grateful for their candidness, vulnerability, and generosity of time. I hope they find it returned in some small way through my confessional narrative in the chapters that follow. If someone said something potentially controversial in a way that could come back to haunt them, I disguised their identity with a pseudonym, or deliberate vagueness, if at all possible. But with many of the death-care professionals I spoke to, their product or services are so unique that the internet (and in some cases, our film) makes anonymity impossible. I followed informed consent protocols, but at times I went beyond them to follow my own protective instincts. I decided to use first names only for consistency but also to treat people equally, from the homeless guy I talked to on the street to the millionaire CEO.

Sometimes my instincts told me to turn the camera off. One example was while filming a man named Rod, whose story appears in chapter 4. Rod had lost his wife several months earlier and became understandably emotional while filming. For me, it just didn't feel right to look at someone's grief so closely, but he didn't ask us to stop, which I had told him he had a right to do at any time. In the moment, I trusted Daniel, who kept rolling. Later, I struggled with my feelings over this scene, and we had to talk it over. Rod urgently and graciously wanted to share his story with us. Was my anxiety of letting him do it a holdover from an age when we were embarrassed to talk about death? Or, as an anthropologist, do I have an obligation to turn off the camera on the most vulnerable scenes of human experience?

Rod's tears were contagious. I welled up too. This happened more than once during filmmaking. And I'm not a crybaby. Was my discomfort about losing observer detachment? I still don't know the answers to these questions.

That's another reason I wanted to write this book. Not to lay out American society and my relationship to it like I am some special authority, but because I feel an obligation to describe difficult truths and internal conflicts. As I finished the manuscript, the Covid-19 pandemic and its political reverberations were sweeping through the United States. Talk about difficult truths and internal conflicts. At first, I worried that I was going to have to rewrite the entire book in the face of a once-in-a-century mass death experience. I started to freeze. Then, I realized two things that gave me the courage to keep going. First, I need to remain true to my original impulse. For the most part, the *cause* of death, whether from a new virus or a toaster accident, does not matter to the story I tell here. My focus is on what happens to the body and the person *after* death. The *before* part is of course important in its own right—the big stories about how we live and how we die—but those aren't the types of conversations I initiated with people. I asked instead: What happens *after*? What do people want done with their body? What happens to us after life? Second, I can't predict the final impact of Covid-19 any better than an epidemiologist. It is going to write its own narrative. It will be years before we understand the full impact of the pandemic on American death practices and conceptions of the afterlife. All ethnographies and film documentaries are works of history—they cover a finite period of time. This book offers a snapshot of American death trends between 2000 and 2020.

In late 2020, I checked in with my key interlocuters to see how they and their businesses had been affected; I have worked updates into the text as needed. More than that, the pandemic has left a watermark on this book because it has touched me personally. Daniel struggled with the lingering effects of the virus for months, as have several of my students and colleagues. Three people that I knew, and was fond of, died from it, two of them "before their time," as we say (though the "right" time can be so unclear). Like everyone, I lived a disjointed life of uncertainty and isolation in 2020 and the first half of 2021. None of us will ever be the same.

I didn't want to write a grim book about death. That is the biggest challenge Covid-19 has presented to completing this work—getting the tone right during a time of devastating loss while staying true to my intent to lighten our fears about mortality. I try to make my struggles visible here.

Perhaps the biggest challenge of all is knowing when to let go of anything. A project. A person. A belief. Or life as we know it. I hope the reader will join me in a process of letting go.

ACKNOWLEDGMENTS

Daniel Zox has been my copilot throughout this project. I will never be able to thank him enough for being game for this adventure. The filmmaking process brought so many moments of awe and wonder that it represents, hands down, one of the most enjoyable periods of my life. This is due in no small part to Daniel's capacious ability to find people interesting, to notice things that even an anthropologist might overlook. He tolerated my ineptitudes and supported me as I explored long-suppressed artistic impulses, though he also taught me that good art is not about beauty. To top it off, he has become one of those rare friends who are like family. And I can always trust him to order me something off the menu that is exactly what I wanted.

In terms of blood kin, my son Asa has tolerated the constant reminders of his own losses throughout this project. Early on, he thought his mother had weird interests, but he also learned how to hold a bounce board. Now I feel supported by the filial pride of a kind and wise young man who is also my best friend. Better than anyone, he understands that throwing myself into my work is what keeps me going. As a result of the pandemic but also, I think, because of this project, I have grown closer to my mother, Arletta. She has listened to my doubts and working-outs, watched rough cuts, helped jog my memory, and sent interesting news items my way. This topic cannot be easy for someone in her eighties who is losing friends and family members at a quickening pace, but she has never told me to shut up about it. In fact, now we talk every day. I also owe an unrepayable debt to my brother Jess, sister-in-law Kim, and niece Allie. Their losses have been deeper and closer than mine. I am in awe of their strength. It was their examples of how to keep the dead close and rewrite the rules for mourning that inspired me to start this journey.

Beyond this tight circle, there are so many others I want and need to thank. Some are colleagues and students who gave helpful feedback, some are the death-care professionals and entrepreneurs who generously gave of their time, others are good-natured strangers who let us interrupt their fun with mortal questions. I also include our sound recordists and other folks who helped on the filmmaking end if not the bookmaking. Others are friends who may not know what they did to help in these last six years, but I do. I will try to thank them all here, although not all appear in these pages or in the film. I'm going to blend them together because that is also what I have liked about this project: death as the great leveler.

I would like to thank, in no logical order: Anwen Tormey, Adolphe Reed, Karon Reese, Steve Stiffler, Tara Loftis, Allie Reese, Sherrie Smith, Ryan Gray, Jeffrey Ehrenreich, Donovan Fannon, Chris Grant, Ross Ransom, Jason McVicar, James Crouch, Paul Thomas, Brent Joseph, Amanda White, Joe Bonni, Alison Kohn, Rob Reilly, Andy Roddick, Lisa Wedeen, Kaushik Sunder-Rajan, Anna Searle Jones, Lauren Berlant, Eilat Maoz, William Mazzarella, Bill Brown, Alex Harnett, Joe Masco, François Richard, Hussein Agrama, Alice Yao, Andrew Zox, Jason De León, Julie Chu, Katina Lillios, Thomas Laqueur, Adela Amaral, Charlotte Soehner, Mary-Cate Garden, Douglas Bamforth, Amanda Woodward, David Nirenberg, Kim Long, David Beriss, Jessica Cattelino, Io McNaughton, Daniel McNaughton,

Genie and Duncan McNaughton, Gidget, Apple, Nyx, Hazel, Bert, Bug, Akos Meggyes, Jeremy Bendik-Keymer, Michelangelo Giampaoli, Davis Rogan, Lee Sig, Rod, Brad Marsh, Dusty Jonakin, Liz Dunnebacke, Darren Crouch, Stephanie Longmuir, Valerie Wages, Eugene Rex, Walker Posey, Jane Hillhouse, Jeff Staab, Juju, Zoë Crossland, Bryan Boyd, Danilyn Rutherford, Sean Brotherton, Tamara Kneese, Abou Farman, Jenny Huberman, Phil Olson, Matthew Engelke, LaShaya Howie, Anya Bernstein, Margaret Schwartz, Matt Reilly, Liv Nilsson Stutz, John Carter, Owen Kohl, Taylor Lowe, Johanna Pacyga, Anna Agbe-Davies, Alison Bell, Andrew Bauer, Barb Voss, Mary Weismantel, Ian Hodder, James Auger, Jessica Charlesworth, Tim Parsons, Cristina Sanchez Carretero, Paul Graves-Brown, Paul Mullins, Chris Leather, Andrea Ford, Karma Frierson, Zachary Cahill, Mike Schuh, Alex Bauer, Ellen Badone, Marek Tamm, Laurent Olivier, Bjørnar Olsen, Þóra Pétursdóttir, Alice von Bieberstein, Yael Navaro, Norman Yoffee, Lynn Meskell, Sharonda Lewis, Anne Chien, Kim Schafer, Benjamin Schmidt, Theo Kassebaum, Claire Bowman, Hannah Burnett, Hanna Pickwell, David Jacobson, Lucas Iorio, John Misenhimer, Justin, Sophia Monzon, Marcus, Jeff Bodean, Amanda Kenney, Nancy Parraz, Angie Avila, Teresa and David Davilla, Maureen Lomasney, Craig Savage, Nick Savage, Veronica Herrigan, John Hodgkin, Veronika Kivenson, Susan Winkelstein, Jermaine Slaughter, Yusu Kanshian, Jerrigrace Lyons, Julian Spalding, Mark Hill, Dana Fox, Tara Coyote, Kay, Maira Lopes, George White, Irene Grauten, Sheila Milberger, Katrina Morgan, Shelly Lever, Sandia Chiefa Winter, Ani Palmo, Esmerelda Kent, Tyler Cassity, Chris Elgabalawi, Jed Wane Holst, Sandy Gibson, Nicholas Thomas, Henry Berton, Dana and Brian Ferguson, Hari Subramanyan, Linda Sue, Cindy Barath, Pedro Tecum, Pablo, Antonio, Moises Vicente, Paige Graham, Katrina Spade, Trey Ganem, Thad

Holmes, Jason Diemer, Emilie Nutter, Jeremy McLin, Stephen Sontheimer, John Pope, Zymora Kimball, Patrick Schoen, Dean VandenBiesen, Richard Baczak, Ruth Toulson, Casey Golomski, Lucia Liu, Stephanie Schiavenato, Roy Richard Grinker, Janeth Gomez, Alicia Heard, Juana Ibañez, Krystine Dinh, Eric, Dakota, Virginia, Alex, Adam Malarchick, Niki Good, Jason Becker, MC Medley, Trevor Aubin, Cecilia Dartez, Taylor Lyon, Jane Boyle, R. Townsend, Elizabeth Hurstell, Karen Wallace, Sabine Brebach, Chad Muse, Darielle Kreuger, Robert Pacheco, Shanna Pahl-Lesch, Joe Lesch, Chris Dunfee, Jason Luce, Chris Dudley, Katherina Saldarriaga, and Rebecca Jenkins.

I also want to thank all the staff not mentioned above at the businesses and institutions that indulged our filming, the wonderful folks at the School of Advanced Research, UChicago students enrolled in Archaeological Experiments in Filmmaking as well as Death and Being, UChicago students engaged in the 3CT's Future Café, and all audience members at my talks and our early film screenings. I am grateful to colleagues at the University of Luxembourg, McMaster University, University of Iowa, IUPUI, University of Florida, CUNY Graduate Center, and Stanford University for their invitations to present the work in progress, a crucial step in getting my thoughts organized.

I humbly acknowledge the following institutions that funded or logistically supported this work: The MacArthur Foundation, University of Chicago Department of Anthropology and its Lichtstern Fund, University of Chicago Center for Contemporary Theory (3CT), University of Chicago Gray Center for Arts and Inquiry and its Mellon Collaborative Fellowship for Arts Practice and Scholarship, the Social Sciences Division of the University of Chicago, and the School for Advanced Research in Santa Fe, New Mexico.

Fragments of the writing have appeared in a handful of academic publications, though toward somewhat different ends. I acknowledge the *Journal of Contemporary Archaeology*, the *Journal of Historical Sociology*, and the editors and publishers of *Rethinking Historical Time: New Approaches to Presentism* (eds. Marek Tamm and Laurent Olivier, Bloomsbury Press). I thank the reviewers of these pieces and the book manuscript for their important work.

I am so happy that editor Fred Appel was willing to go along with a book that was already half-cooked. I also send thanks to the staff at Princeton University Press: Jenny Tan, James Collier, Sara Lerner, Karl Spurzem, Erin Suydam, Maria Whelan, and Kathryn Stevens. I lucked out with copyeditor Amy K. Hughes, who gets it.

I probably got some things wrong. Please forgive me.

AMERICAN AFTERLIVES

CHAPTER 1

The Hole

It was Halloween night in the French Quarter of New Orleans. Daniel, my collaborator and codirector, set up his camera on the sidewalk in front of a costume-wig shop, and the sound guy tested the boom mic. The wig shop was open late that night, busy with last-minute customers. As the sun began to set, couples and small groups of adult revelers, not yet drunk, started to stream past us. We were in the early, experimental stages of making a documentary film. We probably looked like a low-budget TV news crew. We were out to do "man in the street" interviews—or maybe witches, fairies, and unicorns in the street. Whomever we could find. I felt like a nervous streetwalker, propositioning strangers. I was dressed as some sort of vaguely gothic lady in a black corset—hardly the strangest person on the street—but some people crossed over and avoided us anyway. I assume the camera and lights were the scary bit. Others were game to talk.

Early in the evening, one young(?) man walking by on his own paused to humor us. He was dressed completely in black—a suit, tie, and matching trench coat. He had a piece of black hosiery pulled over his head, topped by a fedora. The Invisible Man. I have been told I have a habit of looking too intensely into people's eyes when I talk to them. I passed my eyes like searchlights back and forth over his face, assessing its bumps and dents so I could make a reasonable guess about where his eyes were. Still, as we talked, I couldn't tell if he was looking back at me just as intently or staring off toward a vanishing point just beyond my shoulder.

I warmed up by asking him to tell me his name and where he was from. Trevor talked fast and seemed uncannily prepared for my big question of the evening: "What do you want done with your body when you die?" Without a second's hesitation, he replied, "I would like to figure out a way for me to legally just be put into a bayou. I don't want a grave, I don't want to be cremated. Just put my body in a bayou. Let it go back into the swamp."[1]

When it comes to a ceremony, he said he wants to go straight to the wake, and to be present for it. He said that's what they basically did for a friend of his who had recently died of cancer. They all came over to her house on her last weekend and cooked, talked, and played music before she said she was tired and went up to bed. Forever.

His voice cracked as he finished telling me about his friend. I could see wet spots spreading over his form-fitting mask, even darker than the obscuring cloth. Those eyes I couldn't see started to weep. The invisible man was crying visible tears. I was moved to silence. All I could do was respect his sadness. He gathered himself. "But," he said, "that's how it should be." I thanked him and let him go on his way, hoping he was headed for a party with lighter spirits. I didn't get to my second question—"What do you think happens to us after we die?"

This exchange has stayed with me. It represents the task I have set for myself—to ask nearly impossible questions. And the risk. The risk that I will set off a chain of the most delicate reactions. A trauma, an anxiety, an unhealed grief—or that most universal of existential crises: Why are we here and what

are we going to do about it? In that moment, I felt his grief. It echoed my own. We briefly connected in a way that violates the academic conceit that separates researcher and subject.

Ω Ω Ω

Between 2008 and 2013, I lost four people I loved in the span of five years, as if I had drifted too close to a black hole. That was when I started asking people what they thought happened to us after we died. And what they wanted the living to do with their bodies. A lot of them want to be burned, to go out in a glorious blaze. Fire terrifies me, but many people I talk to say that we are just stardust anyway.

Ω Ω Ω

I am not entirely certain that this book will be considered an anthropological one, much less an archaeological one, except that my profession gave me the arrogance to try to understand human experience by intruding into the private lives of others. But it's the only book I could write. A conventional academic genre about American afterlives in the twenty-first century would not only blur vivid experiences that I am trying to bring into focus but, in the context of the most devastating pandemic to strike in one hundred years, be tactless. I need to honor those moments of connection that I felt with people like the Invisible Man. It would feel dishonest to disappear myself from the emotional events of fieldwork. I hate being photographed, so I do not appear in the camera frame during our interviews, but I will make myself visible here. *I am not invisible.*

It was a couple of years before that Halloween night in 2015 that I started to think about doing a research project on contemporary American death practices. It was my way of dealing with the loss of four loved ones in five years. Each of those deaths was different and felt different. Yet in each case, the body was cremated, and there were decisions made, and ceremonies created, to handle the ashes—scattering, burying, making them into jewelry and birdbaths, placing them in a biodegradable box destined for the river that ran through my childhood. Prior to that, I had never thought much about what happens after life, when the body takes an unrecognizable form as an inert shell, a biological and chemical assemblage on its way to morphing into something else. After the intense phases of grief had passed, I became interested in finding out more about what Americans were doing with the remains of their loved ones, and what this might say about their beliefs about who we are and what happens to us after death. Research for me is a form of emotional processing. I slowly began working on this project, first as a historical investigation and then, after I met filmmaker Daniel Zox, as a documentary film that would capture and complement what I was trying to get down on paper.

As I got deeper into the research, I realized that I had stumbled into a cultural field that was simultaneously falling apart and blossoming. Funeral director after funeral director that I talked to offered a version of what Stan, an entrepreneur who distributes novelty funeral paraphernalia, said to me in 2017: "There have been more changes in the funeral business in the last ten years than in the last hundred."

To this day, the most influential book ever written on the American death scene is British journalist Jessica Mitford's 1963 exposé *The American Way of Death*. Through investigative work in Southern California that retraced some of novelist Evelyn Waugh's steps in *The Loved One*, Mitford documented the ways in which the American funeral industry had standardized a rite of passage and professionalized what used to be a form of family care. She described, and decried, a distinctly American funeral complex characterized by the popularization of embalming, the open casket, fancy caskets, and expensive vault burials. This "tradition" had developed in the 1880s and spread through diverse urban and rural communities in the United States, becoming fully entrenched by the 1920s. In Mitford's view, the American death complex that came to dominate the twentieth century amounted to a big con job. Like Waugh, she thought that embalming reflected American optimism gone haywire— that it expressed a denial that death happens at all.[2] It's time for an update.

Jessica Mitford still haunts funeral directors today. Poet-mortician Thomas Lynch, in his 1997 memoir *The Undertaking*, felt a need to exorcise her ghost, objecting to her claim that "fussing over the dead body" was "barbaric," when, in fact, an embalmer could undo some of the psychic damage inflicted by a more barbaric murderer, citing a horrific case he was called to work on early in his career. As I read his defense of "the dismal trade," it occurred to me that people in other countries may not be as familiar with death by homicide. Perhaps the repair work of embalming and restoration offers precisely the kind of death ritual that a violent society needs.[3]

The United States is also a strongly capitalist society. While Mitford seemed to think that no one should ever make a profit from death, she herself viewed death rituals with a cold, calculating instrumentalist logic. She advocated strongly for low-cost "direct cremation," in which you pick up your loved one's ashes at the crematory in a cardboard box—eliminating the funeral director, whom she viewed as an unnecessary middleman between life and death. In her strong opinion, fussing over the dead was unseemly. It was as if American death offended her British sense of propriety. In my interviews, I have found that funeral directors are still trying to respond to Mitford's critique. Many of the nonprofessionals I spoke to uttered some trickle-down version of it. They don't want any fuss. They don't want to take up any space. They don't want to leave a financial burden. Her ideas have seeped through much of American society and encouraged the transition to cremation. That transition, though, was going slowly until about the year 2000, when it began to explode. Between 2000 and 2015, the US cremation rate doubled, and now nearly 60 percent of all Americans choose this "disposition" of the body (as it is called).[4]

Not only are bodies being treated differently, more people are sidestepping the traditional funeral and inventing rituals of their own. Religious traditions long governed the disposition of the dead, but they are losing their monopoly. Most faiths have become more open to variation in funeral rites, while many Americans now define their beliefs about the human spirit in a highly individualized way, independent of organized religion. In the twenty-first century, death is being reinvented in the United States on three levels simultaneously—the disposition of human remains, new rituals, and ideas about the afterlife.

There has been a tendency to view Western death culture as ordinary, shallow, secular. Contemporary funeral practices were presumed by many scholars to be boring and profane, sanitized and standardized. Today these generalizations are untenable. Contemporary American death culture might be confusing in its innovations and pluralism, but it could not be said to be boring. Even before the Covid-19 pandemic, death was "having a moment" in the public sphere. You can mix your loved one's ashes into a vinyl record that plays a recording of their voice. You can live on through a software program timed to send messages to your family from the beyond. You can have your body frozen, incinerated, buried in a redwood grove, plastinated, dissected for science, or dissolved in chemicals. Soon, you can be composted in a steaming pile of wood chips on an urban lot. Your family can take some of your cremated remains and incorporate them into jewelry, artificial reefs, or paperweights. It is increasingly acceptable not only to personally handle the corpse but to continue to live with a piece of it long after the end of biological life. And it's becoming more acceptable (or once again acceptable) to talk to the dead, to celebrate their birthdays, or to leave a bottle of beer on their grave.[5]

American Afterlives explores rapidly changing death practices in the twenty-first-century United States. It asks: What does the changing face of death tell us about American beliefs and values at this historical juncture? Between 2015 and 2020, I traveled the United States from Vermont to California, Illinois to Alabama, talking to funeral directors, death-care entrepreneurs, designers, cemetery owners, and death doulas about the changes they are seeing and in many cases promoting. I also spoke to people on the street, like Trevor, who were willing to entertain my almost-taboo questions: *What do you think happens to us after we die? And what do you want done with your body?*

This book's premise derives from a long tradition of mortuary archaeology: material evidence of how a society treats its dead can yield powerful clues about that society's values, beliefs, and day-to-day life.[6] This reading of material clues represents a grandiose type of forensics, like Sherlock Holmes reading the psychology of criminals in the cigar ashes they accidentally left behind. Unlike Holmes, an archaeologist can never be entirely certain that they have read the evidence correctly. This book makes no claims that the interpretations offered are the only ones, nor does it offer a complete survey of all that is happening in death care. My focus is on human remains—what is being done with them and what people think and feel about them. Another horizon of big change, both in the United States and internationally, is digital death practices, from video-conferenced funerals to online memorials and several forms of virtual afterlife. These developments have been well studied by others, and fall outside my scope.[7] Rather, I'm interested in *material* afterlives. I take an archaeological approach to contemporary life that uses ethnographic interviews to zero in on the ways in which people relate to objects and landscapes. Traditional archaeologists have to make educated guesses about what artifactual evidence means, but doing a mortuary excavation of the present gives me the advantage of asking people on the ground what *they* think is going on with the changing face of American death. They aren't always real sure either. We fumbled through our questions and answers together. This work is the result of a collaborative dialogue between me and dozens of interlocutors about still-emerging phenomena. Its findings are necessarily speculative but not unfounded. Only after sifting through our conversations and putting patterns into historical context, did I start to have those "aha!" moments that give me the courage of explanation. The conclusions I have come to, and will share in the pages that follow, are more profound and moving than I ever anticipated.

The five years of research that inform this book involved tracking down people who are innovators in death care, or who had professional opinions about where things are going and why. I followed hunches and word-of-mouth suggestions. In extended interviews, often with the same person over a period of time, I collected stories about the individual's life and work and sought to understand the contexts and events that informed their death work. I did not gather opinion surveys or statistical data. That type of information doesn't get you very far in trying to understand *why* people do the things they do. While some readers may find some of the new death options I describe here outlandish, my intent is not to entertain or to shock. My anthropological orientation means that I want to get a sense of collective trends and shared concerns while staying alert for disagreements, diversity, and undercurrents. I could have written a different book focused entirely on the most spectacular, tabloid-worthy death rituals involving celebrities, or John Doe getting buried in his Cadillac (thus making him a posthumous celebrity). But that would give the wrong impression that the new death options I am interested in are eccentricities rather than meaningful cultural practices. I also did not look at medical donation or cryonics, because these represent less than 1 percent of dispositions in the United States. The vast majority of Americans are buried or cremated. Even though I met some colorful characters on this journey, I think of them as representatives of a larger whole. There is no such thing as a typical, everyday American, but the people I have sought out are not doing what they are doing just to get attention. They are cultural influencers, but not in the superficial sense as hawkers of goods. They are tapped into the undercurrents of a desire for something far more significant—a cosmological readjustment.

Ω Ω Ω

People often ask me if I wanted to be an archaeologist when I was a little kid. I didn't. I wanted to be an astronomer. I have thought about this a lot recently because of the number of times people have said to me that we are just stardust returning to stardust. Or something like that. They may not realize that they are paraphrasing Carl Sagan, but maybe he was just paraphrasing common sense. In many cultures, like the Tswana of South Africa or the Onödowa'ga Iroquois, individual stars in the sky are thought to be the souls of the dead.

One of the effects of our bright urban skies is that it makes it hard to see the stars. As if there is a population decline among the dead.

In the summers of my childhood, I went barefoot most of the time. My feet touched the earth. They were often dirty. I made mud pies. My family went camping several times a year. And I slept outside under the stars. We couldn't afford a tent, but I didn't mind and I didn't know any better. Dirt and stars, those were the stuff of the lucky parts of my childhood. Somewhere in there is the firmament of my current path.

My favorite excavation unit is a "1 × 2"—that means it is one meter wide by two meters long. If I'm digging in a public place like the French Quarter in New Orleans, people like to ask: "Are you digging a grave?" It makes me self-conscious, like maybe I *am* doing something macabre by digging up history, moving the fragments of past lives around and making them into new things. But maybe that's what all of us are doing, in our way.

You never know how deep an excavation unit will go when you start. We dig down until we find no more traces of human activity. Where I usually dig, that means sometimes three feet, sometimes six. In some parts of the world, you can go dozens of feet and still not run out of traces of people who lived thousands of years ago.

My favorite phase of an archaeological project is when I can tell the crew to go home as we're coming close to finishing an excavation unit. I get down into the hole, sometimes with my shoes off. I scrape the dirt clean so you can see the different layers of time more clearly. I take photographs and make drawings of what I see—an accumulation of lifetimes. It is dark and cool in the trench. The smell is calming. You can tell that things are simultaneously growing and decaying. And time slows way down.

Ω Ω Ω

In the process of researching, filming, and interviewing, I have met some unusual people and many kind ones. They included thoughtful people doing life-affirming things, like surfing or running a marathon, who stopped to talk to us. I encountered born-again entrepreneurs, visionary proselytizers, quirky makers, and staid traditionalists. Perhaps surprisingly, people's willingness to reinvent death did not skew along the polarized political lines that have defined American public life for the last several years. Some choices might be preferred in blue states more than red ones, but political persuasion did not reliably predict who was willing to get creative with death and, in this way, to work through what they value in life.

The Covid-19 pandemic hit as I was drafting the last chapters of this book, but I had already become convinced that there is a collective existential crisis going on in the United States. People are struggling to figure out what it means to be American in the twenty-first century. It is a struggle happening simultaneously on the spiritual and political fronts. For some people, it means becoming more individualistic, more entrepreneurial, more materialistic but—perhaps counterintuitively—at the same time more spiritual. They give no signs of worrying about a contradiction. For others, it means a return to older, pre-industrial ways of doing things, when we were less alienated from nature, our bodies, and our communities. And then there are those ready to toss everything out and invent radically new approaches that involve reconfiguring our relationships to the dead and to the planet. They want to tear things down to the rafters, to rethink what death means in both physical and metaphysical terms. Postmortem options are proliferating, sometimes pulling in opposite directions. But there is no question that there is a quiet revolution going on. And its roots go all the way down to who we are and why we are here.

All this ferment is relatively new. Throughout the twentieth century, American death practices were remarkably conservative. And also weird. Mitford was right about that. Embalming, viewing, and a concrete cemetery vault constituted the standard American funeral ritual, often regardless of the religious or ethnic background of the deceased. Until quite recently, embalming was rarely practiced in other countries except in the case of public figures lying in state and bodies needing to be transported across borders. Many observers have interpreted the American tradition as emblematic of a national tendency to deny the reality of death. Esmerelda, who makes natural fiber shrouds for green burials, told me that in the twenty-first century, we are witnessing "the death of denial . . . people are *craving* authenticity and anything left of artifice is being *blown apart.*" This craving for authenticity suggests that there is a problem, a void begging to be filled.

"The Denial of Death" is a key theme in existential philosophy. Ernest Becker was a remarkable anthropologist, philosopher, and scholar of psychiatry who published a book by the same title in 1974. Becker argues that Freud was correct that a good bit of human character develops through denial, repression, and transference but that he was wrong about which animal fact of our being is the source of the problem. It is not sexuality but mortality that makes us all a little crazy. Having the conscious capacity to predict our own deaths, we go through all sorts of mental and cultural contortions to act as if it isn't going to happen. We struggle to control our terror of it. Becker points to death denial as the source of many human problems—from anxiety disorders to the compulsion to make war. Coming at it from a neo-Freudian angle, he arrives at the same conclusion as existential philosopher Martin Heidegger did in his magnum opus *Being and Time*: accepting the inevitability of death will make us free.[8]

Becker's thesis about the denial of death is a sweeping, universal one for all of humankind. From an anthropological point of view, that might be its chief weakness. But social critics who were already pointing to some strangeness about American death rituals in the twentieth century took it up as validation. If humans in general tended toward unhealthy habits of denying death, then Americans were overachievers. Jessica Mitford had already made this point in 1963. Elisabeth Kübler-Ross tackled the problem as a clinical one affecting terminally ill patients in her highly influential 1969 book *On Death and Dying*. It was she who gave us the "stages of grief" model that has become a mainstay of pop psychology. "Denial" is stage one. If Americans have been especially prone to denial, the implication was that they were stuck in a kind of arrested development when it came to death.[9]

Eminent scholars concurred. In the 1970s, French historian Philippe Ariès published his own magnum opus on attitudes toward death in the Western world that has become a model for analyzing death through the lens of cultural history. He divided Christian European death into five phases. "The Tame Death" of the early medieval period was one in which death was considered natural, reflecting "the conviction that the life of a man is not an individual destiny but a link in an unbroken chain, the biological continuation of a family or a line that begins with Adam and includes the whole human race."[10] The second phase, the "Death of the Self," marks the beginnings of a more pronounced individualism in the late medieval period, continuing through the Renaissance and the Reformation. The moment of death became a dramatic and anxious rehearsal for the Day of Judgment. People believed they were going somewhere in the afterlife but worried about which destination. "Remote and Imminent Death" characterizes the Enlightenment of the early eighteenth century. With the foundations of Christianity shaken by secular rationalism, the forecast of an afterlife became uncertain and death more frightening for its potential finality.

However, beginning in the Romantic period of the early nineteenth century, Ariès says that some amelioration of this collective existential crisis appeared in the form of a new focus on enduring love between the living and the dead: "The next world becomes the scene of the reunion of those whom death has separated. . . . It is the paradise of Christians or the astral world of spiritualists and psychics. But it is also the world of the memories of nonbelievers and freethinkers who deny the reality of a life after death. In the piety of their love, they preserve the memories of their departed."[11] This phase came to full fruition in the Victorian death cult, with its almost obsessive preoccupation with memorialization through mourning clothes and jewelry, fancy cemeteries, the invention of the obituary, and postmortem photography.

Finally, Ariès identified "Invisible Death," marking the colonization of death by science and industry. By the early twentieth century, family members were no longer the primary caregivers of the dying and the dead. More and more deaths occurred in a hospital setting, and professional funeral directors took over all manner of death arrangements, from collecting the body to erecting a gravestone. In Ariès's view, the new Western faith in scientific medicine's ability to repair the body meant that death came to represent a public failure as much as a private grief. Death became dirty and embarrassing. Outside the professional sanctuaries of funeral homes, communal rituals started to break down. In the United States, embalming rapidly took over as standard practice, and the corpse was sequestered in morgues, funeral homes, and suburban cemeteries. Ariès viewed twentieth-century American funeral practices that he observed in his own lifetime as an extreme case of this phase, calling it a society that behaved "as if death did not exist."[12] Americans were the supreme deniers.

But Ariès was a historian, not an anthropologist. He didn't actually watch people as they went about performing death work or mourning, nor (as far as I can tell) did he talk to anyone about it except other experts. He observed from his writing desk. That kind of distance can introduce distortions. But it is

certainly true that over his lifetime, fewer and fewer people witnessed loved ones in the dying process. And fewer still, outside
war veterans and those in certain professions, ever saw a corpse
until it magically appeared in an open casket, the picture of
sleepy peace. It is also true that even though medicalized death
was growing throughout the Western world, embalming and
viewing made the United States stand out as a bit odd.

In the popular imagination, the idea of American death denial has recently become a kind of self-critique, inspiring new
efforts to overturn this supposedly unhealthy state of affairs in
the twenty-first century through what has been christened the
"death-positive movement." Caitlin Doughty, perhaps the
movement's most prominent spokesperson, created the popular YouTube channel *Ask a Mortician* in 2011 and established the
advocacy and thanatology group Order of the Good Death.
Doughty has published two popular books in which she con-
trasts the dysfunctional American way of death in its dominant
form to more positive funeral practices in other cultural

traditions that she sees as better at confronting the truth and messiness of death. Many of the practitioners and entrepreneurs I sought out consider themselves members of the death-positive movement or early pioneers who made it possible. And almost everyone I interviewed is grateful for its educational work, even if not enthusiastic about all of its tenets. While the death-positive movement is an important side story to what I relate here, for a couple of quite different reasons, it fell outside the center of my focal lens.[13]

First, the more I have delved into the history and practices of American death rituals, the more I have come to question the death denial thesis. I don't think Americans have ever denied death more than anyone else. In some ways, in fact, they have confronted it in bold ways, including through their death rituals. The confusion may derive from the ways in which Americans have long dealt with death that blur the lines between materiality and spirituality. Just because profits and commodities are involved doesn't mean that a funeral rite is soulless. Nor does professionalization necessarily lead to estrangement. Dead bodies around the world are often taken out of the hands of family members and turned over to ritual specialists—that doesn't mean that the fact of death is being covered up in these belief systems. It means that some expertise may be needed to ease the transition between life and death. Somewhere along the line, these errors in logic crept into narratives about American death, and they have been hard to shake. I posit that once we stop leaping to judge practices as "death denying" and stop assuming that capitalism disenchants everything—even the afterlife—then things start to look a little different. And super interesting.

The second reason the death-positive movement is not at the center of this story is because it was late to the party. Many of the practices promoted by death-positive advocates were

emerging a couple of decades before the first social media plat-
forms introduced them to a broader public. The death-positive
movement is finding a ready audience. It is answering, and am-
plifying, a cry for change that was already rising. A major source
for that cry is the hospice movement. Modern hospice practice
started in the United Kingdom in the 1960s and quickly expanded to the United States. In the 1980s, end-of-life care had
become so accepted that it was added to Medicare benefits. The
original aim of hospice was to provide medical and emotional
care for the terminally ill. It has expanded to help dying individuals understand their options and take control over major
decisions that affect quality of life for both themselves and their
loved ones. As a result, hospice has moved increasingly from
hospitals and long-term-care facilities to the home, and the
dying often take an active role in planning their own memorials.
With home hospice, the dying and the dead are returning to the
family. The re-homing of death has become so important to
American family life that one of the most painful aspects of the
Covid-19 pandemic covered by the media in 2020 was the isolation of dying patients in nursing homes and sterile hospital
wards. This recent negative experience is likely to boost the
home hospice movement, which has already played a major role
in making death visible and intimate again, reversing the cultural
shift that Ariès observed for the mid-twentieth century. The hospice movement has reinforced the idea that one has options
when it comes to death care. *What* people opt for and *why* is a
whole other story. That's the one I'm going to try to tell.[14]

Ω Ω Ω

In 1979, anthropologists Peter Metcalf and Richard Huntington
published a book that compared death rituals from around the

world. In their final essay, they turned the ethnographic lens on their own social setting, a move more anthropologists are making today. They noted that the American funeral exhibited a number of paradoxes. The custom of viewing an embalmed body prior to a casket burial was remarkably consistent throughout the twentieth century, despite a continuing influx of immigrants and religious influences. Such assimilation on the part of new arrivals and conservatism on the part of mainstream culture was all the more remarkable, they said, given that the traditional American funeral is fairly "exotic" compared to the other case studies in their book, which ranged from the Nyakyusa in East Africa to the Berawan people of Malaysia. Their intriguing hypothesis was that the American death ritual developed as a component of an American "civil religion" that helped to unify a diverse society. They didn't write it off as just a symptom of denial or as a ritual without meaning. Metcalf and Huntington's conclusions were consciously speculative; they advocated further ethnographic study. Unfortunately, few took them up on it. Forty years later, the unique American death ritual they puzzled over is now dying its own rapid death and so, perhaps, is the nation's civil religion.[15]

Ω Ω Ω

Unexpectedly, this project has meant a homecoming, and a homegoing. I haven't lived in Northern California since my early twenties, but when I started looking for death-care innovators, the quest led me back to a formative landscape. Northern California has the highest rate of cremation in the United States (nearly 90 percent). It is home to one of the largest and best-known "green" cemeteries in the country. And it is the epicenter of the home-funeral movement. Artists, artisans, and gallerists involved in creative memorialization also make the region their home.

So it is not that surprising, I suppose, that I was first buried in Northern California. Fernwood Cemetery is in Marin County, just one county over from where I grew up. Marin is notoriously wealthy, white, and privileged. It serves as a garden community for the elite of San Francisco or their descendants. But the landscape doesn't care—it manifests the same variegated map of yellow-brown hills with oaks shifting into fog-drenched redwood canyons that make up my own home county. Vineyards and aromatic eucalyptus groves crop up in the sunnier patches.

Several years ago, Fernwood Cemetery was a relatively forgotten space tucked amid some expensive real estate. More than a hundred years old (which *is* old by California standards), it safeguarded the bones of Portuguese fishermen and Hispano ranchers. Tyler, who calls himself a cemetery entrepreneur, saw opportunity in Marin County. The region has long been a bastion of left-leaning politics and, despite a hypocritical dependence on the automobile, green consumerism. Nationally, de facto green burials have long been allowed in order to accommodate Orthodox Jewish and Islamic burial customs, in which embalming is prohibited and a simple cotton shroud or wooden coffin prescribed. Now a broader movement toward natural burial has branched out into the general population, from the Carolinas to New England and up and down the West Coast. But it is not yet widely available. Fernwood Cemetery is trying to set a standard and an example. In the green-burial section of the cemetery, bodies must be interred "naturally"—which means chemical-free, without embalming—so that they can contribute their nutrients to a modest landscape of native trees and plants. The "green" section doesn't really look like a cemetery, and it isn't actually all that green. It's more gold and brown, the dominant colors of the native ecosystem for most of the year. It even smells different, with scents of sunburned oak and bay laurel. The natural, low-key aesthetic that Fernwood cultivates in its green-burial section extends to its service style. The staff at Fernwood help make death seem natural with a low-drama vibe. They didn't bat an eye when we asked if it might be possible to film a grave being dug. Sure, they said. If their grounds crew didn't have anything else to do, they could excavate a demonstration grave for us. Emboldened, we asked if we could also film a shrouded body being lowered into the ground to show how it is done. No problem.

Our original idea was to hire an actor. We found a young man from San Francisco willing to do it. But Esmerelda, who was loaning us one of her shrouds, was worried because no one had ever wrapped a *living* person in one. I was worried too. Would he be able to breathe? Would he overheat in the late July warmth? Would this stranger have a panic attack? Would the psychological trip of rehearsing this final part, which we will all eventually have to play, be too much to maintain the divide between reality and make-believe?

The next day, a Fernwood staff member called me to say, "Actually, how about filming the digging of a *real* grave?" A client named Anne had preplanned her arrangements. After a brief illness, she had passed away last night. Her instructions specified no ceremony. There would be no family coming to the grave site. Her executor didn't think she would mind if we borrowed her grave for an afternoon before she was ready for it. Upon hearing all this, which made it all so real, I suddenly knew that I had to be the one in the shroud, in the grave. We couldn't risk the young actor. I had to take responsibility for this experiment. If I couldn't breathe, it would be on me. We didn't know how it would all go down, but at least I had never had a panic attack. In fact, I am quite familiar with a one-by-two-meter pit about six feet deep. A grave is nearly the exact dimensions of the many excavation units I have spent quiet time in. Besides, I was at least thirty pounds lighter than the actor, so it would be a little easier on the gravediggers-cum-pallbearers. Later, I realized that I wanted to be the demonstration corpse because I felt a personal responsibility toward Anne. I needed to make sure we were respectful. On some level, this meant no playacting. I'm not a natural-born actor. In fact, I have a hard time faking feelings or hiding real ones. I was going to be as sincerely dead as I could be without pulling the plug. I was going to put myself not only in her space but in her place.

While filming the scene, the biggest challenge was trying to figure out how rigid or soft to hold my body. If I tried to be stiff, it would be easier on the pallbearers. But I had learned in my research that rigor mortis is a relatively short-lived phase of decomposition that has usually passed by the time of burial. I didn't want to overplay it.

Being dead was an oddly relaxing experience. Once I was wrapped in the shroud, I became an invisible woman. No one was looking at me or evaluating me. All they could see were the contours of my body outlined by creamy muslin. I was carried by four strong Guatemalan men. Their shy murmurs in Spanish to one another made it clear that they took this exercise seriously and wanted to respect me. They worried about me a little. They were gentlemen. I got the feeling that they would have acted the same way if I were really dead. Somehow that was reassuring. They carried me over the rough, sloping ground on a hospital stretcher. I felt swayed like a blind baby in a sling.

The staff had explained the process ahead of time, so I knew they had already laid winch straps out on the grass next to the grave. When we arrived graveside, they transferred me from the stretcher to the ground beside the grave, gently laying my body down on top of three horizontal straps crossing below my shoulders, my hips, and my calves. Then they lifted me with the straps and moved my body over the hole, two men on each side. Once they had my body centered, they gradually began to let out the slack. With each hand-span of length they let go, I descended a little deeper. I started to feel the coolness of the earth envelop me. The sounds of voices, birds, and overhead planes already muffled by the shroud gradually became even more distant, part of a separate world. Ever so gently, my back started to contact the hard-packed dry clay at the bottom of the grave. Then my head. Then my legs. When my weight was finally resting fully on the ground, they slowly pulled the straps out from underneath me. So delicately, it tickled.

And then, I rested. I knew that I would be down there awhile. Daniel was doing a pull-away shot with a drone, and he would do more than one take to make sure we got it right. My face was hot from my own breathing. I don't think I was running out of oxygen, but the air I had was a little stuffy. I wiggled my hand up to my face inside the shroud and opened up a little vent that I would seal again for the close-up.

Daniel wasn't thrilled about me doing this. I had had to put my foot down to make it happen. But he went with it. He and his brother Andrew had to stand with the equipment fifty feet away so they couldn't be seen by the drone's camera. We had tried to rig a system where I could hear him through my cell phone, tucked into the shroud with me. But cell service is lousy six feet under. So we couldn't communicate for that hour. Or was it two? Talking later, we realized that we had experienced completely different sensations of time duration. He was rushing to make sure I wasn't down there too long, and rushing against the setting sun. Time flew by. I was losing track of time in another way. It just seemed to stop. The muffled sounds, the cool air, the lack of light, my immovable body. The best way I can describe it is as suspended animation for long-distance space travel. Or at least what I imagine suspended animation might feel like.

I stayed awake though. While down there, I realized I had the easy part. In my mind, I thanked Anne. I talked to her, told her this was a good place to be. It was peaceful and comfortable. In between the first and second takes, Daniel came to check on me, and I reminded him to please throw the flowers in on top of my body. Earlier that day, I had gone into town at lunchtime to look for flowers that were cheerful and not too cliché. I found some Gerber daisies.

Daniel finished getting what he could before the sunlight and the drone's batteries completely died. It felt like I had been down there a long time, but I also wasn't ready for it to end. I was feeling the most relaxed I had been in a hectic couple of weeks of filming and family visits. Daniel came to tell me that they were done, the shaky timbre of his voice suggesting that maybe he was worried he had taken too long. "Shannon?" I lay still and quiet for a few long seconds, not responding. "Shannon??" He sounded a little worried. I lurched my torso forward, sitting up like a stiff mummy from the movies for a little comic relief. I laughed and got my head free, then unwrapped myself. Before I climbed out of the grave, I asked for a piece of paper and a pen. I wrote a little note to Anne. Then I folded it up tight and put it under a rock that no one would notice. The next day she was to be buried in the same hole. I arranged the flowers across the floor of the grave so they would make a pretty bed for her when she arrived.

When I climbed out of the grave, I was satisfied, but also a little sad that it was all over. It felt like the end of an archaeological dig, when all that is left is the cathartic and satisfying hard labor of backfilling. I yearned to help the crew bury Anne the next day, but we had to move on to other locations and interviews.

I think able-bodied family members should be encouraged to take a hand to the shovel, even if they don't have the experience of a gravedigger, or an archaeologist. With practice, you learn how to pile dirt loosely on the shovel, how to throw it into the pit evenly, and how you need to pack it down every half foot or so with your boots or you'll have too much dirt left over at the end.

At Fernwood, they don't make graves artificially flat like they do at prim and proper suburban cemeteries, or archaeological sites. They let a fresh burial have its natural mound of dirt. The body displaces the dirt. If within a casket or coffin it displaces even more. The newly dead take up volume. The disturbed soil is left ruffled and loose, with pockets of air. But with time, rain, and decay, the grave will eventually settle, healing over and melting into the landscape.

Ω Ω Ω

In my small hometown in Northern California, the community cemetery is tucked away high up on a hill, hidden by redwoods on a dead-end road. You really have to know where it is. Growing up, I was an oddball, but I was not an especially goth teenager. I did, though, spend a lot of time at that cemetery. It was peaceful, and it was a place that stimulated my imagination. Cowboys, Swiss ranchers, and White Russian immigrants are buried there. And I know where to find the empty grave of Ambrose Bierce (an unmarked plot next to his brother's). It lies empty because the master American horror writer made a cliffhanger out of his own life by disappearing in Mexico sometime around 1914. According to his Wikipedia page, Ambrose Bierce's first job was as a "printer's devil," and in the last letter he sent from Mexico he allegedly wrote, "As to me, I leave here tomorrow for an unknown destination." Pretty devilish. It may appear that I diverge here, but historical tendrils that resonate between the past and the present have always mattered to me. And they matter to the American story I am telling here. If you go back just a little way in any account of history, you quickly end up in the territory of the dead. The past is their domain.

I recently learned that scientists have discovered that most of the earth's forests have as much life belowground as above, much of it consisting of a tiny white fungal neural network that connects the entire system. I am not sure why this fact captivates me so much, but I am starting to think that is how we should imagine relations between the past and the present, between the living and the dead.

I started going back to the Guerneville cemetery when family members began dying, though none are buried there. The ramshackle property I called home for most of my late childhood and adolescence had been foreclosed on, so there was no going back there, except for peering through the fence from the road. The cemetery felt like a kind of home, a place I still had access to, that would always welcome me. It encapsulated both my past and the present. And it was a place just quiet enough for feelings to be heard.

In reality, the cemetery has changed as much as I have in the passing decades. The graves and grounds seem less neglected and forgotten now. The space now strikes me as curiously quirky and expressive, like the small town it hovers above. It is the closest thing to a public park that this unincorporated and chronically underfunded community has. Nowadays, many of the graves are decorated with lawn ornaments, homemade markers, grave offerings, and mementos. These votive objects litter many of the fresher grave plots, creating a mosaic of improvised shrines. Pebbles and coins are common (following Jewish tradition) but also seashells, handwritten notes, beer bottles, and toys. This type of artifact scatter is something I have been seeing on the rise all over the United States, but I was startled to see the practice at its most exuberant in Guerneville. Visitors are leaving signs, saying "I was here." People are coming back to cemeteries.

Teenagers may have never left, though. The last time I was at the Guerneville cemetery was when Daniel and I went to film some of these votive offerings. We weren't alone. People came and went, walking their dogs, getting some exercise. One carful of folks arrived to look for an old family grave. Another small group of four young men stayed throughout the afternoon, moving between the protective shade of nearby trees and a sunny plot in the newer section of the cemetery. The grave they kept coming back to was bursting with a miniature garden of herbs and flowers planted on its surface. The gravetenders were dressed in dark, casual clothes. A little on the long-haired and disheveled side, but you could tell they had homes. Just maybe not jobs. When they came out to the garden grave for the third time, I got brave enough to talk to them. Two of them, Eric and Dakota, agreed to be interviewed. The other two stayed in the woods, perhaps naturally shy or a little wide-eyed from the weed they had been smoking. Dakota was dressed in simple dark colors and kept his sunglasses on for the interview. Eric had a few tattoos and some beginning earplugs. He was wearing a T-shirt with an image representing Mac Dre, a rapper murdered in 2004. It depicts Dre as a skull with dreadlocks, a memorial object of sorts.

Daniel set up the camera, and I grabbed the boom mic, doubling as the sound person that day. Without much of a warm-up, I asked Eric, "What do you think happens to us after we die?" He was ready with an answer, faster than most older people I have prodded with the same question.

I believe in a weird version of reincarnation where if you keep messing up in life, like, not being a good person or doing good acts, you're doomed to repeat life over and over again until you figure it out and you actually *do* good deeds and *are* a good person and then you ascend to a higher level and you become one with the universe. And you're everyone and everything and then nothing at the same time. So that's—like—my take on what happens when we die.

I asked him where he thinks he is on that cycle. "I think I'm on the better end of that cycle, to be honest. I really try my best to be the best human being I can be—trying to do things for other people without reward. Just doing it because it needs to be done. And treating people with kindness and love because there's just not enough of it in this world right now."

Eric had even given some thought to what he wanted done with his body.

I've actually thought this out really well. I'm half Swedish so I'm really into Viking lore. I want to go and build my own Viking ship and then have them put me on the ship clenching a sword. And then have them push me out into a lake, or the ocean, and then have someone send a flaming arrow, hit the boat and burn me on the ocean or open water. . . . I think that would be *awesome*. And then everyone needs to party afterwards and celebrate my life.

His friend Dakota pipes in, smiling: "That *would* be pretty awesome."

On the subject of the afterlife, Dakota had a simpler, open-ended answer: "I truly don't know, but I do hold the law of thermodynamics to be very true—that energy cannot be created nor destroyed, so our energy—our entity—itself lives forever after death."

I then asked them why they were there, at the cemetery. "We come out here 'cause my friend's uncle is buried here, and we like to water his plants," explained Eric. He nodded to one of his friends in the trees, who emerged from the shadows once in a while to call his wandering dog back. "And we just kind of hang out. It's good shade on a hot day, so you just hang out and listen to music. You know, send good vibes to his uncle. Enjoy the day. And it's beautiful out here too."

Dakota adds: "I believe this is one of the most peaceful graveyards I've been to. It's not morbid. It's nice just to experience Guerneville here and hang out and enjoy your company. That's pretty much it."

I was moved. On that California trip, I thought these thoughtful young dudes might be anomalies in the national landscape. But the more I have talked to people, the more I have found kindred spirits, though few so young. Maybe the West Coast makes people spiritually precocious, racing ahead. But I have come to believe that Eric and Dakota are an index of things to come. Their worldview does not suggest an abandonment of religious ideas. And they are ritually tending to that grave with more devotion than their parents' or grandparents' generations have probably shown the dead. For them, the afterlife is not a *nothing*. Rather, they give themselves permission to fill in the unknown with their own imagination. Anything goes. It is not uncool to think in spiritual, ethical terms.

Ω Ω Ω

There are other ways in which the filming trip to California felt like an unexpected family reunion. Particularly with mother figures. Two women I met are leaders in different aspects of the natural-death movement. Many would classify them as ex-hippies, although the "ex" part is questionable. During our long interviews and less formal interactions over several days, I got a strong sense not only of them as individuals but of their well-developed philosophies toward life and death. They might fuss about day-to-day matters, but when it comes to the big questions, they exude a sense of existential peace.

Esmerelda can be a little overwhelming. But in a good way. There was a moment in a conversation with her when I discovered that my interview "subjects" were not only teaching me but examining me. We were chatting over tea while Daniel set up his lights in her sitting room, which with its faux animal prints and tropical palms looked a bit like a miniature brothel. We had the talk about where we grew up. I have found that it usually helps to make yourself a little less of a stranger with people if you want them to relax and enjoy the interview. If possible, you share something that might connect your experiences. With Esmerelda, the common thread was being a local and another punk girl. After I explained that I was from Guerneville, she got quiet for a long, awkward moment. In that pause, she must have been imagining what it was like to be me in my present life. Because then, sounding genuinely shocked by whatever sensation this mind experiment was causing, she blurted out: "But how does a California girl *deal* with *Chicago*??!!" I was taken aback. Her dramatic emphasis on the word "Chicago" and her tone of voice expressing dismay, if not horror, had put into words things I could not. I have no right to complain about the extraordinarily privileged life that I have fallen into. But it isn't me. Or at least there's a pretty wide gap between where I am most comfortable and where I have ended up. I teared up inside. Luckily, Daniel was ready, and we moved into the living room before I exposed how much this moment of recognition had unsettled me.

Jerrigrace is a kinetic flow of color and emotion. She wears bright fabrics of greens, reds, and blues that accent her dance-like movements, alternating between busy and serene. She is well suited to her calling, with an ability to find solace in situations that others would find grim. She has a soothing laugh and often expresses a childlike sense of wonder about it all. Jerrigrace helped start the at-home funeral movement in the United States after a close friend and Reiki teacher passed away suddenly in the 1990s. To everyone's surprise, Carolyn had left behind instructions for her friends in the event of her death. On the surface, her request seemed simple—she wanted *them* to care for her body. I'll tell that story (or rather, Jerrigrace will) later. Here I want to skip ahead to Carolyn's cremated remains, which had been distributed among her friends. For a year, Jerrigrace kept a portion of them in a small, Ziploc baggie, unsure about what to do with it. When an opportunity came up to go on a whitewater-rafting trip, she decided to bring the ashes along. As the raft floated in a pool of calm water between cascades, she pulled the baggie out of her backpack. At that very moment, a dragonfly landed on her wet hand. It refused to leave until she had streamed all of Carolyn's remains into the water. In our interview, Jerrigrace told me that in Native American cultures, when a dragonfly lands on you, it means a loved one is visiting you. It doesn't matter whether this tidbit of cultural appropriation is ethnographically correct. It is true enough for Jerrigrace. She sees lots of spirit mediums in the insects and animals who make appearances near a death. For her, these are not coincidences. Listening to her dragonfly story was the only time in the course of this project that I have ever gotten goose bumps. And I had seen my fill of nighttime cemeteries and bright-lit embalming rooms.

Perhaps that tingle down my spine was the trace of a story jumping a circuit—an electric charge conducted through me, traveling from Jerrigrace's patio in Sebastopol back to a tattoo parlor in New Orleans, where a few months earlier we had interviewed Juju, the shop's proprietor. He too had surprised me with his faith in a kind of tribalism. It was one of those interviews that exceeded expectations, but I wasn't sure what to do with it at first. The reason we decided to go in and talk to someone about tattoos was because we were following a hunch that changing attitudes toward death were somehow connected to changing attitudes toward the body, expressed in the piercings and tattoos that have become an unremarkable fashion statement for Eric's generation, or anyone of a bohemian persuasion.

I was not expecting to learn just how much tattoos are about death.

Juju's body is a walking advertisement for his trade. Actually, more like a walking scrapbook, an artful one. He obliges me and goes through his major tattoos, telling the story of each one, where it comes from, what it means. He has a raccoon because he's a "coon ass." He has a Japanese-style tattoo of a mop sweeper, a symbol of the novice in martial arts, representing his apprenticeship as a young tattoo artist. A blue crab symbolizes Louisiana and his time in culinary school. And then: "I have the memorial that I've got for my mother on my hand. It's a compass that points to Mississippi, where we had laid her to rest."

Then he opens an actual book, a large photo album of tattoos he has given people. The tattoos are not arranged in any particular order, but I am surprised to find that around one-third of them are memorial tattoos. Some of them are symbolic, like the one for Juju's mother. Others are portraits—of pets, of babies, of loved ones. He explains: "Getting tattooed for someone who is lost is, you know, accepting the loss and being able to move to the next step afterwards in the grieving process." He helps people with that. He talks about friends torn up by the loss of pets and children especially—the death of innocents is so much harder for us to process. Juju comes across as a care provider. Many people in the funeral industry have been adopting the term "deathcare." A significant portion of Juju's practice could fit under that heading.

Juju calls tattooing a form of therapy—a combination of massage, acupuncture, and the spiritual/psychological type. Soldiers in the Gulf Wars and first responders to Katrina who had seen horrific things—classic tough guys—have been among Juju's most faithful clients. It is how they deal with trauma. Juju's revelations have made me look at heavily tattooed, masculine men in a totally new way. Now I wonder: Are their tattoos emblems of toughness and valor, like medals on a general, or are they really declared scars, admissions of vulnerability? A piercing of the skin that lets you see the pain inside? Juju says, "The difference between being a tattooer—just somebody putting an image down, no meaning to it—and being a tattoo artist is being able to interpret the human struggle and what somebody's dealing with, and being able to translate that into art. *It's going to put somebody where they are.*"

In Western tattooing, death motifs are enduring classics. Juju's own teacher told him that if you couldn't draw a skull with roses, you're in the wrong business. The steady clientele of older generations of sailors, soldiers, and bikers often favored memento mori designs. Now these themes are for women and civilians too. He has developed a local variant that depicts one of New Orleans's iconic aboveground tombs. Juju is as much a philosopher-anthropologist as the rest of us. He says of the popularity of death motifs: "Some folks do it so it reminds them to live every day, I would say, on the good foot—do right and everything. You know, reminding oneself of their own mortality. I think that does put you in a different perspective—a daily appreciation of life."

Juju wishes he could go further as a medicine man, but he's constrained by modern health rules about cleanliness and the boundaries of the body. "Quite often they'll try and bring their loved one's remains to request that we put it in the tattoo ink, but the sanitary and sterile factor comes in. There's almost a tribalist feel to it when people ask." He adds, "I definitely believe on a spiritual level, it's pretty fascinating. It's nice to be able to think about putting a loved one *into* you. It's actually a pretty cool concept."

I had to think about that one. To me, mixing cremation ash with tattoo ink is not as hard to swallow as cannibalism, or eating cremation remains, which is also apparently a thing. In the few years since Juju and I talked, the word at tattoo conventions is that cremation tattoos are becoming more common, if still a little on the down-low. The more I worked on this project, the more I realized that, for a growing number of Americans, honoring the dead means deliberately breaking taboos. It's as if it is a necessary step in redefining the realm of the sacred. And what is becoming sacred are tiny fragments of the body, down to its chemical essence.[16]

Toward the end of our interview, Juju reflects: "I was always telling everybody, you know, tattoos are one of the only things—guaranteed—you are going to take to the grave. I actually had a client whose father had passed. His father's last wish was to save his skin for his family and turn it into a lampshade [not laughing]. But due to state regulations, the family wasn't allowed to save his skin. Unfortunately, it didn't happen for them." The US legal landscape when it comes to death care varies widely state by state. In Ohio, there is now a start-up company established by a couple of embalmers that will preserve tattooed human skin and return it to the family as a keepsake.[17] Such objects made with human body parts have powerful effects that go beyond just triggering memories. They are closer to the old Catholic relics, only your uncle wasn't a saint. Other old words for them are fetishes, talismans, *jujus*. Anthropologists have spilled a lot of ink writing about these sorts of magical objects in non-Western cultures. But really, we don't have to go far away to find things interesting.

Nine months after we filmed Juju, I returned to his shop. This time, for a little therapy. I wanted a dragonfly wing on my hand to remind me of those fluttering nearby in another realm.

Ω Ω Ω

In 1907, French anthropologist Robert Hertz published an enduring comparative study of death rituals around the world. He argued that one universal feature they share is that they are designed to "conquer death" by preventing the social fabric from being torn apart by loss. They work to mend the hole that a death leaves. For many Americans, neither organized religion nor the national tradition with an embalmed body is doing a great job at healing the hole anymore.[18]

This book is about changing practices in American death care and what these tell us about American society—how death care reflects beliefs and values concerning the body, the person, and the way the universe works. I focus on material practices in particular, and what people say about them, to provide an account of the emerging popular philosophies that are both metaphysical and ethical. While in some places I will make a strong case for American exceptionalism, some trends are global in nature, particularly in cosmopolitan centers with an increasingly agnostic middle class. Overall, these material practices relate to a shift in ritual practice away from religious funeral rites. This does not mean that death is unmarked by ritual. Rather a space has opened up where people are experimenting and inventing their own meaningful practices that heal the hole.

My process has been to follow new artifacts and emerging practices to see where they lead. Sometimes they lead to subplots about religious minorities, the cultural influences of immigrants, and enduring racial inequality, but I did not set out to try to create a family photo album of American death diversity. Perhaps it sounds strange coming from an anthropologist, but I wasn't all that interested in tradition. I was interested in change. One of the most significant dynamics occurring today among US residents is an openness to ritual suggestion. Mexican Day of the Dead altars, African American grave-tending, Jewish "green" burial, Hindu cremation, the legacy of AIDS, Muslim shrouding, Indigenous healing ceremonies, and Mahayana Buddhism are all making their way into a heterogeneous mix of new death practices. It is impossible to accurately trace and fully credit the influences of these traditions. But they're there. I beg the reader's indulgence as I use the oversimplification of "American" in order to try to grasp what is happening on the national level. My primary sources were not the bereaved or the dying but death-care professionals and entrepreneurs. The latter skewed white and male, consistent with a system that favors them with investment capital. But their clientele could be as diverse as the crowds at Disney World. What could be more *American* than Disney?

Ω Ω Ω

Daniel and I conducted our first set of interviews at the 2015 meeting of the National Funeral Directors Association in Indianapolis. We wanted to get oriented to the death-care scene by learning from conventional funeral directors. As it turns out, most of the people we talked to that weekend were anything but conventional. I will introduce several of them in the pages that follow, but one in particular stands out as a spokesperson for how death care relates to a new American existentialism.

Brad is a tall, balding man in his late forties or early fifties with kind eyes and a kinder voice. He does not have a long history in the death-care industry, but his demeanor seems well suited to it. It is actually harder to imagine him in his earlier careers as a nuclear submarine officer in the US Navy and then a top-level executive for the Walt Disney Company. Brad was with Disney for twelve years before coming to death care, five of those at Epcot Center: "My first day was the day of 9/11. I had never run a Disney theme park before, so quite a challenging time, but we got through it."

We missed Brad's conference seminar on the future of the funeral business, but he was generous with his time afterward and allowed us an extended interview. Brad now works for a company that owns thirty-six funeral homes and six cemeteries in thirteen states. When Brad is speaking, his explanations are so natural and sincere that I only realized later, when going over the footage, that in the early part of the interview he was delivering verbatim, carefully crafted mission statements. He says, for example, that his company's vision "is to capture, acknowledge, and share life's purpose, and we believe that every loved one has a story that needs to be told. Hans Christian Andersen had the quote: 'A human life is a story told by God.' And we believe that very strongly—that that story should be told creatively, uniquely, and in a very personal way. Using technology is a part of that."

When I got him to talk about his background, he cautiously started to go off script: "If you think about it, a funeral is an experience. So, my background from Disney was creating experiences, and what I wanted to do was essentially reinvent the funeral experience." Funerals as entertainment? Or akin to entertainment? I was intrigued but puzzled. Though it makes a kind of virtual sense. "One of the key elements we use is our multisensory experience room." I'm not sure about my transcription. Maybe he meant that to be capitalized—Multisensory Experience Room? Do they call it "the MER"? He says Disney taught him that for a directed experience to be memorable, you need to engage all the senses. In the Multisensory Experience Room they use high-definition projectors and screens, surround sound—and a scent generator. I didn't even know this technology existed. With a little online research, I found that a scent generator is a piece of optional equipment for virtual reality setups. According to Brad, the purpose is, "so that we can take you to different locations for your service. And locations that were particularly meaningful to the loved one." The way he says it, *The Loved One* should definitely be capitalized.

At that moment, I suddenly became worried that we were making an accidental mockumentary. Echoes of *The Loved One*, Evelyn Waugh's satire about the intersection of Hollywood and the Los Angeles funeral industry, were almost too rich to be real. Later, following one of those fungal roots of history, I looked into Waugh. Sure enough, during a visit to the United States that inspired the novel, the haughty Brit *did* hang out with Walt Disney. Going down that rabbit hole was my way of trying to account for the uncanny impression left by this tour guide through the new American afterlife. Brad was like the Willy Wonka of death. I pictured the Multisensory Experience Room as a Wonkavision transporter. In the most soothing bedtime voice, he said, "For example, we can take you to the beach, to the golf course, to the mountains, to a Zen garden. We can re-create the kitchen where the person maybe baked cookies." These special rooms are in the funeral home. What the rooms are intended to do—and the scent generator, especially—is trigger memories. When he asks people what they remember about *The Loved One*, he says they often reminisce about smells—perfume, cigar smoke, the old-timey scent of a grandparent's house.

I guess my dad would have smelled liked baloney and Pall Mall Reds. I'm not sure I want to relive that. Especially since that unfiltered smoke contributed to his kidney cancer.

I asked Brad about language. I noticed that he was carefully consistent with the term "deathcare" (a neologism). He said Disney World had taught him the importance of language— they talk about cast members and costumes, not employees and uniforms. In reinventing death care, his company has changed other terminology as well. What is sometimes called a "rental casket," used for a viewing before cremation, they now call a "ceremonial casket." And instead of calling memorial events "services," which has religious overtones, they call them "gatherings." He and his associates are not "funeral directors," they are "arrangers." He said people don't want to be directed, they just want someone to help make their wishes come true.

After we finished talking to Brad in the convention's stuffy pressroom, Daniel and I took a walk on the exhibit floor. Among the more attention-grabbing products are a stack of personalized caskets. I don't mean cheaply customized with a Marine Corps appliqué or a Patriots cloth liner, the kind of standard "personalization" options that have become available in casket catalogs. I mean that the caskets themselves have a personality. One is a faithful replica of Thomas the Tank engine; another is a pint-size model painted hot pink for a Disney princess. These are tearjerkers, but also cute. Then there is a large black casket sporting a silk-screen image of Louis Armstrong, the words "jazz club" outlined in colored LED lights, and an ornamental trumpet attached to the lid. For the hunter in the family, another casket is lined with camouflage cloth and sports a glued-on rack of antlers. These are one-of-a-kind pieces, reminiscent of the fantasy coffins created by Ghanaian craftsmen.[19]

The couple who run this boutique casket company are almost as colorful as their products. The wife (and business manager) is hard to miss with her bright pink hair and go-go boots, especially in the sea of dark suits on the showroom floor. She reminds me of a younger Sharon Osbourne. The husband (I'll call him "Mr. O") is the craftsman. He has a big beard and walks with a friendly cowboy swagger. I can't use their real names because a big bouncer dude working for a reality television producer interrupted us and wouldn't let me film an interview— they had signed an exclusive contract. Off camera, we talked enough for me to gather that they got into this business after Mr. O lost a close friend and fellow hunter twenty-five years ago. He was dismayed by the generic funeral service that followed. Its trappings left him cold. The blandness of it all seemed to erase the uniqueness of his friend. He wanted to remember his buddy as he was in life. Mr. O thought he could do better. Personalized caskets became his calling, adapting skills he had developed customizing cars and making musical instruments. He says that in his line of work, it helps to be an artist. While working on a piece, "I get in touch with my soul, to the people that passed. It's a passion for me."

This passion to make death better through a material practice is shared by a growing number of Americans. In remaking death, they are giving new meaning to their lives. This book is about them.

Ω Ω Ω

As I will argue in the chapters that follow, Americans began radically reinventing death with new rituals after 9/11. The Covid-19 pandemic may open a whole new chapter, yet to be written. Major catastrophes with high fatalities have a way of reconfiguring our relationship to death. President-Elect Joe Biden noted in his November 2020 acceptance speech that American history has been shaped by "inflection points." There have been several important inflection points in American death culture. The roots of the embalming ritual lie in the disaster of the Civil War, in which at least 750,000 Americans died. The Spanish flu pandemic of 1918–20 took nearly the same number of American lives. Extending a panicked medical logic, embalming came to be seen as a necessary sanitation measure, codifying a practice that became the dominant custom of the twentieth century.

With rising life expectancies in the twentieth century, death became a stranger. Americans told one another to "move on" after the body was in the ground. Funeral directors came to see the embalming and viewing ritual as a way to psychologically speed things up. I argue that what had developed by mid-century was not so much a denial of death as a suppression of grief. Pausing too long on loss was a threat to a social system based on optimism and economic productivity. At a Covid-19 press conference in March 2020, President Donald Trump stated that death is a "terrible concept"—a pithy summation of Cold War America's thoughts on mortality.

But for many Americans, something changed after 9/11. It is as if the televised mass trauma of the collapsing Twin Towers jolted us away from our attachment to the beautiful corpse, to once again embrace the principle of "dust to dust." We had no other choice. So many victims were already dust. And perhaps more importantly, for several weeks, time stood still. Within that pause, as the rubble and dust plumes came tumbling down, something germinated. The spontaneous fence memorials at Ground Zero made it permissible to publicly mourn in a way that had not been permissible since the Victorian era. And as the search for identifiable remains stretched from weeks to months, and then years, the socially acceptable timeline for grief also shifted. And the US cremation rate started to soar.

After 9/11, popular culture experienced an explosion of forensic television shows in which the exquisite details of the corpse were confronted in high definition, from *Bones* to the *CSI* franchise. Searching for answers, Americans engaged visually with the corpse—needing to confront it, to understand its secrets. The tiniest bits of body matter seem to hold clues to difficult questions. Not least, "Why did this happen?" and "Where did they go?" And then there were zombies. Lots of zombies. From the *Walking Dead* to spontaneous zombie apocalypse parties in the streets. Of all the zombie movies in existence, more than half date to the early 2000s. Americans became glued to the spectacle of decay. Perhaps it signals an acceptance that rot happens, and will happen to each of us, unless we opt for the sooty cleanse of cremation.

People love to point out that cremation is simply cheaper and account for its growing popularity that way. But this form of disposition has been available since the 1880s, yet it did not take off with earlier economic downturns. Besides, this is a bizarre argument. In most cultures, funerals are among the most important (and therefore expensive) rituals of community life. With embalming and a vault, in 2019 the average American funeral costs around $10,000, while the average American wedding costs more than $30,000. And you only die once. Embalming, viewing, and fancy funerals are still highly valued in Black communities in the United States. As one urban funeral director put it to me, you have to show respect for the person in death because they didn't get it in life. Her statement is all the more poignant in the wake of the Black Lives Matter movement. The question is not why Americans pay so much for funerals but rather why anyone would think that death care is a "waste"—of money, of space, of time. Applying such economic thinking to an event meant to recognize the value of an individual is really kind of mind-blowing. Carried to its logical conclusion, it implies that the person has no social value. That's a spectacular internal contradiction for a society built on the cult of individualism.

An attempt to resolve this contradiction may be the major driver behind some of the new death practices I describe in this book. Cremation is double-edged. It can mean a pale reduction of meaning, down to a mere transaction. But it is also igniting a ritual revival for those who want it, allowing everyday citizens to become their own shamans and mediums. Cremation has been good for the dead too, nurturing a new kind of material afterlife.

The slow disaster of the climate emergency is also having a direct impact on contemporary American death practices. Green burials of an unembalmed corpse with a simple shroud or biodegradable coffin are hot. Demand exceeds supply, as local governments and cemetery operators have been slow to respond.

Nine months into the pandemic, I checked in with several of the people and businesses that appear in the book. I needed to know how they were doing. And I needed to know if I had to scrap what I had written because the death world had been turned upside down. Instead, from traditional funeral directors to those purveying some of the more unusual mortuary objects,

I heard the same two things: business was (sadly) up, and the trends that we had discussed in pre-pandemic times were only accelerating, not changing course. Most of the practices I describe in the pages that follow are not only still valid for Covid times but strong indicators of where things are going. The exceptions are practices like DIY (do-it-yourself) home funerals and extreme embalming, which have been put on hold for the same reason that conventional funerals have been—the social-distancing measures needed to keep funerals safe for the living. During peaks, gatherings were limited to ten people, regardless of family ties. One funeral director told me that at those times she felt a tension in the air of the funeral home, where instead of guiding people through a difficult time, she had to police their grief so they didn't slip up and take off their masks or start hugging across family pods. A friend who is an Anglican priest told me it is hard to provide comfort under these conditions. She noticed longer graveside services taking the place of church rituals, and little hospitality afterward. She missed funeral sandwiches. One of the common pandemic accommodations that funeral directors and clergy have made is to offer Zoom and Facebook Live participation for guests who cannot be present. But technical glitches are common, and there are always guests who aren't tech savvy, don't have a reliable connection, or just don't find it a satisfying experience.

In terms of disposition choices, there are some early indications that the cremation rate has sped up in hard-hit places like New York, and among Blacks and Hispanics, who earlier had been slow to adopt it. One funeral director told me that he thinks more of his clientele of color are selecting cremation because they don't see the point of a small funeral—the idea is a big send-off. Another told me that there is such job precarity, that many simply can't do for their loved ones what they want.

It's hard to say whether these particular trends will stick, but people appear to be compensating for the lack of comforting get-togethers and ritual displays by embracing memorial objects they might not have considered previously. Nick, owner of Memory Glass (featured in chapter 3), told me that he thinks his business is up for this reason, even beyond the rising death rate. When each person can have and hold a similar object made with the remains of their loved one, he said, "it brings people together." Funeral directors have noticed that orders for items like memorial T-shirts and blankets blazoned with portraits of the deceased have also gone up.

Cremation may be growing faster at the expense of conventional burial, but not at the expense of green burial. Janeth, the manager of Fernwood Cemetery, told me that at the beginning of the pandemic they had braced themselves for a rise in cremation, but it just didn't happen. She said a couple of other interesting things. "I have seen more people coming in and questioning their own mortality." Younger people are preplanning, an effect of the pandemic that has been noted nationally. In her area, these clients lean heavily toward green burial. She was particularly moved by a nurse who came in on a day off from the front lines. She told Janeth, "I don't think I'm going to make it. I think I need to prepare for myself." The reality checks of 2020 were harsh, but Janeth also noticed families putting more effort into working out the details of arrangements. Anguished by the separation from loved ones (a pandemic restriction regardless of the cause of death), "there's such a loss of control, not to be with them in the hospital, and I think the living feel this need to reconcile—a need to offer some care." The pandemic may be teaching Americans to care for their own dead again.

My hope is that this book will help people face their own mortality so they can embrace life more fully when it's good, and that it might help them find new ways to communicate with those who have crossed over.

Ω Ω Ω

In the chapters that follow, I will take the reader through a process of decomposition. We begin with the whole corpse (chapter 2, "Flesh") and learn about the peculiar history of American embalming, the current transition to DIY funerals and green burial, and the new practice of extreme embalming. The continuity that shines through these variations is the magical, healing properties of the corpse in American practice. In chapter 3, "Bones," I look at the rise of industrial cremation and its impact. I focus particularly on the artists and creative entrepreneurs who are making art, jewelry, and other objects with pulverized human bone. I take a close look at the objects they are making and how they challenge our conventional understandings of what a "person" is. From there, we move down the scale of particulate matter to "Dirt" (chapter 4), to contemplate the changing American deathscape, or where and how the dead are being returned to the earth through practices such as ash scattering, human composting, and conservation cemeteries. Many people I interviewed expressed their desire to "become a tree," and there are several new ways to do this. An interest in the regenerative potential of our corpses reflects a growing material ethics. In chapter 5, we arrive at the level of the spirit, where I introduce some Americans who are intent on finding new ways to disappear into the air. I ask others what they think happens to us after we die. And I take a stab at the big questions: What is happening to the American death ritual? What does the American afterlife look like in the twenty-first century? And what does all this say about who we are becoming?

CHAPTER 2

Flesh

The last person I expected to see at the funeral was Leah.

Like most people, by early adulthood I had had some experience with death—an emotionally distant, chain-smoking grandmother who died in her reading chair; the father of a girl I used to babysit by a horrific suicide; and a high school classmate killed by inexperienced teenage driving on a winding country road. Although I have clear memories of my emotional reactions to each of these events (numbness, anger, shock), I would not say that they were life-changing. With Leah, it was different.

Leah and I had been raised together in our puppy years. When I was a toddler, her mother looked after us while mine worked. In one of the family photo albums, there is a picture of us as naked hippie two-year-olds in an inflatable swimming pool, giving baths to our dogs. Even after my family moved away, Leah and I had many playdates over the years at her house in a small California town that has since been engulfed by vineyards and wealth. I remember especially the lovely overgrown garden behind her family's Victorian cottage. I loved being there. Her mother often made us macaroni and cheese, served in white lotus-flower bowls on the picnic table. We would get into trouble sometimes, like by being too rowdy when her mother was trying to meditate in the house. We'd then be sent outdoors where we got into bigger trouble, but out of sight. One time (I think we were around eight) we hid in some oleander bushes and threw rocks at passing cars. One of the cars stopped and an angry man got out and tried to chase us down. Fueled by a new kind of terror, we ran as fast as we could into the deeper cover of a stand of eucalyptus trees and stayed crouched on the ground until he gave up. I thought he was going to murder us. We were late to dinner that evening and got scolded, but we accepted it like a balm of safety, exchanging looks of survivor solidarity.

Leah was five months older than me and acted like it. She was beautiful, one-quarter Chinese American and the rest glowing, tan-and-blond Californian, like her tennis-player dad. She was verbal and bossy and seemed to know what makes people tick. I was quiet and plain, except for a copper mess of hair, often lost in my own world. She was the girlie girl; I was the tomboy. We had fights, we made up, we grew apart. I don't know if she ever realized that I looked up to her. She knew how to get people to do what she wanted, while I mostly felt bewildered by the human world.

For all these reasons, Leah was the closest thing I had to a sister. Although we had not been in touch since I had gone away to college, I always assumed she would be there, that someday we would catch up. Implicitly, our connection was for life.

We were in our late twenties, doing our own things in different parts of the country. I didn't even know she had been sick. On short notice, I flew home from New Orleans.

I don't remember much about the funeral home except that the interior was off-white and the ceiling hung oppressively low, forcing a kind of repressed suburban hush. The bits and pieces

I can recall about the event are like a surreal dream. While Leah might have been having the real out-of-body experience, I wasn't far behind. I couldn't feel my feet. I floated numbly through space. At the same time, it was all shockingly normal. In the lobby, my mom and I encountered a poster board set up on an easel, displaying a photo collage of Leah's life. I stopped to look and catch up with phases of her life that I had missed. Like the birth of her daughter, now four. I hung back from the mingling crowd, just as I would have during childhood, not sure how to act or what to say. I knew I would have to talk to her mom and couldn't wrap my head around the black hole that she must be feeling.

And then I saw her. Leah, not her mom.

She was lying peacefully in a casket. I don't remember many of the details (rosewood? white satin lining?), but I do remember that her blond hair looked permed and puffed up in a 1980s style that was looking a bit dated by 1996 but not entirely out of character for her cheerleader style either. And she looked—*alive*. Healthy, glowing even. I wanted to touch her to see if she was real. It was impossible to believe that she had wasted away from cervical cancer.

The doctors had caught it too late to extend her life past twenty-eight years. Some freak spin of fate had determined that that was all the time she was going to get. This was not in the unconscious script I had written for our lives.

On seeing her, my insides emptied out, went somewhere else. I became a husk. The whole tableau seemed so weird, so wrong. Her body was not providing the clues I needed to catch up with the news of her illness, to comprehend how her family must have been preparing for this ending for the past few months. Instead, I felt like I was being lied to. That she hadn't died of cancer. Maybe this was all being staged as a bit of elaborate theater. I staggered and sat down in a pew, staring into space—avoiding her face—and waiting for the service to begin. My disbelief was broken by the laughter of children. Leah's daughter and another preschooler had suddenly appeared and started running in circles in front of her mother's open casket, much like we would have done as wild things. At that moment, I thought, this four-year-old might be the only other person in the room who understands how I am feeling. She doesn't think this is real either. After the vaguely Protestant ritual of spoken words, I saw Leah's mom gently laughing with departing guests. She was the model of poise and grace, as she always has been. But her composure—her lack of visible pain—only deepened my unease. She, too, seemed to project an image that said everything is all right. *But how could that possibly be?*

I got up the courage to say goodbye to Leah, one-on-one. I walked up to the casket and paused to take in her face. Perhaps an anthropologist's sense of respect for other people's traditions, or my curiosity, got the better of me. After I walked away, feelings started to rush in. I wanted to wail and tear at my clothes. I wanted to completely lose my shit. I was not prepared for *any* of this. And I was completely confused by the lifelike appearance of Leah's body. All the more so because another part of me—the part that was *not* in denial—knew that it would soon disappear forever.

Ω Ω Ω

Contemporary Americans hold some very contradictory ideas about the body. We are our bodies, and we are much more than our bodies. Although genetics give us a limited palette at birth, today's culture not only tolerates body modification but encourages it as a way to realize our "true selves." Americans experiment with, express, and transform their identities through hairstyles, cosmetics, plastic surgery, piercing, exercise, diet, tanning, tattoos, and sex reassignment surgery. This "our bodies/ourselves" belief system is brought to the fore when contemplating the inanimate body left behind by someone we knew and loved. In some ways it may be reinforced, but it is also placed in doubt. The corpse is both familiar and strange— uncanny, caught between two worlds. Something remains of them, but something has departed. *Remains* is a good word, really. And so is *departed*.

The options for what to do with the body (the cadaver, the corpse, the loved one) after death, from cremation through green burial, are professionally referred to as forms of "disposition." The root of the word is the same as disposal, but most of us have a hard time thinking of the nonliving body as trash to be disposed of. Even if that is exactly the problem that cemeteries and cremation were designed to solve. What is to be done with a collection of organic materials that are no longer useful to their owner, but which are, to put it indelicately, noxious to others? "Putrescibles" is a word the waste industry uses for flesh and bodily by-products that rot and smell to high heaven. "Disposition" can be used as a synonym for a rearrangement, something dis-positioned, out of place. Where do we place the dead? Are they and their remains always "matter out of place," as classic anthropological theory would put it—a disruption to the social order? "Disposition" also has the meaning of temperament or inclination ("she has a sunny disposition"). What is our temperament toward mortality? What is our inclination toward death?

The best clues we have to answer these questions come not from what people have to say about death but in what they *do* about it. Most importantly, how they treat the dead body.

Ω Ω Ω

When Daniel and I arrived at a training session for Final Passages on a hot summer day in 2016, we saw a group of people spread out in patches of shade bordering a large backyard. Most of them were women dressed in loose, colorful clothing. Some were quietly talking in small groups at tables on the back deck as the communal vegetarian lunch was coming to an end. A string of Tibetan-style peace flags swayed above their heads in the occasional breeze. Other participants occupied the shade of a large tree across the yard. They were working on decorating a long cardboard box—a cremation coffin—painting it freestyle with tempera paints and adding feathers, stickers, words, symbols, and floral designs per their own inclination. One of them joked that it was like collaborating on a giant adult coloring book. Wind chimes and the chirps of birds surrounded quiet human activity. Beyond them, the large open yard faded into more trees, its vague edges posted with several stone statues of Buddhas and other deities not of this Northern California world. At least not originally. Out of earshot from the workshop, an old willow protected a gauzy day tent set up for naps or meditation. Just in case you needed a retreat from the retreat.

While this idyllic buzz was going on, Jerrigrace, the leader of the workshop and founder of the educational nonprofit Final Passages, fussed busily in the background. Final Passages trains people in the legal, logistical, health, and spiritual dimensions of DIY funerals.[1] She and her partner, Mark, were setting up for the afternoon training session. They were moving props, furniture, and supplies around the outdoor classroom. In the center of the yard they assembled a massage table under a shade tent. When everything was ready, they took a break to reset and to demonstrate what Jerrigrace had described to me in an earlier conversation.

Mark, with his long gray hair tied back and his feet bare, climbed gracefully onto the massage table. He lay down on his back and closed his eyes, his feet turned out in Shavasana, the "corpse pose" that marks the beginning and the end of most yoga sessions. As I watched them from a few yards away while Daniel filmed, the scene reminded me of a painting I had seen at the International Museum of Surgical Science in Chicago, in which a near-naked man appears laid out on a table in prep for some sort of cutting, his eyes half-lidded. That painting itself seemed to quote a genre of Renaissance paintings called "the Lamentation of Christ," in which Jesus is laid out for anointing and shrouding. In those paintings, you are forced to engage with the body in its horizontal, vulnerable wholeness. The tacit relationship between the prone body of the image and the standing body of the viewer invites touch.

Jerrigrace is the one standing. She approaches Mark. She asks him how he is doing and if it is okay for her to touch him. He says yes in a quiet voice. Slowly she begins to scan her open hands over his body, hovering about two or three inches above it. She occasionally lays her hands on him, pausing for several moments, and then continues the scan. His eyes are closed, hers are open. She smiles broadly as she works. It looks like love. This is the quietest and calmest that I have seen her in the two days of training we had been filming. When teaching, Jerrigrace performs like a conductor, managing the attention and responses of her students. But this is her on a different channel. When she finishes, she asks Mark, almost in a private whisper, "How do you feel?" Sitting up slowly and blinking his eyes open, he answers, "Reborn!" She laughs and says he is a clown and how lucky he was to get a free fifteen-minute Reiki session.

Though, she adds, maybe it's just payback for the foot massage she got that morning.

Soon they are fussing again with towels and bottles for the afternoon session on body washing. They call everyone back to the shade tent, and instruction begins again. Jerrigrace explains in a loud, clear voice how to apply dry ice, how to set up a laying-out table, how to wash the body, and the best essential oils to use for anointing—and why all these things matter. She has years of practice. She has been doing this for over twenty years, but she is not doctrinaire. She encourages her students to be flexible and to do what works best for them and for the family they might be assisting. She prefers to call what she does, and what she is training them to do, as "assisting family-directed funerals." It is not so much about where one does it (the home versus a funeral parlor), nor that it saves money to do it yourself. What is most important to Jerrigrace is that this alternative practice provides the family an opportunity to *touch* the body.

Reiki is the way Jerrigrace found her calling as a doyenne of the home-funeral movement. She leads these training sessions several times a year all over the country, although most are concentrated on the West Coast. She has presided over more than four hundred home funerals but interest has grown so much in recent years that training others now takes most of her time. She helped found the National Home Funeral Alliance to advocate, train, and educate people about home funerals. The movement is growing quickly. But, she asserts, "I don't call this a trend. I call it reclaiming. It's a reclaiming of something we all used to do. We all knew how to do it, and we just forgot. We all went to sleep. . . . It's just a path that grew over with weeds, and what we're doing is cutting the weeds back and reopening the path."

She told me this during an extended interview a couple of days after the training workshop. We met on the porch of the

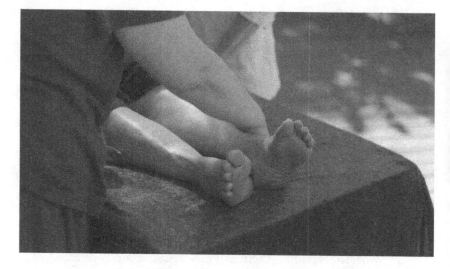

modest cottage she shares with Mark in another small Sonoma
County town. There are Buddhist statues and wind chimes
there too.

Jerrigrace has been doing bodywork of one kind or another
for nearly forty years. Moving from living bodies to dead ones
was a natural and, as it turns out, not all that dramatic shift. She
was working as a masseuse when she became interested in Reiki
in the early 1990s. She began attending sessions with a Reiki
master and nurse named Carolyn. Carolyn led a Reiki group at
her house once a week. According to Jerrigrace, Carolyn had a
unique equanimity and sense of humor. They quickly became
close friends. It felt like one of those friendships that would last
a lifetime. It did. It just wasn't as long a lifetime as Jerrigrace had
assumed it would be. She was shocked to get a call from a mu-
tual friend in 1994 informing her that Carolyn had passed away
suddenly, probably from an asthma attack. A further surprise
came when Carolyn's friends met at her house that night to
share in their grief and learned that she had prepared her final

instructions. She had left them a note. What she wanted was for her friends to bring her home and care for her themselves. She did not want her body to go to a funeral home. Carolyn had done her research and knew it was legal, but otherwise this was uncharted territory for everyone. When they got her home the next day, they opened the body bag with some anxiety. They were relieved to find that her eyes were closed. She had a peaceful expression on her face. After they removed her from the bag, the next step seemed natural to this group of bodyworkers—to lay their hands on her. Carolyn's friends performed Reiki on her corpse.

Jerrigrace explained to me that the Reiki practitioner first scans the body with hovering hands, searching for hot and cold spots or places that make the hands tingle. The practitioner is a conduit for "life-force energy"; they can add it, reduce it, and move it around as needed. Invented by a Japanese monk in the 1920s, Reiki is based on the Chinese concept of *qi*, the basis for acupuncture. Jerrigrace remembers, "Amazingly, we felt a lot of energy coming from her heart, and her head, [even though] she had been in the morgue all night. And that's when we really knew that life is still happening after the last breath, after the heartbeat stops." Over the next three days, they washed and dressed Carolyn, arranged her body with meaningful artifacts like gardenias (her favorite flower), a bird's wing, a piece of driftwood. They invited more friends to visit. Some rituals were individual and impromptu, some were agreed upon by the group. On the third day, the circle of friends loaded Carolyn's body into a Volkswagen Vanagon and took it to the crematorium. The whole experience had brought them closer together, and they didn't feel quite ready to disband. Those who could joined a celebratory lunch while their friend's body was reduced to dry, crushed bone. They picked up her remains at the end of the day. They were still warm, Jerrigrace remembers. Like her body had been.

Jerrigrace names several coincidences that happened over those days that allowed her to be present for all stages of Carolyn's postmortem care, and moments when she "just knew what to do," as if she had done it before. Sometimes she felt Carolyn watching from above. It felt like an initiation, for herself as well as for Carolyn.

Ω Ω Ω

I am struck by the parallels between Jerrigrace's up-close and personal observations of death and what the French anthropologist Robert Hertz described one hundred years ago in *Death and the Right Hand*. Hertz wrote his now-classic study of death rituals as a precocious young scholar before dying himself in World War I. Hertz, too, declared, "death is an initiation." From his armchair, Hertz gathered accounts from Indonesia and Malaysia and other non-Western cultures. He recorded a dizzying variety of customs, some quite exotic to his audience (like endocannibalism, and the intentional use of vultures), but he found others that closely resembled the familiar rites of Judeo-Christian Europe. What interested him most, however, were some common patterns underlying this diversity of death rituals. While anthropologists today are extremely cautious when it comes to making claims about universals in human behavior that ignore the influence of cultural context, some of Hertz's insights have endured and had a profound impact on our understanding of both death and ritual.[2]

Regarding the corpse, Hertz noted that most of the societies he studied understood the early phase of bodily decay to be a dangerous one for a soul caught between two worlds. The freshly deceased is a being in transition from one type of life to another. Cultures have come up with different ways of managing this liminal, or threshold, period. Death rituals in nonindustrial societies often required several phases, sometimes separated by a year or more, but there tended to be two primary ones. For example, among the Olo Ngaju of southeastern Borneo, the dead were laid out inside houses in the village while the family observed a series of rituals and taboos. This special period lasted until the flesh had safely decomposed. Then the community would hold a great feast and everyone would return to normal routines. Caribs of French Guiana would place the dead person in a pit, seated on a stool, surrounded by food and weapons; the body would not be disturbed until the flesh had melted away.

These practices involve gradually separating the living and the dead emotionally and physically, but also isolating the grief-stricken from the rest of the living. Hertz called this the exclusion phase. It was then followed by an integration phase, in which the dead enter a new, unseen society in the afterlife, and the living mourners are welcomed back into everyday society. Hertz observed that cross-culturally, "Death has long been looked upon as a transitory state of a certain duration. . . . We cannot bring ourselves to consider the deceased as dead straight away: he is too much part of our substance, we have put too much of ourselves into him, and participation in the same social life creates ties which are not to be severed in one day."[3] Crucially, Hertz realized that physical death and social death do not happen at the same time. "Social death" in this case refers to that time when the person ceases to play an active role in the lives of the living, imaginatively or otherwise. The body might be perceived as dying quickly or slowly—decay itself can be seen as a continuation of the dying process—but the spirit has its own timetable. Sometimes it leaves as soon as the person ceases speaking and breathing. In other cases, it lurks nearby for hours, days, weeks, even years, until a proper integration ritual has been performed. If reintegration does not go well, you get ghosts.[4]

Influenced by his mentor, the famous French sociologist Emile Durkheim, Hertz viewed society as akin to an organism. He argued that death rituals help a society heal itself from the wound that a death causes. Rituals are like sutures that aid healthy scarring. Another metaphor might be that death rituals are attempts to reweave the social fabric, to mend the hole left by the loss of one of its members. Whichever metaphor one prefers, repair requires both ritual and time. In contemporary American society, there's a lot of talk about a need for "closure" after a death. How many people pause to think what this implies—closure of *what* exactly? a chapter? a case file? a door? a wound? a hole? Funeral directors insist that the corpse plays an important role in achieving closure. Are they acting out a variation on Hertz's theme?

If there are three principles that guide Jerrigrace's practice, they are: death is a process, not an event; the dead body has healing properties for those left behind; and when it comes to ritual, follow your gut. I don't know if Jerrigrace reads hundred-year-old anthropology texts, but she does claim to be influenced by other cultures.

The first point, that death is never instantaneous, has both a biological and a spiritual dimension in Jerrigrace's understanding.

Many people around the world believe that it is important to keep the body at home for at least three days, and over these twenty years I now fully understand why. The body goes through all kinds of change, and we can visually see it, but we can feel it too and sense it with our body. The body visually changes. At first it seems like there's this beautiful glow around the body. In fact, one of the things that happens . . . is the person gets a smile on their face or just a very peaceful expression. . . . . By the third day, the body's starting to look more like a shell, like the bodysuit we were renting when the spirit has flown. You just sense that that life force is gone. It's waning slowly, but by that third day, it's gone. The eyes look different—they may sink in a little bit. The facial expression may change. But it helps families to know that it's time to release the physical body.

In family-directed home funerals, Jerrigrace uses this three-day timeline to guide ritual stages. And she's not wrong about it being a common standard around the world, including historically in the United States and much of Europe. Many people have an image of the "Irish wake," but the practice of a multiday, bodyside vigil was once widespread throughout Europe and its colonies. Only at the end of the nineteenth century did it start to wane. The practice of multiday viewing and visitation is one of the reasons we have funeral *homes*. They were places where out-of-town mourners could rest overnight and where friends and family could prepare and serve food. Or, as one funeral director in New Orleans told me, to party all night long. Ritual stages and hospitality drawn out over a series of days were once standard and expected elements of the American funeral. According to Jerrigrace, a funeral should last about three days because it takes that long for a body to cool down and lose its life force. This unrushed goodbye also gives family and friends time to touch the body and, through the body, to accept an inevitable transformation.

When I asked her if there were ever cases that she would hesitate to undertake for a home funeral, she says that if the individual had been badly mangled in an accident—dismembered—she might say no. But, "I would really check it out thoroughly. I think it is *so* important for people to be able to touch even a part of their loved one, like a hand, or a foot. Just to touch them and know it's their person. That can be very healing and help them process the death. So I would do whatever I could."

Jerrigrace believes in meaningful coincidences. Another woman I spoke to had said almost the exact same thing several months earlier—how even a small body part can have healing properties for the bereaved. I have come to think of this as "corpse therapy." Perhaps surprisingly, a belief in the curative power of the dead body is an article of faith that Jerrigrace's DIY funeral devotees share with conservative professionals in the death-care industry—especially those practitioners of the arcane practice of embalming.

Ω Ω Ω

In November of 2015, we were in a very different context, in a very different part of the country. The National Funeral Directors Association was having its annual meeting in Indianapolis, Indiana, and the PR department had agreed to let us film. They even set us up with a few interview contacts. One of them was Beverly. We spoke to her in the noisy exhibition hall where vendors and funeral directors were busy networking and making deals. Nearly half of the floor space was given over to displays of late-model hearses, from luxury to sporty numbers. Several funeral directors told us that this is the most popular part of the showroom. But being new to a death trade show, we were more transfixed by biodegradable urns, memorial jewelry, and cemetery reconnaissance drones.

Beverly dropped an anchor of calm among the hubbub when we met her in a busy aisle between booths. She shook my hand—warm and gentle but firm. She was dressed in a dark, mannish suit, her steel-gray hair cropped short. Her manner is direct and reassuring. But she's not motherly. She comes across more like a gym teacher or a highly competent nurse. Care is her profession, and she communicates this remarkably effectively through her body language and words. She deals with a lot of bodies and a lot of emotions in her line of work. Perhaps this has honed her attunement to both.

I asked Beverly what changes she has noticed in the death-care industry over the course of her career. She doesn't immediately answer. Instead, she suggests that a future correction is needed. She wants the field to "go back to basics . . . our body language, our tone of voice, our words and phrases. You know, historically in our profession we've used the word 'removal' or 'transfer,' but we need to change that, you know: 'we are going to come and bring your mother into our care.'"

Beverly inherited her family's funeral business. Her father came to it more by predilection. From an early age, he was fascinated by death. He created his own personal pet cemetery, complete with little handmade caskets. He also drew pictures of his friends in caskets. I have encountered a few death prodigies like him over the course of this project, but fewer than you might think. What Beverly said next was something I heard many times, in different iterations: "I believe a lot of us are called to this. We look at it as a ministry. It is an honor." But I think she was called to this ministry differently from her father. She was called to care for the living affected by death. Her father was called to care for the dead themselves.

On the topic of change, Beverly mentions, as does almost every professional I talked to, the mass movement toward cremation in American society in the last few decades. She suspects that this shift has to do with the fact that we have become a more mobile society. People no longer live near their families or hometown cemeteries. Cremation makes the dead more portable. Or perhaps disposable. Direct cremation is a change that she laments:

> It seems like there's a little transition here of families not having the body present. But it is *so* critical. That is part of the grieving process. I think it is important to have an open casket if you can because there is the reality of what we do— that this has happened and you need to see the loved one. In mortuary school, they train us to create a pleasant memory picture.

She believes that embalming and restoration should be applied wherever possible, even in cases of physical trauma. "It is important for a funeral director—an embalmer—to give her or his talents to create that person back."

Her words puzzled me. "Create them back" sounds like embalmers are creating a revenant—a zombie, or a returning Christ.[5] But as Beverly continued to explain the craft of restoration to me, I began to understand that she means creating them back in appearance to a time before suffering and trauma. This is the source of the special power that the embalmed and restored body has to heal the living. "A person, say, that is real emaciated, that's lost a lot of weight—what a talented embalmer can do is use tissue builder and kind of bring that person back where it almost erases that hard time they went through with that loved one, and they're almost transported back when mom was up and going. We get her hair done, her makeup." Of course, the embalmer cannot erase those experiences for the dead, who are beyond suffering, but they fade the memory of it for those left behind. The language about embalming creating a "memory picture" circulates widely in the funeral business, but what Beverly helped me understand is that it is a doctored picture—a repaired memory. The embalmed corpse comforts by attempting to *erase* certain bad memories, not by creating a lasting, frozen portrait of the moment of death.

Even in the cases of shattering physical trauma, Beverly advocates for the medicinal properties of the dead body, although this is a somewhat different kind of healing power—one that purportedly helps survivors accept the reality of death (the "acceptance" stage in Kübler-Ross's grief scheme). Regarding this healing power, she strongly agrees with Jerrigrace's position, although she focuses on the sense of sight rather than the sense of touch. And she tells me a story that Jerrigrace later echoed about how it doesn't even have to be the whole body—parts will do. On Christmas Day some years ago, a man, his wife, and their daughter were flying into Beverly's local airport in his small private plane when it crashed. Both parents died, but the daughter in the back seat survived unscathed. Her brother had missed the trip due to work obligations. He struggled to accept what had happened. His mother's body had been disfigured but, Beverly said, "the father's body, you couldn't see at all." The son was bewildered and distraught—how was it that his parents were gone but his sister looked like she hadn't been on the same plane? He asked to see his mom and, according to Beverly, understood and accepted her visible death. But then,

> nothing would do him but to see his dad. So we took the family out, and what we did is . . . [she pauses, searching for words]. You know, the body was so mangled from the

wreckage—his left foot was pretty well intact. And we took it out of the body bag, cleaned it, and we put a nice little velvet throw over it. And I can still see him today sitting on that end of that daybed, just rubbing his dad's foot. Now for some people that would be gruesome, or "how could you do that?" But I knew that he probably wouldn't be able to go on if he didn't. He could see his sister. He could see his mom. But he had to see something of his dad—that this really happened to me.

Even a severed body part will work to cure death denial. In this case, though, it is not our own mortality that is the problem, as Ernest Becker held in *The Denial of Death*, but the death of another. In this common narrative in the American funeral business, there is something about the familiar flesh of a loved one that makes it easier to let go—to believe in death. It represents someone/something to show love to, talk to. But also, according to pop psychology, a method for overcoming the denial stage of grief.

Most of the traditional funeral directors and embalmers I have spoken to insist on the healing properties of viewing the dead body, or the power of a "memory picture." However, among all the nonprofessionals I have spoken to, I encountered only one young woman who voiced a desire to be embalmed and viewed. She seemed nonpartisan on the subject but thought the tradition would bring comfort to her Catholic family. More often, laypeople say they are "creeped out" by the whole embalmed body and open casket thing, although the social pressure to go along with a traditional funeral may not allow them to give voice to that discomfort. My own reaction to Leah's embalmed body was something in between. I did not find her corpse scary, but I in no way found it reassuring. It didn't work the way it was supposed to. It made the whole fact of her death from cancer *harder* to believe. It was unreal.

Ω Ω Ω

One of the funniest moments we experienced while filming was on that Halloween night in New Orleans in 2015. A middle-aged couple stopped and agreed to talk to us. The woman was dressed as some sort of heavy-metal goth groupie. The man's face appeared to be melting under gray-green makeup. He wore a blood-spattered shirt and limped suggestively. A zombie. After some small talk about zombie problems, like forgetting where you put your fingers, I hit them with one of my stock questions: "What do you want done with your body after you die?" The man suddenly broke character and got serious. But he didn't seem offended by my question. It was more like he appreciated that somebody had finally asked. He talked about how he had recently dealt with the deaths of his parents. That experience had helped him get clarity: "I think the ritual of burial and viewing of the dead body is the most morbid thing that anybody *ever* came up with." So, one finding of my research is that zombies take a firm stand against embalming.

Highly variable reactions to the ritual of viewing the embalmed body today suggests that Americans are having trouble reaching a consensus about what they consider to be morbid. The wide gap between the faith that embalmers have in the healing properties of their practice and its declining efficacy among the public is, I have come to believe, another reason for the rise of cremation. Many people now find the open casket scary and far from comforting. This is a significant historical shift. Until recently, embalming was an integral part of a traditional funeral suite that dominated death in America despite the country's ethnic and religious diversity. In the mid-twentieth century, embalming and casket burial accounted for 95 percent of all dispositions. Even today, the American embalming rate far outpaces that of any country in the world. It remains particularly strong in Black communities, in Catholic communities (regardless of race), and in the US South (also across racial lines), although it is gradually declining among these groups as well. Until very recently, embalming elsewhere in the world was largely reserved for purely practical reasons— for medical dissections, transportation over long distances, or for public figures lying in state. Globally, the American pattern from circa 1900 to 2000 was extraordinary, and peculiar.

Scholars and social commentators have pointed to the embalming ritual as evidence for a propensity to deny death by re-creating a lifelike body, another case of American exceptionalism. Historian David Sloane calls it the "death taboo." But Beverly told me that viewing or touching the embalmed body does quite the opposite—that it helps overcome death denial. I will return to this puzzle and how I have come to doubt strong versions of the "death denial thesis," but first I want to dig into the historical roots of embalming to better understand how Americans became neo-Egyptians in the first place.[6]

Ω Ω Ω

Historians who have studied the US case all point to the Civil War as a watershed event in American death culture. During the war, a crude type of embalming began to be practiced in field hospitals as a way to limit putrefaction and facilitate the return of fallen soldiers, mostly to Northern families. These bodies were picked up from battlefields sometimes weeks or months after death. The aim of this early embalming practice was not the restoration of a "memory picture" but to stop the emanation of fluids and odors in nonrefrigerated train cars—to slow down decay of whatever flesh remained. It was pragmatic and material. The symbolic power of viewing the preserved and *restored* body traces to the very end of the Civil War. President Lincoln's embalmed and cosmeticized body was placed on a funeral train that made several stops on its two-week journey from Washington, DC, to Springfield, Illinois, in the spring of 1865. It was an unprecedented spectacle. The waxen, sleeping corpse of the president was viewed by tens of thousands of Americans in person, multiplied by thousands more via lithographs and newspaper accounts. How much this corpse viewing was driven by respect for the martyred president, versus fascination with the novelty of embalming, is impossible to say. But the second motivation should not be discounted, given that demand for cosmetic embalming soared after the war among Americans who could afford it. During this same period, "Egyptomania" had captured the American imagination. The display and ceremonial unwrapping of Egyptian mummies was itself a popular spectacle in the nineteenth century. It may strike us as odd now, but the same fascination with potential revenants fuels movie box office sales today. The link between Egyptomania and the rise of embalming is no trivial coincidence. Early embalmers explicitly referenced their art as being inspired by the Egyptians, only in America, "everyone's a pharaoh." Several embalmers I interviewed referred seriously to ancient Egyptians as their forerunners, if not forefathers.[7]

Embalming requires specialized training, equipment, and techniques, which led to the professionalization of death care at the end of the nineteenth century and the rise of a standardized industry. Prior to the Civil War, bodies were washed, dressed, and laid out by family members or experienced members of the community—in both cases usually women. In other words they were "family-directed home funerals." Birthing, raising children, tending the sick, and caring for the dead all constitute the intimate bodywork delegated to the domestic sphere. Corpse care was once distinct from "undertaking," which referred more narrowly to the occasional gig work undertaken by carpenters and draymen to build coffins and transport the body to the cemetery in a horse-drawn cart.

After the Civil War, the specialized bodywork of embalming and the other goods and services related to death started to be taken over by male professionals. Hence the evolution from "undertaker" to "mortician." "Mortician" is a word invented at the end of the nineteenth century that mashes the Latin word for death with the suffix from "physician." These new death workers wanted to be understood as a special kind of doctor. While this rebranding was undoubtedly a pitch for dignity, it can also be understood as an overt move by members of this new professional class to assert themselves as a type of healer. By the end of World War I, the transition was complete. Professional organizations, mortuary schools, certifications, and protective legislation had enabled the complete commercialization and standardization of a major life event that families used to handle themselves.

But still, to understand why Egyptomania and the spectacle of Lincoln's corpse led to such rapid public uptake of embalming in the United States at the end of the nineteenth century, it is necessary to go back even earlier. Long before embalming was invented, there was a widespread custom in the United States of viewing the dead body before burial. This visual engagement with the corpse by family and friends would usually take place during the typical three-day wake in the family parlor, even as the body started to smell and decompose. When a body had to be buried more quickly due to weather, disease, or travel, attendees would still often pop open the coffin lid at the graveside in order to take one last look.

The custom of viewing the corpse during a pre-funeral wake or vigil by family and close friends is not uncommon around the world and across the major religions. It is at least tolerated among Buddhists, Hindus, and Christians, and sometimes expected, but rare among Jews and Muslims. But in most cases, the coffin or casket will be closed for the main ritual. In fact, the closing of the casket often ceremonially signals that the public funeral rite is about to begin. By contrast, in the early United States, visual engagement with the corpse became a centerpiece of the ritual. By the late 1700s, English travel writers thought the American fixation on getting a "last look" was bizarre enough to note it in their journals with some repugnance. Well before modern embalming techniques were invented, entrepreneurial coffin and casket makers were designing models with a glass panel set over the face to facilitate this visual connection between the living and the dead. (For the uninitiated: a coffin is a tapered box with a separate, nailed lid while a casket is a rectangular case with an attached, hinged lid.) This need for visualization also drove one of the first applications of the daguerreotype through the fad of postmortem photography in the Victorian era. Death portraits began to decline in the 1890s just as embalming in the United States was taking off, leading some scholars to suggest that embalming satisfied the same visual impulse. This genealogy would help explain why embalmers refer to their work as creating a "memory picture."[8]

Still, we are left with the question: *Why* did Americans have such a compulsion to visually witness and preserve the dead? None of the answers death scholars or funeral directors have offered put the question to rest. Two explanations cite the dominance of Christianity among settlers, enslaved people, and immigrants in the colonial and early national periods. Although American Protestantism was, and is, extraordinarily diverse, Evangelical movements have dominated since the First Great Awakening (1720–40). Historically, Evangelicals held a strong literal belief in heavenly recognition, that "individuals who had known each other on earth would be able to identify each other in heaven."[9] This might have made it quite important to burn an image of a loved one's appearance into memory—at the wake or through a peek into a coffin. Or, if you could afford it, to capture a memory picture via a death mask, painted portrait, or photograph of the beloved.

Another explanation sometimes offered is a more practical one, also cited for cremation—that a society scattered over such a vast territory needed to buy time for family and friends to make the journey for the funeral rite. If this is a sufficient explanation, then embalming should have also become a go-to preservation technique in other large territories with dispersed settlements, like Australia or imperial Russia. But it did not. If embalming was just about preservation, then refrigeration technology would have put an end to it by the 1930s.

Another, more unusual explanation for corpse viewing refers to the nineteenth-century taphophobia panic. "Taphophobia" is the fear of being buried alive. It was in this period that several clever inventors came up with coffins outfitted with breathing tubes and bells so that someone who woke up underground could alert those in the graveyard that they weren't yet done with this life. Similarly, a popular explanation of the *wake* is that its purpose is to verify that the person is not actually going to *wake up* again—people watched the body for signs of life. The physical transformations that Jerrigrace describes, as well as the smell that she alludes to (with her injunction to use a lot of aromatherapy), would have been sure proof of death. Conversely, a fog forming on glass (another benefit of the glass-topped coffin) or a mirror held up to the mouth were signs of shallow breathing by the merely comatose. Of course, embalming would certainly eliminate any fear of being buried alive. After your body has been exsanguinated, you are dead beyond a reasonable doubt. But the idea of being embalmed alive holds its own special horror. There's no evidence that Americans were more prone than anyone else to this rare phobia.[10]

While none of these explanations quite satisfy, it is irrefutable that for the last two centuries most Americans have shared a keen need to *see* the dead—shriveled in a coffin three days after death, unnaturally preserved by embalming fluids, or with their spirits captured through the lens of a camera. Until recently, the whole corpse has been the sacred object that grounded the American funeral ritual, overriding most ethnic and denominational differences.

That said, most Americans share a popular misconception that embalming is practiced as a form of medical hygiene. Laypersons assume it is required by public health codes, but the conditions that might mandate embalming are exceedingly rare. In fact, due to the incisions, body manipulation, and bloodletting involved, embalming presents more health risks than it prevents. During the Covid-19 pandemic, the World Health Organization recommended that the practice be suspended. The United States as ever decided to go its own way. The US Centers for Disease Control allowed the national tradition to continue, albeit with special guidelines and extra personal protective equipment (PPE) for death workers. Although embalming is slowly dying out, it is an American cultural practice protected—against the advice of scientists—as a religious freedom that no religion demands. This peculiar fact supports the theory that American embalming is best understood as a national ritual. Although its historical roots are multiple, its culmination is singular. So what does embalming *do*? What is its ritual purpose?[11]

Ω Ω Ω

Modern arterial embalming goes back to late eighteenth- and early nineteenth-century European efforts to develop a way to preserve cadavers for medical dissection. Tubes are inserted into incisions made in the body to access the circulatory system. The tubes connect to a special pump that then pushes chemical preservatives in and blood out.[12]

I have seen a variety of embalming rooms, from a DIY setup in a Home Depot aluminum storage shed in a backyard to a hyperclean, fluorescent-lit, state-of-the-art operating room. More typically, embalming rooms are tucked away in the funeral home basement and look like a place where amateur science experiments take place. The fact that blood and other bodily excretions, as well as any overflow of toxic embalming fluids, drain directly into the sewer lines underscores the fact that if there are sanitary reasons to embalm, they are more to control for emotional types of pollution than for biological ones. In fact, it is much harder to get sick from dead bodies than from living ones. Or, as the World Health Organization succinctly puts it: "The widespread belief that corpses pose a major health risk is inaccurate." With few exceptions, most diseases do not long survive their hosts. However, there is a small threat that some viable bacteria or virus in the blood or excrement can enter the drinking supply through embalming runoff or seepage from unembalmed burials. Generally, the medical hygiene procedures that embalmers follow are to protect themselves, not the public.[13]

Exaggeration of the contaminating potential of the corpse, although expressed in pseudo-medical terms, is strongly reminiscent of the dangerous liminality, or in-betweenness, that Hertz observed in nonindustrial societies in the early period after a death. The dangers that the corpse and its detaching spirit present to the living are often expressed in magical terms. Given that the scientific basis for embalming is tenuous at best, perhaps Americans have been more magical in their thinking about death than we have appreciated. Mary Douglas, an anthropologist famous for her interpretation of human symbolic behavior, notes how rituals are often predicated on controlling states or substances that members of a culture considered polluting and dangerous. One of her insights was that the line between physical and social contamination is thin to the point of being one and the same. She demonstrates this proposition by looking at the cultural logics expressed through phobias, taboos, and purification rituals involving dirt, blood, and food. A perceived threat to the biological body represents a threat to the social body and vice versa. Individuals who are in some sort of ambiguous or neither/nor state when it comes to accepted social categories in a given culture—menstruating girls, trans people, strangers, lower-caste workers—are considered sources of dangerous contagion through their bodily fluids or through touching other people's food. They are often viewed with disgust and fear, though those who view them this way aren't necessarily able to articulate *why*. They may be kept forcibly segregated from the rest of the group, or they may be made "safe" through purification and integration rituals.[14] We have seen that interaction with the dead body of a loved one is supposed to have magical healing properties. Is it perhaps also the case that, being neither a person nor a thing, the dead have dangerous properties? Is fear of bodily decay another type of magical thinking? Is embalming actually a purification ritual?

Ω Ω Ω

As a group, embalmers are the most interesting people I have ever met. Some are earnest and intense. Others are laid-back and ironic. But all, after they open up a little, come across as compassionate and philosophical. They are forced to think about big existential questions by the nature of their routine work. They quietly observe dynamics of American families in revelatory moments of duress. Acutely aware of the stigma of their profession, they perch on the edge of their own society, looking in. They have a lot of thoughts about tradition, social bonds, and cultural trends. Not that different from anthropologists, really.

Bob is enjoying retirement but keeps a hand in the small community funeral home he owned and operated in a working-class Chicago suburb for over fifty years. A well-known mentor in the metro area, over the years he has trained many an apprentice embalmer for the local mortuary college. We met in the office of the modest neocolonial funeral home that he sold a few years ago to a big conglomerate that controls about 20 percent of the US market. As with many of these acquisitions, they didn't change the facade or the family name. Its executives know that reassuring familiarity is what most people want in a funeral home. The struggle between big business and the little guy is real in today's funeral business, but that's a story I can't do justice to here. I refer the reader to the hit HBO series *Six Feet Under*, which got a lot of things right about this ongoing story.

Bob answers my questions with avuncular good spirit in an old-time Chicago accent you rarely hear anymore. He has seen the composition of his community change over the years. He says different ethnic customs make it interesting. If he had served only one group in all that time, he would have gotten bored. Italian, Polish, Lithuanian, Mexican, and African American families make up his diverse base. He has performed Muslim, Buddhist, and Shinto services, but most of his clientele are Catholic, and they still want something "traditional," with a wake, viewing, visitation, formal funeral service, and burial. In the case of Chicagoland's large and extraordinarily diverse Eastern Orthodox Christian population (in Bob's suburb, primarily Syrian and Serbian), the deceased's body is usually present for a wake, and cremation is banned. While the Vatican lifted its prohibition against cremation in the 1960s, and many of Bob's Catholic families are immigrants from places where embalming was rarely practiced, members of these communities seem to have adapted to embalming as a necessary accommodation to the traditions of their new home. Bob says that funerals are major social events for the communities he serves, gathering friends and families from dispersed neighborhoods and suburbs to assert their connections through tradition. This is as true for immigrant groups as for African Americans, who also tend to prefer embalming and an open casket during the service.

Karla Holloway and other Black scholars have noted that embalming has played an important role in ensuring that Black bodies can be brought back home to the community. Vitally, the "homegoing" ritual allows the deceased to be "honored with visitations that indicated respect and esteem" that might have been denied them in life. The demand for dignity in death is felt as keenly as ever in the wake of police brutality brought to light by the Black Lives Matter movement. Although large in-person funerals were put on hold through much of 2020, they will likely experience a resurgence, including deferred celebrations once it is safe to gather. But in those cases, the body will not be present, which may be felt as an additional loss. As Holloway says, "a laying-on of hands, touching, kissing, and expressing one's grief by viewing the remains have traditionally mattered deeply. . . . [Embalming] resided easily within African American traditions that respected the emotional power of the presence of the deceased."[15] Although enduring differences in the American experience of death are significant in their own right, the retention of embalming and viewing among African Americans could help us understand how it might have once worked for a larger swath of the population.

If the family is going to spend any time with the body, Bob says, that means embalming "99 percent of the time." Bob encourages it for liability reasons, because you don't want anything "macabre" to happen. "Visitation usually equals embalming, so whatever the final disposition is, whether it's burial or cremation, it doesn't make any difference. We're safer, the family is safer. Everything is done the way it should be." For Bob, embalming is a safety practice, but his words suggest that it is about the *emotional* danger of leaking fluids, gaping mouths and eyes, and that heavy, warm odor of decaying flesh. And about his legal safety. He hints that he doesn't want to give families any cause to sue him for emotional distress. Embalming is an intervention meant to address the tremendous anxiety that the natural biological processes of death seem to trigger. Are Americans particularly squeamish about decomposition?

After talking in his office awhile, we headed down to the basement area, accessed through a service elevator for easy transport of bodies and caskets. The space is clearly not intended for the viewing public. Down a short hallway, a workshop dedicated to repairs or adjustments to coffins sits across from a stockroom with boxes of crucifixes and ornate keepsake

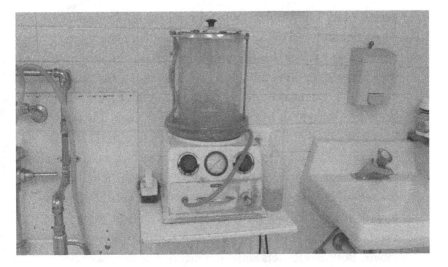

urns that look like they would be right at home in a grandmo-
therly knickknack cabinet. Supplies overflow into the hallway,
where cardboard boxes stamped "infant casket / made in
China" teeter in stacks. At the end of the hall, there's a break
room with a kitchen.

While Daniel and I waited for Bob to tidy up the embalming
room, I noticed a tattered educational poster in the hallway list-
ing "Medical Examiner Cases." These are special deaths that
may require an autopsy. The long list of causes of death (nearly
one hundred) transfixed me. I expected to see "homicide" and
"suicide," but I also see death by "tooth extraction," "fireworks,"
and "accidents in mines and quarries," as well as the somehow
sadder "alcoholism," "exposure," and "hunger and thirst." I was
struck by all the many ways that our stories can end, and the
way the last chapter gets told by our remains.

Bob had thrown some things into a large plastic garbage can
and pulled it out of the room, asking a passing staff member to

get rid of it. "No problem, not contaminating," he said to us by way of an unasked-for explanation. Of course, this made me want to peek at the contents, but Bob was inviting us to look elsewhere. The embalming room is functional but not pretty. The Formica counters and linoleum floor are showing their age, unhelped by the unforgiving fluorescent lights. Along one side of the room is a plumbing fixture that looks like a janitor's sink with extra hoses. Next to that, on top of a small medical cart, sits a vintage embalming pump with bright orange tubing connected to a clear tank that gets filled with embalming fluid when it's in operation. White enamel, with oversize dials, it looks like a contraption from a 1950s sci-fi movie. Built-in cabinets and countertops line the back wall. A collection of cheap shampoo, hairspray, and makeup sits on the counter, along with a small boom box. I wonder what kind of music the staff play as they work. It is easy to imagine Bob listening to Cubs games.

He steps into the room and turns toward us. We're standing in the doorway, and Daniel is balancing the camera on his shoulder. We've laced Bob up with a lapel mic. Without a hint of theater, Bob asks, "So, you want a little embalming lecture?" I nod yes.

Very simply, our circulatory system is a closed system. If you remember in the old days, when you had a radiator in your house with the warm water that came through, and down in your basement somewhere you had a heater that was heating the warm water. The heating system—the pump that's pumping the water to make it circulate, that's your heart over there. The rest of it, all the radiators and everything, that's your circulatory system, whether it be artery, venous system, or little capillaries, etc. And this is embalming.

He elaborates on the different types of fluid that you select according to the person's cause of death, age, weight, and so on. Size is very important. There are different types of fluid for petite people and large people. You don't want to under-embalm, or over-embalm, he says. He gets a little more brass tacks: "OK, to inject the fluid, you choose a vein to let the blood out over there [he points to a basement drain on the floor]. A lot of people are like 'oh my God, it goes down the drain over there!' Yes, it does. There's a lot of other things in our society that are going down the drain, but I don't want to get into that . . ." Midwest humor.

Bob goes on to explain the different techniques he has to use in the case of an autopsy or a severe trauma. Sometimes he's forced to recommend a closed casket, especially when the body was not discovered for days or weeks: "It's just chemistry, what's going to happen to a human body left out. Embalming will stop that. We're not building pyramids in this country. We don't care if it's going to last from the Egyptian times. We are not God, but we're able to do many magical things."

When I started this project, I had no idea I was going to run into magicians and ancient Egyptians.

Ω Ω Ω

Michael is another professional embalmer. We met in the living room of the flat he shares with his husband in one of the quiet, hill-less San Francisco neighborhoods that fade into the coastal fog. As we enter the foyer, I notice a small altar on the floor with an ankh, a statue of the cat god Bastet, a scarab beetle, and two urns with the heads of Horus and Anubis (the Egyptian god of mummification), along with some other objects I don't recognize but that clearly have Egyptian referents. In the living room, we set up for the interview, with Michael sitting in an over-stuffed vintage chair with damask upholstery covered with floating cherubs. Tiny angels.

Michael transitioned into embalming when he realized that he could bring together his experiences in health care and beauty. In former lives, he had been a dental technician and a makeup artist. He said, in his slow, careful way: "My craft is an unusual craft. I knew right from the beginning that I could be useful." After receiving his mortuary school training and certification, Michael started to work with the same large conglomerate that now owns Bob's funeral home. As I learned from other funeral directors, in major urban areas the big companies quietly transport the bodies to central processing facilities in industrial zones, where teams of embalmers and restorers do their work before the bodies reappear for their special events back at the funeral home.

Soon Michael was doing one hundred embalmings a month. He developed a specialty in post-traumatic restoration for cases like gunshot wounds. The pace was exhausting and at odds with his sense of craft and care. Like Beverly, he sees what he does as a calling, though he's more like her father. Michael serves the dead, not the bereaved. It is, he says, "much more than work. It is an opportunity to be with an individual, and this is their last—[he pauses]—what people are going to see." I wonder what he was going to say—last party? last photo shoot? last memory picture? But he changed his mind. Perhaps because he is still trying to work out his role, and the right language, in a rapidly changing field. In our interview, Michael repeatedly refers to the deceased person in his care as the *individual* rather than "the loved one." Many directors of small funeral homes double as the embalmer, so they care for both the dead and the living. But others, like Michael, are specialists who rarely interact with the family.

Eventually, Michael left the large corporation for a small start-up that handles both embalmed and natural (or "green") burials. He is comfortable with both methods but has become concerned about the environmental and health impacts of embalming. While the new generation of chemicals is less harsh than the old formaldehyde solutions, they can still penetrate and burn living skin. Once in the ground, the fluids and fumes will gradually dissipate. He explains that the soil acts like a natural filter, although concrete vaults in conventional cemeteries create barriers that let the toxins pool and collect, until they are reopened to add a spouse, or they inevitably crack under the slow pressures of the elements.

Despite his altar to the Egyptian gods (which we did not discuss), Michael says that modern embalming is *not* a form of mummification for eternity. The preservation it provides is temporary—a matter of years, maybe decades, but not centuries or millennia. I have come to realize that this is another big disconnect between professional and public understandings of the embalming practice. Most laypeople seem to assume that embalming will prevent decay of the body indefinitely. The actual time frame, as with any archaeological deposit, depends on local environmental conditions—soil chemistry, design of the vault and casket, moisture content, and seasonal temperature fluctuations. Embalming might delay the inevitable, but it does not stop it. Materially, its primary purpose resides in the funeral ritual.

As our interview winds down, I ask Michael what the most difficult part of his job is. His answer matches what every other funeral director I have talked to says: children. He tells a story about handling his first embalming of a little one. In one difficult hour, he imagined what it would be like to be a father with a child, and then to be a father without a child.

Across the country, in a small Southern town, I interviewed another embalmer who *is* a father. Jeffrey's daughter is a strong-willed adolescent, as became apparent from the barrage of text messages that kept interrupting our conversation. Jeffrey is refreshingly frank about the social changes affecting the funeral industry. In his region, green burial is rarely mentioned and cremation is growing more slowly than the national rate. But there are other changes happening. He says fewer and fewer people take the time to come to funeral services. It's not necessarily by choice. People are moving away to cities in other states. Families are scattered. Added to this, the low-income (and largely Black) folks who make up the largest segment of his clientele do not have the types of jobs that provide paid bereavement leave. Even close family members can't afford to take time off for a tradition that once spanned three or four days of family visits and multiple ritual stages, from wake to burial. Today, he says, death often gets only about forty-five minutes of focused attention by friends and family at a memorial service. Less time than a TV episode. Jeffrey says this is a symptom of the overall time compression that Americans live under. Services are, "becoming smaller and smaller because, as a culture, we're not allowed—we're don't have the liberty of—as much time off as we used to, and people are forced to make the choice nowadays: 'Do I want to spend my days off at my great-aunt's funeral, or do I want to spend these days off with my kids?'" The sparse attendance is often embarrassing, but he tries to joke: "Maybe grandma was a bitch!" He checks himself quickly to explain that humor is a coping mechanism in the industry. "It's our way of letting go of the stress. You gotta laugh when you can, because you're gonna cry the rest of the time. It's very stressful to deal with death care on a daily basis." He was one of the only conventional funeral directors I spoke to who was willing to admit this. Most of them have had a lifetime of practice in buttoning up.

Jeffrey is willing to help people in his community in any way that seems reasonable, although he tries to keep quiet about some of the special requests he has honored. "I find it fascinating that a lot of people like to put items that were special to the deceased in their casket with them. That happens a lot. We learned in history that the Egyptians liked to do that. And that's still today very prevalent in our society, because anything and everything that you can think of, I've seen put in a casket with people, from liquor to photographs to marijuana to even, one time, a seeing-eye dog."

There they are, the American Egyptians again. The dog had died at the same time as his owner, but Jeffrey doesn't explain further, except to say he doesn't want this to become a trend. He asked the family to keep it mum. Anubis the jackal god accompanied dead kings into the afterlife. And the Egyptians mummified their pets. Jeffrey, by the way, is also a doting father to a large, pointy-eared Doberman.

As we were wrapping up the interview, Daniel asked Jeffrey if there were any stories or moments in his career that stood out. Jeffrey turned more serious and started to tell us about one, a special request of a boy named Caleb that he honored with difficulty. Caleb's parents called up Jeffrey one day and explained the situation. They said that throughout his struggle with leukemia, Caleb had been involved in his own treatment. He always asked questions about what was going to happen and how it was going to feel. As treatment options ran out, Caleb could sense death was near, and his curiosity switched to the embalming room. He wanted to visit, to see where his body would go. He wanted Jeffrey to explain everything that was going to happen. At first this freaked Jeffrey out, and he tried to talk the parents out of it, but once they had explained that this really was one of Caleb's last wishes, he agreed.

> I took him on a tour of the funeral home. I made sure that there were no cases in the embalming room, and I showed him in the door. I didn't take him in, but I showed him what the room was and everything. And it wasn't but about three days later that my phone rang at night, and it was his mom and dad. He had passed away, and he was in his room in his Batman pajamas. And I went and got him and took him back to the funeral home. The hardest thing to do was to leave him in that embalming room and turn off that light because I just remembered a few days earlier holding his hand and standing in the door, explaining to him what was going to happen. And that is probably the hardest thing I have ever dealt with.

Jeffrey couldn't get through those last couple of sentences without choking up. He grabbed a tissue (they are always nearby in a funeral home) and wiped his eyes. Then he broke into a big smile and joked that he wouldn't charge us extra for that performance. But I know it wasn't an act. He seemed to surprise himself. People probably don't ask him about his job very much. They don't want to know.

What is remarkable about Caleb's story is not the inevitable melancholy, but his brave confrontation not only with death, but with the fate of his body afterward. Here was an eight-year-old child as far from being in denial as one could be.

Ω Ω Ω

In New Orleans, people are proud of doing things differently from the rest of the country, including death. The city is famous for its raised tomb cemeteries and jazz funerals.[16] That said, the city is heavily Catholic, if not in reality, then in cultural influence, which has meant a very slow rise in the cremation rate. One New Orleans funeral director told me that it was still only at 30 percent, meaning most bodies are embalmed unless the family follows conservative Jewish or Muslim practice. But embalming doesn't have to be boring. Death is changing in New Orleans too. Only differently. New Orleanians not only continue to look death in the face; they encourage it to look back.

I spoke to Patrick in the expansive Victorian house that is the mothership of his family's mortuary business. Patrick is a fifth-generation funeral director. His great-great-grandfather started the business according to a classic pattern, transitioning from livery service after a major yellow-fever epidemic in 1874. Patrick's ancestor entered a new profession rising fast out of the bones and ashes of the Civil War.

Patrick walks us through the multi-parlor home, pointing out various antiques, each with an interesting provenance or story. But the reason I wanted to interview Patrick was not because his business epitomizes a classic Southern funeral home worthy of Hollywood, but because he had recently helped arrange a quite unusual funeral. He is happy to talk about the final chapter of Mickey Easterling's story. "She was sitting up on her park bench—it was a wrought-iron bench from her backyard. She was fully dressed. She had a diamond pin on, and she had her little cigarette holder with a cigarette, [and] the boa. She was a New Orleans socialite, and she just wanted to host her last party. You almost have to see it [to understand], 'cause it *does* have a little shock value." He said this last sentence with a coy smile, suggesting something a tad naughty.

Mickey Easterling had been embalmed in a *wakeful* position. Some funeral directors whisper the name for this new technique:

"extreme embalming." Quick research indicates that the trend started in Puerto Rico in the mid-2000s. It remains a novelty in Latin America and has appeared in the United States, to my knowledge, only in New Orleans. I am interested that it exists at all. Extreme embalming is an example of how quickly death practices can flow across national and ethnic lines.[17]

Ms. Easterling was not the first, nor the last, New Orleanian to be embalmed this way. Uncle Lionel Baptiste, a beloved jazz musician from a well-known musical family in the Afro-Creole neighborhood of Tremé, led the way in 2012. For his funeral, Uncle Lionel was embalmed in a standing position, supported cleverly by a fake streetlamp. Known for his dapper dress, he attended his own visitation in a cream-colored suit, a bowler hat, and a brightly colored necktie with a matching pocket kerchief. According to a newspaper account, "His head was cocked slightly to the left. He appeared ready to step from behind the velvet rope and saunter off to Frenchmen Street, where he reveled in dancing and drinking beer. 'He looks better today than when I saw him the Thursday before he died,' said Storyville Stompers tuba player Woody Penouilh." These very special arrangements had been designed according to the wishes of Baptiste's son, who said he wanted the service to reflect his dad, who was "an original." He had promised his father he would send him out in style. A sense of fun and humor were de rigueur. Although the media tried to milk the "shock value" of Baptiste's funeral, as Patrick called it, there was a notable absence of negative reactions from attendees: "I was looking for him to move. . . . That's something I've never seen before. It's perfect. It's a wonderful, strange thing." The Charbonnet Funeral Home also runs five generations deep. The senior director said that in his fifty years of experience, he had never embalmed a body like this before. He declined to share his trade secrets but quipped: "You have to

think outside the box. And so he's outside the box. We didn't want him to be confined to his casket."[18]

While I presume there are extra fees involved for the services of extreme embalming, subjects do not have to be public figures like Uncle Lionel or Mickey Easterling. Before her death, "Ms. Mae" was not well known outside the backwater New Orleans neighborhood where she lived most of her fifty-three years. After she died in a hospital following complications from a stroke in 2014, her niece, whom she had raised as a daughter, took charge of her final arrangements. When I asked Zymora what moved her to make the unusual choice she did, she told me that she needed a little more time with her aunt, and also that she was special, and her wake needed to reflect that. At the funeral home, Mae's body was set up at her own kitchen table in her Saints football jersey, smoking a cigarette, and drinking a Busch beer. Guests were invited to sit and visit with her, taking "visitation" to a new level. As we talked together about a year after the funeral, Zymora kept slipping into the present tense.

She was just different. She had a big heart. She can be the funniest. She can be the meanest—but in a good way! Her personality is really indescribable. And I know what she wants. She loves her family. She loves to party. I organized a whole party. I had tables set up with beer, shot glasses. They took shots of alcohol at the funeral. It was a party, but she was just deceased and not physically there. I wanted happiness, and it was happy. Mae was loving. She was a teenager. And I missed that.

I have puzzled over Zymora saying that her aunt was "not physically there." This suggests that she does not identify Mae with her body. But Mae was (is) present in some other way that helped create the party. Perhaps Ms. Mae's corpse and spirit are different entities that were starting to separate in the ritual process that Hertz had observed in other cultures. Ms. Mae seemed to be, at least in some imaginative way, witnessing the event. Zymora said, "I know she's not going to forget this." Rather than being creepy (at least for the friends and family who responded favorably to the event), Mae's corpse in its in-between state facilitated a joyful event, and it bought time for a longer goodbye. It had the semblance of a party that would have been a natural for Ms. Mae when she was alive.

The need for more time is felt especially by those who have lost someone prematurely or unexpectedly. The next case of extreme embalming in New Orleans occurred in 2018, of a young man who had been gunned down at the age of eighteen. For his service, also arranged by Mr. Charbonnet, Renard Matthews was propped up in a chair, facing a TV screen with a PlayStation controller in his hands. His family wanted to remember him doing something he loved. It was a memory picture, or maybe a memory sculpture, that placed him in a happy time before the shooting.[19]

Ω Ω Ω

If you really want to deny death, wouldn't you run away from the corpse? Wouldn't you close the casket, cremate quickly, or substitute a photograph of the person as the centerpiece of the memorial service? Or have no service at all? In fact, all these alternatives to embalming and visitation are trending right now. I have learned that the relationship between American funeral practices and death denial is more complicated than has been assumed by most scholars and culture critics. While for many people, viewing the embalmed body in an open casket may not accomplish the magical healing work it once did, some intriguing facts emerge from looking more closely at this exotic American custom.

Embalmers sincerely believe that interacting with a restored, peaceful-looking corpse is therapeutic. As Bob intimated, embalming is a purification ritual meant to neutralize the dangerous emotional effects (misunderstood as medical ones) that the dead can have on the living. Mourners need to not be rushed into accepting the inevitable—meaning putrefaction. Decay would make the body look less like the person they knew, which would throw everything off. As Michael said, it's all about the individual. The body-person is the sacred object of the funeral ritual.

Embalming is a kind of healing magic, according to traditional funeral directors, because it helps friends and family overcome the denial that a death has occurred, creating an opening to the final stage of grief—acceptance. It buys the living time to gather their thoughts and say goodbye. It gives them an opportunity to see and talk to their loved one. The benefits of corpse therapy are also promoted by Jerrigrace and her allies in the home-funeral movement, even if their go-to method of temporary preservation is dry ice rather than formaldehyde.

American embalming was just the latest technological practice introduced to satisfy a pronounced need to visually engage with the dead. Americans, one way or another, have literally been looking death in the face for over two hundred years. Embalming was a dramatic innovation within an older tradition we could call "death witnessing." Witnessing honors the dead by contemplating and honoring their unique body-soul. In that lingering look, the relationship between the dead and the living is prioritized over a godly one.

The magic that embalming and restoration performs is not about making a mummy but, rather, about manipulating the perception of time. I can see Robert Hertz nodding his head in the anthropological afterlife. Embalming is a way to stretch out the ambiguous liminal period between biological and social death. Sleep is the middle ground. The dead are always (well, almost always) embalmed with their eyes closed, and caskets are designed with pillows and satin liners. Embalming magically reverses time to a period before suffering and before the event of death itself. It slows time way down, allowing for multiday rituals and deferring the onset of decomposition. The embalmed deceased, hovering in an in-between state between two worlds, is not-quite-dead-yet. This lingering, however it is accomplished, helps social and emotional wounds to heal through a gradual departure. It is not that Americans have used embalming as an illusion to deny death. Rather, they developed it as a ritual to slow death down—to take a lingering look and say a long goodbye. For all its twentieth-century exoticism, the national ritual of embalming and viewing actually put Americans in good non-Western company. The funeral rite was doing precisely what old-fashioned functional anthropology said it should be doing: holding people together.

CHAPTER 3

Bones

My most treasured piece of jewelry is a little glass vial attached to a gold chain. Inside, visible through the glass, is one ounce of Jessa. Her mother, my sister-in-law, filled the cork-topped vial herself. When I look at it, I often wonder what her frame of mind might have been as she handled her daughter's ashes. I think of the necklace more as talisman than memento mori. It is not a morbid thing. Its purpose is to remind us not of death but of life—of Jessa. With it present in my hand, I can more easily address her in my thoughts. My niece exists in many objects and places now, spread out among her family and friends. I've worn the necklace a couple of times, but most of the time it dangles from a framed photograph of Jessa, a beautiful selfie that she took shortly before she died. She looks like a tender teenage blossom.

Ω Ω Ω

"Is the camera off? Is that thing off?" Adam asks me, pointing to Daniel's camera. Daniel flips a switch and steps away from the tripod. Adam is by turns charming and grumpy in our interview at his suburban funeral home. I had asked him what he thinks about the trend toward cremation. He pauses and looks at me grimly: "It's industrial incineration." He knows that most of his clients aren't all that interested in the truth of the matter.

"Retorts," as they are called in the business, are large incinerators built of stainless steel, aluminum, and kiln brick, equipped with conveyer belts and computerized button controls. They spew enough particulate matter out of their smokestacks that the Environmental Protection Agency regularly monitors them. Sometimes the local fire department shows up if the smoke gets too black. Although some funeral homes and cemeteries have crematories on location, these days they are more often located in urban industrial zones alongside welding shops and airports. And embalming facilities.

Crematories are sites of centralized mass processing. They have refrigerated holding rooms where bodies wait their turn. During business hours, hearses and reefer trucks come and go, delivering bodies from several (sometimes dozens of) funeral homes. Retorts fire at 1,500 to 1,800 degrees Fahrenheit (about 800–1,000 degrees Celsius) using natural gas or propane. They are cousins to incinerators made by the same manufacturers used to dispose of medical and other waste. The cremation process takes forty-five minutes to two hours, depending on the design of the retort and the size of the person. One of the largest retort suppliers reports that its average "destruction rate" is one hour per hundred pounds. But the retort is not a magical machine that transforms the corpse into the precious dust that we have come to expect. Human labor is required. The crematory attendant uses a rake to verify that the casket or coffin (usually no more than a cardboard box), clothing, and flesh have disappeared and that the bones are dry and ready to crumble. The larger pieces, such as the skull, may need a little help with a metal poker. The bones emerge from the retort in large, recognizable fragments, as they do in traditional outdoor pyre cremations in other parts of the world. In traditions where the bones are destined for an urn, box, or other container, an additional step involves breaking up the larger pieces by hand so that they will fit easily into their final resting object. After cremation and funeral urns started to be embraced more broadly in Europe at the end of the nineteenth century, the grinding process was also industrialized through the invention of the cremulator, a grinding mill that crushes the bones into the consistency of fine gravel and sand. Cremulation obliterates anything visually referencing a recognizable human being, which soon became a desirable side effect.[1]

Perhaps it is about taking the biblical idea of "dust to dust" as literally as you can. In English, we colloquially refer to the output of the industrial cremation process as "ash," but technically, it is roasted, pulverized bone. Ash from wood or coal consists primarily of carbon residue, while in cremation most of the body's carbon gets burned away. "Bone dust" would be more accurate. Some people have started to call the end product "cremains," but most death-care professionals I spoke to find this neologism distasteful. As with embalming, there are a lot of public misconceptions about cremation, above all that it is greener and less wasteful than a traditional burial. In fact, most retorts require a significant amount of fossil fuel to operate. Combustion and the burning off of organic material result in emissions of carbon dioxide (the main greenhouse gas) with a mix of other harmful gases (sulfur dioxide, nitrous oxides) and particulates that can include heavy metals. After things have cooled down, what remains is mostly phosphate (48 percent), calcium (25 percent), and a medley of sulfate, salts, potassium, silica, and trace amounts of a long list of metals depending on the person's age, diet, region, and medical history. Pacemakers and surgical implants are routinely removed prior to firing because they can jam up the cremation process and even cause explosions. Smaller items like dental fillings or jewelry left on the body are picked out with a large magnet before everything is put through the cremulator.[2]

Ω Ω Ω

Cremation can be romantic. In 1822, the poet Percy Shelley was cremated on a pyre on a beach in Italy by Lord Byron and friends after a boating accident. In death as in life, Romantics wanted to bring back what they thought were the nobler practices of ancient Greece and Rome. The embrace of cremation by educated Europeans started to chip away at cultural (and largely Christian) biases against it, but cremation did not take off until the later nineteenth century. And then, for quite different reasons. Industrial cremation was promoted to address a perceived crisis in England and continental Europe over smelly, overcrowded urban cemeteries. Early experiments applied the new technology to the bodies of the indigent. While the Sanitary Movement did not contribute to the adoption of embalming in Europe as it did in the United States, it did support the expansion of cremation, which increasingly became the "clean" disposition option preferred by non-Catholics in continental Europe, the United Kingdom, and Australia in the twentieth century. However, this genealogy is probably a bit too neat and Eurocentric. Historian David Arnold argues that another significant factor in its adoption was the strident defense of traditional cremation by Indian Hindus, Buddhists, and Sikhs against critiques of the colonial British government. The debate led to a greater public awareness of cremation and a practical need to accommodate the Indian diaspora.[3]

Cremation as a human funerary practice runs deep into antiquity. Archaeological evidence indicates that ancient Australians were practicing cremation at least twenty thousand years ago, possibly much longer. Cremation ash is ephemeral and easily missed on archaeological sites. It will blend into the other layers of dirt and trash in the ground unless preserved within cinerary urns or chests. Cremation was likely practiced in Asia long before the rise of Hinduism and Buddhism (four thousand and twenty-five hundred years ago, respectively), two religions that have encouraged and sometimes prescribed it. In the Near East and Europe, archaeologists have found evidence of cremation urns and containers dating to at least five thousand years ago. More recently, in imperial Rome, cinerary urns filled with burned bones could be works of art, crafted in marble, alabaster, or glass. Elites placed urns in ornate cemetery tombs, where family members could commemorate the dead on important occasions, especially the Roman Day of the Dead. Among plebeians, urns could take nearly any container form, from a rectangular wooden box to a wine bottle. In Bronze Age and Iron Age Europe, Anglo-Saxons and other "barbarians" practiced cremation before Christianity and its peculiar cult of the revenant dead wiped out this form of disposition (it was thought that cremated bodies could not be resurrected on Judgment Day). Protestantism, neo-paganism, secularism, and the influence of immigrants from the colonies opened the way for cremation to return to Europe in the nineteenth century. The revival of cremation also meant the return of fancy Roman-style urns. Shelley would have been pleased.[4]

The story of modern cremation is one part historical revival and one part industrial innovation. But the desire for a more "authentic," or perhaps Romantic, version of cremation is growing in the United States. In line with the home-funeral or

green-burial movement's critique of embalming and commer-
cialized death care, advocates would like to see less technology
and more family autonomy. They see open-pyre funerals as
more in tune with the natural elements as well as ancient human
practices. Eric in Guerneville loved the idea of a Viking ship
cremation. His desires are not uncommon among younger
Americans. A student and fellow archaeologist was kind enough
to let Daniel and me interview him at the beginning of our film
collaboration. My intent was to use Joe as a guinea pig in a practice run, just to figure out what the hell I was doing—how to
stand next to Daniel but stay out of the shot, how to help him
with staging and sound, how to move a conversation along
while making sure it would still be editable later. Joe ended up
being one of the most charismatic people on camera that we
ever interviewed. He also surprised me, like Eric did, with how
much he had thought about what he wanted.

> I would like to be immolated. I would like to be burned. I've
> always felt a fascination with, and an attachment to, fire. Ex-
> cept for random fires (forest fires, accidental fires), most fire
> is social. Most fire [is so] people come together to cook, to
> eat, to stay warm, to say goodbye. If you want an opportunity
> for your friends to come together, in a place of warmth, when
> you have passed, I think that rather than in a sterile hall in a
> funeral parlor, [it should be] on the bank of a river some-
> where with a little bit of wine and a fire—I can't think of a
> better way to say goodbye.

As Joe noted in our conversation, this death option isn't actually legal yet in most of the United States. It is more difficult
to control an open fire and to account for all the human remains
when they are mixed up with a cord of wood. The tiny town of
Crestone, Colorado, has become famous as a center for spiritual

retreats in the Hindu and Buddhist traditions—and the hippie tradition. It is also the only place in the United States at the time of this writing where open-pyre funerals are permitted, through the Crestone End of Life Project. Interest has been so high that organizers quickly had to institute a rule that their services were available only to residents and landowners of Saguache County. There's now a small population boom in the area. Meanwhile, in Missouri, Democratic state senator Jason Holsman sponsored a bill in 2019 to make it the first state to legalize open-air cremation entirely. In an era of political divisiveness, the measure passed both houses, but it was vetoed by the governor for not detailing enough how "health and safety concerns" would be addressed. Holsman's bill was nicknamed the "Jedi Disposal Act," after funeral-pyre scenes in the Star Wars movies. But he cited other cultural influences: "The Vikings, the Native Americans, the settlers. . . . I personally would like to have the end-of-life process be an open-air ceremony. I don't want to be put in a kiln; I don't want to be put in the ground. And right now, the crown, the government is telling me that I can't do that. And I think that's un-American." Holsman's opinion that the government should not dictate how we care for the dead suggests that very American ideas about civil liberties are now coming into conflict with civil religion. A kind of funereal anti-Federalism. He did stress to his fellow legislators, however, that passing this law would put Missouri in a unique position to grow a cottage industry for a national market. Entrepreneurialism is never far behind in America.[5]

Industrial crematory operators have not been entirely deaf to the demand for religious freedom. One of the modern accommodations they have made for Hindus and others who believe in the importance of witnessing the cremation has been the introduction of viewing rooms where, from behind a window, the family can watch the body enter the retort. It has also become fairly common to allow a family member to activate the start button on the machine—the equivalent of being the torchbearer.

Technologies for reducing the dead to manageable remains continue to evolve. Given the fossil fuel consumption and resulting pollution emitted by incinerators, engineers have been working on other solutions. Alkaline hydrolysis is sometimes advertised as "green cremation" or "water cremation" because it does not directly involve fossil fuel and smoke. Now approved in a handful of states, it is a process that dissolves the soft tissues in a heated bath of an alkaline solution (the opposite of acid). Another method still under development is Promession (a term trademarked by its inventor), which involves freeze-drying and then shaking the corpse until it shatters into thousands of pieces. All this ingenuity speaks to a remarkable need to process human bodies through accelerated means. One motivation is to get through the icky part of decomposition quickly, but another may be so that the family can have the remains back as soon as possible to perform death rituals. As with embalming, the disposition ritual is about controlling time. While embalming slows down social death, cremation speeds up biological death.[6]

Ω Ω Ω

The classic curvy urn form is based on a similar container type used in classical times for oils, ointments, and other products, called a "ginger jar." With a removable lid, it is a vessel designed for storage of accessible contents. Archaeologists will tell you that storage of food and other necessities, an underappreciated human practice, has driven much of human cultural innovation, allowing us to imagine and plan for the future and manage risks in times of disaster or scarcity. Storage or hoarding also provides the means for controlling supply and demand and thus amassing wealth. It's all a futures game.

In the case of the cremated remains of a loved one, however, for what possible future are the remains being stored? In other societies, an urn with dry bone might have been a convenient way to preserve a bit of the ancestors who were asked to play a part in occasions on the ritual calendar. But ancestor worship doesn't square with the supposedly anti-idolatry religious majorities found in the United States. Sure, cremation is the cheaper option, but with the emotional intensity that comes with the momentous event of death, it seems unlikely that it all comes down to money, even when that is the explanation offered by those planning their own arrangements. As with embalming, few people have paused to ask what modern cremation practice means for those who undertake it. The history of industrial pro-cremation movements in the West makes clear that it was tied up with debates over nuisance problems in densely populated cities. In making their case, proponents often tried to gross people out, helping them to imagine the disgusting process of decay that would inevitably liquefy their loved ones underground through the seething activities of worms, grubs, and invisible bugs. At the peak of sanitation fever at the turn of the nineteenth century (circa 1880–1920), this was an effective strategy. Cremation was also, though, tied up with religion and anti-religion. Stephen Prothero documents how it was embraced particularly by anti-Catholics in the United States, but was also the disposition of choice for atheists, spiritualists, and several competing flavors of Protestants, all for different ideological reasons. Cremation has never been just about cost and convenience.[7]

What happens after cremation? There is no dearth of stories about urn accidents involving cats and children, and the awkward follow-up: to vacuum or not to vacuum. Our discomfort makes for good comedy, as in scenes about ash accidents in movies like *The Big Lebowski* or *Meet the Parents*. I think we laugh because we don't know what we're doing or why we are doing it. Cremation may be a good example of a little-discussed anthropological phenomenon: the half-assed cultural practice. Americans have for decades been bumbling around trying to come up with rituals, etiquette, and rationales for a material practice that was decided upon with little thought for the aftermath. Although cremation is essentially "industrial incineration," as Adam put it, or a form of waste disposal, it is exceedingly difficult to treat human remains, even in the sanitized and convenient form of cremation ash, as inert material. What to do then?

In the Victorian period, Roman-style urns became popular in both cemeteries and domestic spaces. Urns were used as ornamental planters in gardens and "ginger jar" porcelain urns were often among the knickknacks on cluttered mantelpieces of the middle and upper classes. Just when these tchotchkes started to be used to keep the remains of loved ones at home is a little harder to trace, although references to them start to crop up in literary culture by the early 1900s. Still, most funerary "urns" advertised in mid-twentieth-century trade magazines were in the form of wooden boxes. Although cemeteries quickly adjusted to the rising popularity of cremation in the 1960s by offering columbaria, or wall niches, and in-ground urn burials (still the only destination of cremated remains approved by the Catholic Church), a parallel movement to "take it with you" sprang up. Or rather, to take your loved one with you. Those urns on the mantelpiece were ready receptacles. But how many boxes of ashes simply got placed in a closet, mostly forgotten?

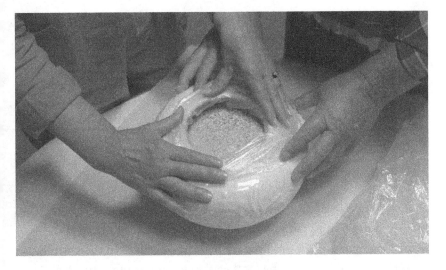

When a widow dies or when a house gets sold, an unsettled estate may include the unwanted inheritance of human remains. According to the Cremation Association of North America, the destiny for cremation remains breaks down in about equal thirds in the United States: one-third are deposited in a cemetery, one-third are scattered, and one-third are brought home in a box or urn. Of those who bring ashes home, more people say they keep them there "because I don't know what else to do" than say they do it "to keep my loved one close."[8]

Around 60 percent of the urns that are purchased are kept at home in the United States, at least for a time. The rest are deposited in cemeteries. Today the funerary market offers a dizzying range of choices, from one-of-kind art objects to mass-produced, biodegradable urns. Maureen runs a small art gallery called Funeria located in Graton, California. She has curated what may be the most unique collection of contemporary urns in the world. Gallery visitors will find, arranged on pedestals and shelves, beautiful carved-wood ginger jars, a blue ceramic dog, a tiny Etruscan tomb, and a boat reminiscent of Charon's vessel that crosses the Styx. Maureen has pursued an interest in design her entire life, although not following the most conventional of paths. As a child she sketched imaginary bomb shelters. By midlife she had developed a career designing exhibit spaces for trade shows. In the early 2000s, she started sponsoring design competitions and juried shows for artist-designed urns. Maureen says she sees urns as another kind of shelter. But they are also a kind of packaging.

> When I saw that there was an abysmal lack of beautiful designs in urns, I thought, well, what is a life? It's all about packaging. Packaging is how we present ourselves to the world when we're alive, the clothes that we choose for ourselves, the entertainment that we choose that reflects our taste, the books we read and share—those are all reflections of who we are as individuals. When we're gone, however, what's left of us?

Of course, this self-packaging is subject to significant cultural influences that shape popular choices, and consciously or unconsciously constrain our personal style. Or even provide the rules of "good taste" that we can willfully choose to break. Maureen notes that Victorian mortuary culture, with its gothic, all-black aesthetic, did not offer many choices to people of the time, but it is even less appropriate for contemporary Americans: "That really doesn't reflect contemporary taste and character. We're a colorful people. We're vibrant and exciting, and we do lots of different things."

Some of us also have a sense of humor. One attention-grabbing piece in her gallery is the *Urnamatic*, which appears to be a readapted vintage vacuum cleaner. It offers one way to make the best of those mantelpiece accidents, winking toward them and suggesting the whole absurdity of ash keeping. My favorite, though, is a gumball machine filled with clear plastic spheres—the kind that dispense small throwaway toys. Instead of toys, twenty-five cents will get you "a little bit of Uncle Joe," as Maureen says. The spheres are intended to be filled with ash (there's just newspaper in the demonstration model). The artist's idea is that at a memorial service, any friends or family members who want to, provided they have a quarter, can take home a little bit of Uncle Joe to keep or to scatter wherever they wish. Clearly, this option wouldn't be appropriate if Uncle Joe had been a humorless prude.

Although tombs, urns, and burials are often on the minds of archaeologists, I have not found that people in the death-care industry think that much about archaeology or the ways they are creating a material record for the future. Maureen is an exception. As a girl, she was fascinated by the archaeology galleries at the Metropolitan Museum of Art in New York—especially the ones with sarcophagi and wrapped mummies. She hopes that someday the urns in her gallery will be found "in the rubble." She means this in a good way. "It's going to tell future archaeologists who we were. We're not just going to be remembered for our cell phones and our technology. We'll be remembered for beautiful craftsmanship, great imagination, and care." I hope Maureen is right about our archaeological future. But Funeria serves a niche market. And it faces major competition in the fast-growing trends of ash scattering and objects that incorporate, rather than contain, human remains.

Ω Ω Ω

Some types of ash scattering are involuntary. It is a different type of rubble that brought Lee to apply her own art skills to the dead. Lee was working at her computer programming job in the Twin Towers in lower Manhattan when the planes struck on September 11, 2001. She made it out. Many co-workers did not. Some were atomized, their remains raining down on the people below. It was mass incineration. A traumatic, involuntary funeral pyre.

Of the 2,753 people reported dead, more than 1,000 have never been identified. Too little remained. Too little could be separated from the rubble. After the attack, Lee gave up her tech career and moved back to Ohio. There she rediscovered her love for making art. Eventually, she opened an art glass studio called Glass Remembrance that makes custom pieces incorporating cremated remains. Her work captures and keeps what would be lost in scattering, voluntary or otherwise—small bulwarks against total annihilation.

Lee is one member of a new movement in the United States that follows out an impulse to transform some organic essence of the deceased person into a new object. Some people call these objects "keepsakes" or "memorial objects," but this makes them sound like mere souvenirs. They are clearly so much more powerful—simultaneously more visceral and more metaphysical—than that. I sometimes call them "death objects," but that fails to get at their vitality. It is hard to come up with the right words. While apparently inanimate, they are designed to play an active role in the lives of those left behind. Some people talk to them, even bring them along to family events. They stir up thoughts and feelings. In short, they facilitate an ongoing relationship between the living and the dead. And although some of them might appear identical to others made in the same factory or workshop, these death objects are understood by their makers and their keepers as absolutely one of a kind.

The options for incorporating cremated human remains into various types of objects are proliferating even faster than urn designs. Among the most popular are those that involve some sort of secondary firing. This suggests a two-part transformation— the first to purify and reduce, the second to forge something new. Intentional phoenixes. Crucibles of destruction and creation.

Lee is not the only one making glass objects, although hers stand out for being custom art pieces. Cremated remains can be easily incorporated into ceramics as well. In fact, there is a history of "bone China" from England in which crushed animal bones were mixed into clay and fired at high temperatures to approximate the recipe for Chinese porcelain. We are animals too. You could say this is a functional repurposing of our biomatter, though that's not how these pieces are marketed. A designer in New Mexico made a set of dinnerware with a human glaze. He has since moved on to create ceramic objects he calls Parting Stones. His company offers to "purify" cremation remains so that they can be touched and displayed in a collection of twenty-five to thirty smooth white rocks of various sizes. The pitch on their website addresses the anxieties we might have about handling human remains in a cruder state, as well as the possibilities for nurturing a healthy relationship between the dead and the living: "Solidified remains let you feel a meaningful connection with your departed. No more uncomfortable ash."[9] Parting Stone bluntly sells a purification ritual—a transformation of dangerously potent and polluting human remains into a more easily managed sacred object. And there is the appeal of permanence. We *can* be turned to stone. I am reminded of stories of petrifaction in myths and fairy tales (and Harry Potter), when the life force of someone gets trapped in something solid and unmoving through a magical transformation. Perhaps that's not far off.

Maureen is right about the packaging. Americans are increasingly choosing post-life packages that reflect who they were when they were alive. In the death industry, this is called "personalization."[10] This term can refer to a coffin designed with the logo of your favorite sports team (the American equivalent of a clan totem), or a 3D-printed urn in the shape of your favorite vintage car. Actress Carrie Fisher's ashes reside in a giant Prozac pill. Prince's ashes are stored in a miniature version of his Paisley Park house and studio. Now he is always home. More and more, objects considered iconic of the person are determining the packaging rather than any shared aesthetic. The entrepreneurial response to this personalization trend may be behind the proliferation of options more than the artistic impulses of people like Maureen or Lee. That said, traditional funeral directors are often more conservative than their clientele, working within a business culture that prioritizes "human dignity" according to principles that the people they serve may not share. Several of them told me that one of their major tasks is to educate people about the need to show dignity for human remains and what that means. The death-care industry does not just respond to cultural currents but attempts to shape them. And sometimes it fails.

Even if they decline to offer the most attention-grabbing products, most of the death-care professionals I talked to express the importance of personalizing urns, coffins, and other objects to reflect the personality and tastes of the deceased, not those of the living. Whether unique or mass-produced, though, how much of the *person* is captured in the packaging?

Ω Ω Ω

When human remains become an integral component of a memorial commodity, the line between subject and object blurs.

As I talked to people about these "objects," I noticed that the speaker will often slip from talking about "it" to talking about "him," "her," or "them." Even entrepreneurs who try to stay agnostic about the realm of the spirit fall into this habit.

"Personhood" is a much-used and much-debated term in anthropology, but it marks something that we might otherwise take for granted—that the definition of a "person" is fluid and culturally defined. We need not look far to grasp this point. The abortion debate has been said to teeter on the definition of when "life" begins, but this characterization is patently false. Most biologists recognize that cells in a petri dish are a form of "life" as long as they can reproduce themselves, but few people have a problem terminating a small colony of E. coli. Rather, the crux of the human abortion debate turns on when a *person* begins.

A person and an individual are not necessarily the same thing. Within anthropology, it is generally recognized that not all cultures share the concept of the individual. Individualism, rugged or otherwise, is so fundamental to the American worldview that it can be a challenge to comprehend how culturally particular it is as an ideology. That said, even within the modern United States, different types of ethical and political individualisms compete with one another, from far right conservatives to libertarians and identitarian liberals. But individualists generally agree that each human being is unique, has rights, and that their personhood is bounded by an equally unique biological body. Under individualism, body and mind are integrally connected to one another and to the consciousness that we subjectively experience inside our heads as "the self."[11] In the United States, individuals are important legal entities whose rights are protected against those of the group. In broader cultural terms, we talk about the "identity" of the individual in ways that often reference visible physical characteristics—age, sex, race, body type, etc. All this is to say that personhood in the United States has historically been based on the idea of the unique, embodied individual.[12]

In other societies, personhood may not be predicated on *either* the individual *or* the human body. Persons—or parts of them—escape their bodies all the time through dreams, possession, magic, and, of course, through death. They become ghosts and ancestors, or bits of them break off to reenter the world reincarnated. Further, belief systems across the world formally or informally recognize animals, tree spirits, rivers, and sacred mountains as persons.

Anthropologist Marilyn Strathern offered the concept of the "dividual," as opposed to the individual, to explain how Melanesian people conceive of human personhood, which is as a manifestation of different social relationships. Her theory helps explain why in some societies the individual is more important than the group, while in other societies quite the opposite is true (so-called individualist versus corporatist, or egocentric versus sociocentric societies). These terms express key differences in how personhood is conceived, best put by another anthropologist, Karl Smith:

> In the simplest terms, the individual is considered to be an indivisible self or person. That is, it refers to something like the essential core, or spirit of a singular human being, which, as a whole, defines that self in its particularity. To change, remove or otherwise alter any part of that whole would fundamentally alter the "self"; she/he would then be, effectively, a different person. By contrast, the dividual is considered to be divisible, comprising a complex of separable—interrelated but essentially independent—dimensions or aspects.

In a dividual belief system, there is a part of me that is a sister. That part of me is quite similar to the equivalent part in someone reading this who is also a sister. As a dividual, I am an amalgam of different social relationships. I am as unique as that combination (sister/mother/teacher/writer/neighbor), but my personhood will inherently change over time as my relationships and roles evolve. In an individual system, the person is thought to have a unique core essence (spirit, soul, personality) that is indivisible and endures throughout the stages of life. While the person may develop and adapt over time, such changes are more likely to be associated with the aging body than with changing social roles. In a classic individualist worldview, a singular person can feel "trapped" inside their body, but in the contemporary United States, this distinction becomes blurred. Identities are so glued to physical appearance that the person in some ways *is* their body, or at least it is very hard to detach. This close association between personhood and the body under American individualism is another way to account for the importance of viewing the corpse in the traditional funeral—mourners are engaging with the person by interacting with their body.[13]

In the dividual worldview, identity is not fixed. And most importantly, the self is composed of recombinant parts. The result is a "partible self," or one that can be divided up and redistributed. In English, the most common use of this archaic adjective can be found in the phrase "partible inheritance." After someone dies, their wealth is divided up and distributed among their heirs. Is it possible that their personhood could be too?

Ω Ω Ω

"So, this one here is Peter," Craig says as he holds up a sphere of clear glass with a cloudy center. A little larger than a baseball, it fits perfectly in his hand. It looks heavy but not fragile. Craig is a gravelly-voiced, attractive man in his early sixties. With snow-white hair and a well-trimmed goatee, he looks a little like a wizard. Peter was one of his best friends; he died suddenly in 1997. Peter's cremated remains are trapped as a swirl in the center of the orb. Peter was the prototype for the hundreds of glass objects found in various states of production in the small industrial space where we are meeting—a business that Craig and his son Nick started in Southern California in the wake of the 2008 financial crash. Growing out of a makeshift operation in Craig's garage, the business has been growing steadily, keeping pace with the doubling of the US cremation rate between 2000 and 2015.

We walk through the office to the back workshop where the orbs and pendants that form the bulk of Craig and Nick's business are made. The air simmers from the nonstop work of the furnace, glory hole, and cooling kiln. Glassworking occurs at about 2,000 degrees Fahrenheit (1,100 degrees Celsius), a few hundred degrees hotter than cremation. Pontil rods, workbenches, shears, and other tools of the glassblowing trade lie scattered around the shop, as they would be in any art glass studio. But there are subtle differences. One is the extremely methodical and repetitive process that the handful of employees at Memory Glass follow as they produce up to two hundred objects per day. Breaking down each stage of manufacture into a discrete and uniform step, production is as carefully controlled as it would be in an assembly plant. But the manufacturing process is still *manual*, by hand. Their process lies somewhere between industrial production and craftwork. Another thing you wouldn't find in a normal glass studio is a curious locked cabinet along the back wall. While giving us a tour of the shop, Nick opened it to reveal rows of carefully organized, brightly colored bins about the size of tissue boxes. Each bin contains a single, small prescription bottle and its associated paperwork. Nick opens a couple of the bottles to show me the contents. One bottle contains dark granular matter that looks like coffee grounds. Another holds a fine milky powder. Nick says that every set of remains has a different texture and that colors range from black to gray, brown, and pink to even blue. "Everybody's individuality makes its way through and past death," he says. This individuality is a common article of faith among those in the death-care industry and among clients interested in the objects that Memory Glass forges.

While personalized grave markers and designer caskets offer one way to emphasize the individuality of the deceased, cremation objects do this by repackaging the individuality of the person's body, taking consumer personalization to a whole new level. As Nick says, "There are options to have your own version of death." Death can be customized. But these new products/ creations/entities also take *personhood* to a whole new level— and into a new medium. Such "objects" suggest that American conceptions of personhood are undergoing a fascinating transformation.

Nick had no prior experience in glassblowing or art, but he is the third generation of a family of entrepreneurs. His father, Craig, says the family has been secular, or nonreligious, for these same three generations. Although Memory Glass is Nick's baby, its origin story comes from his dad. Before becoming a successful real-estate developer, like many baby boomers, Craig went through a phase living as a hippie in the woods with a small community of artists and social experimenters. That was how he befriended Peter. After Peter died in a boating accident, his girlfriend wanted to do something unique to honor him. An artist and glassblower, she had the idea of taking some of his ashes and incorporating them into a glass globe. Her act

became the inspiration for a successful business ten years later. Peter is now spread around, distributed in different objects.

Back at the conference table in their reception area, Nick and Craig show me their prototypes. Peter is there, of course, but also the original Together Forever design, which contains the mixed remains of Nick's grandmother and grandfather. "Once in a while, we wonder if they are happy together like this," says Craig, making fun of his parents and testing me for a reaction. I note that there is only about a tablespoon of remains visible in this piece, as with their other models. I ask Craig what he did with the rest. His son shoots him a bemused look, and Craig looks a little sheepish. It turns out, the rest of his parents' ashes ride around in his truck, tossed in a box behind the seat. He keeps them there, ready for some unknown destination. He's not sure what else to do. He says he could just throw them out, into the trash. Cremation is, after all, a form of "waste disposal," he says, but he likes to keep them close and talk to them.

Nick holds up a more unusual piece, shaped like a breaking ocean wave, with opaque blue glass and a white inclusion representing sea foam. They made this custom piece for Craig's brother Rusty, who died suddenly and unexpectedly while visiting Craig a few years ago. The mood has shifted. Craig has no jokes to tell about finding his brother's body on the floor of his bathroom. Squinting with remembered pain, he said, "It's not something you ever forget." Rusty had been a lifelong surfer. Nick explains the glass wave: "It was sad to see him go, but we're happy to see him around like this, in something that is fitting."

The personal direction our conversation has taken prompts me to ask them about their own views on spirituality and the afterlife. I don't get a very straight answer. I suspect they hedge in part because they want to respect the spiritual beliefs of their clients, some of whom believe that the orbs contain some spiritual element of the deceased. Craig says that he just didn't like the idea of an urn sitting up on the mantelpiece. He prefers an orb. "It's unobtrusive. No one has to know that that is Peter." While we talk, Craig slips back and forth between referring to the orb as "Peter" and saying that it is just a bit of matter and memories. When I press him, he says he believes what continues after life are "memories" and our DNA, which itself, he suggests, encodes memories across generations. Trained as a biologist before his entrepreneurial turn, this sort of science-y afterlife makes sense to him.

When I ask Nick what he thinks happens to us after we die, he claims to be agnostic but admits that he has had some strange experiences. At any one time, the remains of hundreds of individuals occupy the building, and he says he can feel their presence. He then tells me a story about one set of remains they tried to shape into an orb five or six different times. Each time they placed an orb in the cooling kiln, it shattered. They tried making technical adjustments with the temperature, or the flux, or the timing. But still it kept happening. Their shop has developed such fine-tuned control over the process that an occurrence like this is quite rare. The failures were starting to unnerve the staff, so Nick called the funeral home that had sent in the remains to ask if there was anything distinctive about the cremation process or the individual. They could point to nothing unusual. The man had died in a car accident. Though he didn't die from the impact. He had died from lacerations caused by the shattered windshield. Nick concluded that this man's spirit did not want to be encased in glass. Although he says there is no way of knowing exactly what happens to us, after this experience he became convinced, "that there is an afterlife that we are a part of."

I am intrigued by Nick's language. There is an afterlife, but it is not the great *beyond*. It is right here with us. And we, the living, can take an active hand in crafting it.

Memory Glass guarantees that its products contain the unique and traceable remains of your loved ones. Thanks to the big conglomerates that dominate the death-care industry, the company can receive orders from over two thousand funeral homes across the country. The company goes to extreme lengths to control, verify, and track the remains throughout their process. An employee assigns a unique number to each sample as soon as it is received and uses this to track it through a detailed logging system for the different stages of production. Small security cameras are set up in every work space where remains are handled. If there is ever any question about the identity of any set of remains, they can pull up the recorded workday as proof. This concern with preserving and verifying the unique identity of human remains runs throughout the death-care industry. Legally, only one body can be cremated at a time, and it must enter a cremation retort in some sort of container so that there is no mixing or ambiguity about whose remains they are. An ethical and legal cordon surrounds each deceased person throughout all stages of handling, from retrieval at the place of death until the remains are either buried or released to the family. Mixing the cremated remains of individuals, as Memory Glass does in its Together Forever product, is something that family members can direct, but this choice represents something like a sacred right. Or rite. If a death-care worker did the mixing on their own initiative, or through negligence, it would be viewed not only as an act of desecration but as a crime. American law regarding the human body is a fascinating study in materialist thought. Technically, you "own" your body as property. After you die, your next of kin owns it. In between, you are property in the temporary care and custody of professionals who must protect it through a careful chain of custody.[14]

Memorial objects can blur into a type of forensic evidence. Memory Glass also makes small, wearable glass pendants, available in a variety of sixteen bright colors on the visible spectrum. Although customers select identical-looking products from the online catalog, each piece becomes one of a kind when a small amount of the remains they provide gets folded into the hot glass. To stamp this unique identity more visibly, for fifty dollars more, Memory Glass will etch the fingerprint of the deceased onto the cooled pendant using a laser cutter. Funeral directors collect the fingerprint in their preparation room before cremation. Each of these pendants is thus "encoded" with not just one but two biological signatures of the deceased. I say "encoded" because, as Craig notes, the knowledge that this piece of jewelry is made from a dead person is secret. No one needs to know. It is a private relationship between you and the dead.

Ω Ω Ω

An impulse to capture the code of an individual person and store it, even cherish it, cuts across different materials. Back on the floor of the National Funeral Directors Association convention, we met a salesman at one of the standard blue-curtained booths with displays of information and wares. Ben is a representative of a relatively new company that has developed a method for extracting DNA strands and attaching them to a stable, visible substrate that can be stored at room temperature. Normally, DNA handling requires a powerful microscope and lab-controlled freezers set to −112 Fahrenheit (−80 degrees Celsius). But DNA Memorial's target market is not the laboratory. Rather, it sells directly to the general public. The human DNA samples it repackages can be taken from either living or deceased subjects.

DNA Memorial's basic product, the Home Banking Vial, costs about $300. Ben showed us the floor sample, removing what looks like a jewelry box for an engagement ring from an acrylic display case. He opened the petite box ceremoniously to reveal a small glass vial, its authentication certificate attached with a tiny black ribbon. It looked like something from an eighteenth-century apothecary. Or a wizard shop.

I asked him why someone would want this product. "We work in the funeral industry now because ancestral DNA does have medical and genealogical value. So this is the last chance to save it, because, of course, cremation does destroy the genetic record, and after burial it is very difficult to retrieve. So we are really giving families the last chance to save the genetic record." The company claims that this miniature archive can provide an important source of medical information and genealogical history. Families will be able to better trace inherited disorders but also their "good traits" and potentially contribute to future gene therapies.

Ben expressed his enthusiasm in terms of both past ancestry and future technology. His perception of time, and the value of his wares, stretched far beyond the duration of an individual lifetime. But he also expressed the worth of his wares in familiar economic metaphors: "In a way, this is like a bit of an investment—because it does increase in value over time." He explained that people who understand the research value of DNA are on board immediately. But those who associate DNA with television crime shows are more wary (because it could be used against them?). Yet others get carried away with "misconceptions ... [and] talk about cloning." When I asked him if he tries to correct these misconceptions, he didn't exactly answer the question, but he noted that it usually takes a decade or two for scientific discoveries to trickle down to the general populace.

Ben then showed me other objects in the display case. His company is willing to provide customers what they want. This means they produce objects that have different kinds of value. Their first wearable product, which was his favorite, is a silver pendant necklace with a metal-capped vial. It is smaller than the Home Banking Vial but still displays a visible, fuzzy white thread suspended in some sort of liquid. It's "the real deal," he says—viable DNA that can be extracted at a later time. A miniature time capsule or human storage vessel.

I thought, "in case of emergency, break glass." It looks like one of those small glass time-delay fuses in vintage cars and old appliances. I know this only because my dad was an electrician. This artifact has its own peculiar resonance for me. But more generally, it suggests that to understand what is going on with American death right now, we need to understand how people think, act, and feel through objects.

Ben had some other wares to show us. One is a tear-shaped glass object with a white and a red swirl, reminiscent of Memory Glass's orbs in size and aesthetic. And there is a necklace with a glass heart pendant, with the DNA mixed in, barely visible. As Ben shows me this one, he explains, "just as DNA is unique to every individual, these pieces become *as* unique. So these are very sentimental pieces. The DNA is of course not still viable but it is mixed in there. These are all handmade and do come signed by the artist." While the Home Banking Vial has scientific value, these solid-glass pieces embedded with unusable genetic material are "sentimental." He encouraged me to try on another piece from the case—a ring with a royal blue stone in a gold setting. It looked like a petite graduation ring. But the opaque glass contains the unique code of a singular person. I forgot to ask who I was wearing. I was too much in awe. Not of some magical presence of a person (maybe that would be there if my dad's DNA had been inside) but of the fact that anything that precious could be bought and sold. DNA Memorial successfully sells notions and feelings. In that sales booth, I bought the idea that you could hold a miniature blueprint of a dead human being in your hand—their essence. And that, just perhaps, this person has a future, as well as a past. They also exist, in some partible state, in the now. On my finger.

Ω Ω Ω

While DNA Memorial is still a young start-up gambling on a speculative future, a company called LifeGem has been engineering its own mix of science and sentiment—and objects with a much deeper future—for the past twenty years. Dean had no prior experience in the funeral industry. Before founding LifeGem, he designed parts for the auto industry. The idea for his company came about from a preoccupation that had followed Dean's brother for years. He was not afraid of dying. Rather, he was terrified of being forgotten. This fear arose during childhood, but it stayed with him, even as he pursued a career as an airline pilot. Dean, a trained geologist and industrial engineer, at some point realized that the carbon of the human body could be captured and used to create a synthetic diamond.

Although cremation sends the vast majority of human carbon into the air, if not overdone, small amounts from the marrow and soft tissues will remain. Recovering this carbon is not straightforward. It requires special instructions to the crematory and a multistage purification process at the LifeGem lab. But LifeGem technicians can usually isolate enough of a sample (about two hundred milliliters, just shy of a one-cup measure) to make a diamond. They don't need (or want) remains of the whole body. Their process depends upon the partibility of the dead.

LifeGem transforms human remains into synthetic diamonds through a patented process that uses extreme heat and pressure to exponentially accelerate the natural geological process of converting base carbon to diamond. This general method has been used since the 1950s for the manufacture of diamonds for industrial applications. The same process has been used since the 1970s by the jewelry market to create alternatives to blood diamonds. To be clear—these are not cubic zirconia. Mineralogically speaking, they are "the real deal"—diamonds.

LifeGem's operation is located in a quiet industrial park near O'Hare airport in Chicago's Northwest suburbs. When you walk into the nondescript single-story building, there is no fancy showroom. Instead, you are greeted by a wall of sound. You know instantly that you are in the presence of hardworking machines. A thick glass wall encloses a half dozen machines.

The room looks like a medical lab and sounds like a blast furnace. The machines it houses are specialized furnaces and diamond presses that can exert nine hundred thousand pounds of pressure per square inch and an unfathomable amount of heat: 5,432 degrees Fahrenheit (3,000 degrees Celsius). During our walk-through, Dean explained that when a press finishes a diamond, the plates explode apart with a sound like a gunshot. It turns out that he didn't need to explain this, because one went off unexpectedly while we were talking. I jumped out of my skin and my ears rang. Dean apologized and seemed surprised himself. And a little embarrassed. Dean and his staff follow a meticulous technical process, but as at Memory Glass, there are limits to human control. Normally, they anticipate the completion stage for a diamond in process and wear industrial ear protectors during the expected time window. Making a diamond from human scratch is an expensive, slow, noisy, and hot process. And slightly dangerous.

Americans form the primary customer base for LifeGem (80 percent), followed by people from Japan, Canada, and a few other countries in Asia. The diamonds the company produces range widely in terms of size and color, and they cost between $2,500 and $25,000. The process takes patience. It requires a minimum of sixteen weeks for a tiny inset diamond to grow and could take up to a year for a larger diamond. LifeGem carefully tracks the human remains from the moment of arrival, assigning them a unique specimen number. Along with the finished diamond, the company returns any unused remains to the customer with a certificate of authenticity that includes a microscopically etched number that has been entered into a global diamond registry. Each diamond truly is unique. The carbon substrate comes from a person who lived an irreplicable life. The object made with their bodily substance bears a one-in-the-world identification

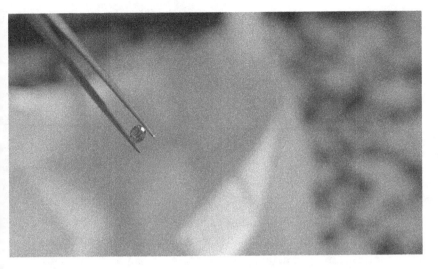

number. Their DNA, though, is thoroughly destroyed in the crucible.

I met a lot of interesting people while pursuing this project. Dean was different in a different way. Soft-spoken and precise, he talks like an engineer—not a salesperson, a visionary, an artist, or a care provider. He became the most animated when he talked about the idea that humankind can improve on nature. When I asked him why he thinks we value diamonds so much, he said that it is not only because they catch the light and sparkle like no other material, but because they are the hardest substance known to humankind and (under natural conditions) take millions, if not billions, of years to form from soft carbon. He says nature makes them randomly—by mistake. But his diamonds are all about intentional design.

It was the De Beers company that created the advertising slogan "A diamond is forever." LifeGem pushes this a step further—to the romantic implication that your *loved one* "is forever." Its process creates a very long afterlife in object form.

LifeGem diamonds are the most durable goods on the planet. They will outlast not only human memory but quite likely our entire species. The time frame of a LifeGem diamond is not ancestral time or a science-fiction future but geological time. Perhaps that is as close to eternity as we will ever come.

Diamonds are among the most expensive raw materials in the contemporary world economy, but Dean resists thinking about them in the way that diamonds are usually valued—as a cross-cultural symbol of wealth. Some people approach diamonds as a good way to store money, as they retain their monetary value even as currency values rise and fall. Solid as a rock. But Dean maintains that LifeGem diamonds are different from other diamonds. "A natural diamond or a traditional diamond in the jewelry profession can be viewed as an investment . . . but for our product, basically, it's a very personal material. It really is not made as an investment or something you would resell. I always joke: you know, nobody wants a diamond made from *me*."

These diamonds mess with our ideas of value. They are treasured because they last nearly forever and each one is utterly unique. But made from a once-living human being, they are also *too* unique to be exchangeable. They are expensive but truly priceless because there is no market for them. Diamonds are normally high-status items worn to communicate wealth and taste, but these particular rarities are not just about conspicuous consumption. As Craig said about Memory Glass orbs, "no one has to know." You can wear a LifeGem diamond, and it'll look pretty. But its value derives not from the potential of investment (a form of storage) nor from the potential of exchange (converting to money or other goods). These precious commodities are curiously resistant to normal economic thinking. Exchange value is based on relationships in the living world. The meaningful transaction here is between the living and the dead. The act of transforming your loved one into such a durable and costly little object proclaims that person's high value—their preciousness—but to you and no one else. *And* it expresses a wish that they will live on forever in some form. Or at least for two billion years.

Dean says that the most important common denominator of his clients is a close loving relationship with the deceased. Most of his clients are women who may already wear diamonds. The trace of remains that forms the seed of their diamond might be from a spouse, parent, child, or pet.[15] Some terminally ill clients decide on this transformation ahead of their biological death. Testimonials on the LifeGem website make it clear that these are not mere keepsakes, though that is the word Dean uses. For some clients, they clearly represent a new embodiment of the person. They refer to their diamonds as "Stan" or "Mom" and talk about how the unique properties of their diamonds (blue, rose, square-cut) reflect the personality of the departed. Several testimonials attest to the importance of having something *more* than memories, or as one woman put it, "it is lovely to have something tangible." According to one daughter, "When I first saw it in all of its beauty, tears came to my eyes, because I felt as if my mother's life essence was contained within the diamond." These objects can even activate the imaginative possibility of the dead participating in ongoing lives. One young woman wrote: "My grandma will be with me forever, when I walk down the aisle, when I take that amazing vacation. . . . You all have given me the opportunity to do the things I couldn't do before, because I wanted my grandma with me when I did so." Almost all of LifeGem's customer feedback refers to the healing properties of the diamonds in helping with grief. There is something therapeutic about transforming the dead into a material object. While engagement with the corpse—another material object—is said to help with healing in the short term, the curative properties of cremation objects extend through time. They aren't about "closure." In fact, quite the opposite. They are about creating an opening—a portal between the living and the dead, the means for an ongoing relationship.

Dean, like almost all of the entrepreneurs I have interviewed, treads these spirit waters carefully. He tries not to judge clients who express mystical ideas about the properties of their human diamonds. But he did say that he thinks we are witnessing a new blend of science and spirituality. I think he's right. Although this blend might depend more on scientific *notions* than scientific *facts*—like the notion that you could clone your grandmother or that DNA survives cremation or that our personhood is biologically determined.

Ω Ω Ω

Many Americans seem to be embracing the anonymity of these new death objects. They can disguise their loved one as an unremarkable piece of jewelry, or place them on a shelf with other collectibles, and no one has to be the wiser. There is something private and intimate about these objects. But do they also signal some lingering embarrassment about death? While I think the "death denial" argument has been overstated, it is not wrong to say that many Americans suffer from a profound social awkwardness around death—not knowing what to say, or what to do, when someone passes away. Many of us who have had significant or frequent losses share the experience of being made to feel that we are being "morbid" if we talk about the dead person, or that we need to see a shrink if we are still celebrating their birthday several years later. Maybe that's why so many of these new cremation objects are kept on the down-low. The dead are present, but to most beholders they are invisible, camouflaged as a commonplace commodity. That is one way that cremation objects are magical—they are something other than what they appear to be. Some people, though, are finding new ways to invite the *visible* dead into their lives.

"Dusty" is his real name. Dusty is a self-taught artist who creates portraits of the deceased by mixing a natural oil paint from their own cremated remains. We first met him at the same convention where we met Ben of DNA Memorial. Their booths were just yards apart, but Dusty was getting more attention because he had just won the award for "best new booth." Even he seemed surprised by this sudden acceptance. Most of the funeral directors I have interviewed point out the conservative nature of the business. Until recently, the traditional industry tended to vigorously resist new ideas.

We later met up with Dusty at his studio in Memphis, Tennessee, which occupies a tiny bedroom in a house stacked with half-finished art projects and the usual clutter that comes with two small children. His kids were excited to see us and wanted to be in the movie, but we eventually got things quieted down so that the mic could capture the sound of Dusty grinding bone with a mortar and pestle as he prepared another painting. He painted as we talked. Dusty is friendly, curious, and approachable—he comes across as a happy, open book.

The portrait he was working on was based on his prototype. The subject is Donny, a close friend whose life was cut short when a car hit him as he was walking home from work one day. Painting was Dusty's way of working through the pain, but he also knew that Donny would have thought it was cool. Donny's wife received the first cremation portrait. This new one was for Donny's mother. At first, like many people, she had found Dusty's

paintings odd, if not creepy. But over the years since Donny's death, she had warmed to the idea.

As a teenager, Dusty worked for his family's multigenerational floral business making deliveries to local funeral homes and cemeteries. Those old contacts provided his first paying customers for Cremation Portraits. Business has grown so quickly that he now does the majority of his orders through funeral homes rather than directly to clients. His base price is $200. He knows that funeral homes jack it up, but it keeps things simple. A skilled portrait artist who can work quickly from a photograph, like a sketch artist at a carnival, Dusty can produce several portraits a day. For someone who used to live paycheck to paycheck, it's a decent living. And it's steady.

Like others who make cremation objects, Dusty keeps careful track of the remains through the individual's name and shipping information, and he provides a certificate of authenticity. Most of his orders are for a single portrait made from an eight-ounce cup of baked and pulverized bone. Occasionally he receives orders for duplicates to be distributed to different family members. If families have held onto the ash in an urn or the nondescript box from the crematory, they might be opting for this transformation many years after the person passed away. So maybe there was a purpose to the storage function of cremation urns after all—waiting until a right-feeling solution came along. Or maybe the right kind of afterlife.

While the individuality of cremated remains gets obscured in the crucibles of glass and diamond creation, the color and texture of a person's powdered bone contributes to the visual effects of Dusty's portraits. They range from black to gray to brown, and from a fine dust to a granular, chunky mix that destroys his brushes. Like most artists, he welcomes the properties and constraints of different materials and works with them to achieve different effects. Each of his portraits is doubly unique. On the invisible spectrum, their base material was sourced from a singular human being. On the visible spectrum, the portraits capture a person's appearance at a certain moment of time, and with a density and style of brushwork that varies with each commission. Dusty stresses how important it is to capture the individuality of the person. It is especially important to get the eyes right and the expression of the mouth. He says that if he didn't have confidence in his ability to render a realistic likeness based on photographs, then he would not be in the business. You can't fudge this kind of work.

When I asked Dusty why he thinks his business is flourishing, he cites, as did Dean, the decline of religious influence in American life. But he also pointed to a desire for more unique forms of memorialization, especially among clients under fifty. But there is something more radical about Dusty's creations than personalization. And "memorialization" isn't the right word either. I keep turning over something he said to me: "It is not just a representation of them, it *is* them. That's Donny on the wall."

Ω Ω Ω

While his choice of medium might be unique, Dusty is far from the first to use the likeness of the deceased to form a memorial object. Death masks were once a thing, from ancient Egypt to Renaissance Europe. Soon after death, a likeness of the person's face would be captured with a plaster or wax mold, which in turn could be used to cast a more permanent material. This was the technique used to make Napoleon's famous bronze death mask.

I met Stan, who runs a small distribution business out of his home in a small New England town, on a late summer day. He specializes in novelty cremation options, from personalized urns and jewelry to some more unusual items. After we talked for a while about how he got into the business (he was once a funeral director), he showed me some of his inventory.

I don't know what kind of expression passed over my face as I encountered the bodiless head of former president Barack Obama. Behind my professional mask, I was feeling a mix of fascination and repulsion. Of course, there were no blood and guts involved. What I was seeing was a life-size replica of Obama's head created by a 3D printer that had been fed a photographic image and spat out a heavy plastic replica. The resulting object has a removable lid that lifts off like a toupee. The demonstration model was empty. Stan said that he had featured this custom urn on his website as a prototype to advertise his new 3D-printed options for what we might call extreme personalization. It had been a little controversial. Of course, the idea is not that you would put your loved one into Barack Obama's head but rather into a computer-generated likeness of their own head. Like Dusty's cremation portraits, there is a doubling here—the idea that the person could be present both visibly in their likeness and invisibly in their bony essence.

Ω Ω Ω

At the moment, the easiest way to take a tangible part of your human loved one with you is through cremation. The most common explanation for the explosive transition from whole-body burial to cremation in the United States has been its relative low cost, followed by the spatial mobility that has broken our relationships to family plots and hometown cemeteries. But I think there are other, more meaningful explanations. Viewing of the embalmed body is not working the healing magic it once did for a majority of Americans. It is an arcane enough practice that one needs to have been initiated into the cult. If you don't understand the ritual process, it will leave you cold. Cremation, on the other hand, does not come as a package with an associated ritual. It is a form of disposition that separates bodywork from beliefs. Even though it may be the option of choice among atheists and secular humanists, there is nothing about cremation itself that prevents spirituality. In fact, it allows people to invent their own rituals and their own sacred objects.

Many Americans, starting with the baby-boom generation, are resisting the great leveler that is death. They want their inimitable personalities to be recognized after biological death. To respect the deceased, we celebrate how they were different from everybody else. Belief in a singular, indivisible personhood persists and cuts across ethnic and religious groups. American individualism has only become more pronounced as consumer society tells us more and more loudly that we are what we buy. We are "packaging" as Maureen says. Tastes in material goods are widely understood to express something revelatory about our identity. The general push for personalization in funeral paraphernalia should not surprise us. Though what it suggests is that personhood continues after biological death.

In the case of the objects made with human remains, there is something more going on—a way in which personhood is becoming more *divisible*. I have come to believe that objects made from cremated remains materialize how Americans are reimagining personhood, however inchoately. It is about essence rather than identity, substance rather than packaging. These objects also point to a profound shift taking place in the relationship between the living and the dead. The individual person has long been equated with their body in American belief, as reflected in postmortem photography and, later, embalming. But now wholeness is no longer so important. In an emerging worldview that blends science and the unknowable, matter and spirit, there is an enigmatic but vital part of the person understood to be present in the smallest fragments. Even dust-size particles of the body contain something essential about them, whether it is DNA or other intimate molecules. And if we can preserve that part, the person will in some manner remain present with us. They will continue to exist in another form. Possibly for a very long time.

This is a kind of partible personhood that is not about being the sum of our different social roles as it is in Melanesia. Rather, it is about the relationship between our bodies and our mysterious selves. A growing number of Americans believe that our unique personhood is not so much expressed in our exterior packaging as it is encoded in our bones. And if our personhood remains in the material traces of our body, then once the whole body is no longer viable, the "person" can be divided, shared, transformed, and redistributed. Maybe even recycled.

CHAPTER 4

Dirt

I think it happened when I was driving around in a van after Hurricane Katrina and the levee breaks, surveying the devastation to the New Orleans landscape after the water had finally receded, in early October 2005. I was volunteering for the State of Louisiana to help assess damage to the historic fabric of the city. On those twelve-hour days, working with other volunteers and emergency professionals on "windshield surveys," conversations to pass the time flitted from the absurd to the intimate. We were trying to process our losses and feel our way through a profound disorientation. Somehow, we got on the topic of what we wanted done with our bodies when we die. Maybe it came up because we were floating through a fog of death. The smell of rotting flesh suffused the entire city. It has marked the memory of everyone who was there in those early months, as I am sure it has survivors of wars and other mass disasters. Mostly, the sickening stench emanated from meat that had been left to rot in domestic refrigerators for three months but also from dogs and cats that had perished. And humans. At one point, we had to pull back our survey of architectural damage in the Lower Ninth Ward when we realized that the recovery teams had missed someone.

As heavy as this ether felt, I remember the conversation that day feeling lighthearted. And I remember what I said. I had never considered it before, but the answer was ready at hand: I wanted to be buried. I'm fine with decomposition. I've seen a lot of it. Plus, as an archaeologist, I thought it would be unfair to my future colleagues if I didn't leave them something to puzzle over. My request would include that I be buried with certain artifacts as clues. My burial would become a time capsule, a message in a bottle from one archaeologist to another. It is a kind of futurity I can imagine with greater confidence than any other kind of afterlife.

Ω Ω Ω

Eleven years later, it is a late summer afternoon in Northern California. The wind is whipping us, bringing with it a fog that dips over the yellow and green hills like dry ice. I am stumbling over rocks, climbing up a scratchy hill, trying to keep up with Chris as he walks and talks us through Fernwood Cemetery, with Daniel and the sound guy not far behind. Chris has long legs and a boyish charm. He is extremely nervous about being interviewed. Maybe that's why he keeps looking away, keeps wanting to move on and show us something else in the thirty-two-acre parcel that he helps maintain. When he does stop to talk, he has to hold his floppy hiking hat onto his head with one hand, and the mic mostly just picks up the brushy whooshing of the wind. Chris has a bachelor's degree in environmental sciences with a specialty in GIS (Geographic Information Systems), both of which have come in handy in his role as the cemetery's grounds manager. He has created a mapping system using small, numbered brass pins placed across the grounds. They mark unmarked graves or the sites of future ones.

We pass the Jewish section of the cemetery, which at first glance looks like a scrubby patch of native plants—scattered California live oaks, golden-brown oat grass, and dark green coyote bush. Following the body of Jewish law and tradition known as Halacha ("The Way"), Orthodox and Conservative customs prescribe burial of an unembalmed body wrapped in a shroud or placed in a plain pine box without metal or other inorganic elements. Next to this section lies the Lower Meadow, the first area set aside for people who want a green burial according to a different belief system that revolves around Mother Earth but materially follows the same principles. It has now been joined by six other green sections, distinguished by their microclimates and vegetation. Farther up the hill, Chris leads us through the "traditional" section of the cemetery, its geographical heart and a tumble of tombstones of different eras and styles set among non-native cypress, willow, and palm trees. People have left flowers in cement vases built into some of the graves. The plastic ones are sunbaked to pale hues. There are gravestones engraved in Portuguese and in Chinese characters. As it peters out, we turn onto a path that will take us to the Ancestral Forest, a densely shaded area farther up the hill with mature, fragrant bay laurels and twisting oaks. Although we are racing against the fast-fading sunlight, at least the forest provides a windbreak, so I can hear Chris's answers to my questions.

More than just a cemetery that offers a new product in the form of green burial, Fernwood is a test case for how a death-scape can be used to regenerate life. A microcosm of California's diversity, the cemetery is home to at least five different ecological zones, each with its distinct mix of sun, wind, moisture, and vegetation. "The wildlife habitat certification is something that we take a lot of pride in," says Chris. "We're allowing it to return to a natural state. The certification requires certain elements that tie really nicely into green burial." These requirements mean that the land can't be fertilized or watered and that the cemetery follow a plan to remove invasive plant species, allowing the natives to rebound.[1]

Fernwood's program of habitat restoration has effectively extended the adjacent wildlife range of the Golden Gate National Recreation Area. The cemetery is home to many bird species, from songbirds we hear all around us to the more visible turkey vultures and red-tailed hawks that soar above. Great blue herons and egrets come up from Coyote Creek to forage and hunt gophers. And, indeed, coyotes roam the grounds in the quiet hours as do foxes, bobcats, and deer. One morning, one of the cemetery employees saw a mountain lion sunning herself next to a headstone.

Chris explains that a green burial means no embalming, and no metals or plastics are used for the markers, mortuary furniture, or grave goods, as archaeologists would call the materials associated with an interment. A biodegradable wood or wicker coffin or a natural-fiber shroud surrounds the body. The graves are hand-dug, if possible, to reduce the carbon footprint (most cemeteries these days use small backhoes). The reason the Jewish and green-burial sections do not at first glance look like a cemetery is that the only markers that are allowed are naturally occurring stones placed at the head of the grave, although these can be engraved if so desired. No plantings are permitted, but Chris and his team encourage families to scatter native wildflower seeds on the fresh mound of dirt. I did see some red Indian paintbrush and golden California poppies sprouting cheerfully out of one grave.

Before starting her own business making burial shrouds, Esmerelda worked at Fernwood during its early start-up days.

"It was like a cartoon haunted cemetery, in a way. It was very overgrown—very wild. It's just a very special, magical place." When Chris arrived a few years later it was, he says, still "a wild, rough, uncut piece of land." It took years of landscape management to make it *more* wild, more native. The aim of Fernwood's restoration program, however, is not to create an isolated nature preserve. Rather, it is designed to be a welcoming habitat for humans as well. Chris calls it a "burial park," which is something different—something more—than a cemetery. "We get dog walkers, mountain bikers, families, hikers, or people just coming to visit a loved one at a grave, and everyone comes together and uses this place in harmony. And it gives the community a way to use green space in a place where they probably wouldn't have expected to have found it." In our time filming there, we often had to stop what we were doing and step aside for all these lively humans. Fernwood Cemetery is not a dead space.

I asked Chris what he would like done with his body. He says that he has changed his mind a few times since coming to work there, but now, "being buried next to a tree, and becoming part of the tree, I think that's probably the most beautiful way to go. And that way you can have a place for loved ones to come and swing on your limbs and pay you a visit. I think green burial is amazing. Embalming? I mean, who would want to put that in their loved one? Why not just return to the system from which we came?" Chris's way of expressing things echoes the innuendos around cremation objects—that the dead person has an existence that persists past biological or legal death. A loved one is still connected to their corpse, which is why you wouldn't want to do harsh things to it. But gradually, the entity within— Chris called it, noncommittally, "your soul or whatever"— loosens up and lets go, making it possible to transition into something else. It is this transition that cremation objects

attempt to engineer. In the case of green burial, the transition means becoming other living things, from an iconic California oak with limbs twisted in a frozen dance to the microbes enriching the dirt below.

The idea of transforming cemeteries into actively used green spaces is the brainchild of Tyler, the co-owner and CEO of Fernwood, although he is in good company with green-burial activists and other cemetery operators at the vanguard of a movement to re-naturalize death.[2] We met in a stunning mid-twentieth-century building designed by the renowned architecture firm Skidmore, Owings and Merrill that sits at the foot of the hill near the entrance to the cemetery. The building exudes something like Japanese modernism, entirely appropriate for the mix of Westernized Buddhism and tradition-busting entrepreneurialism that characterizes Northern California. The concrete and glass building looks nothing like the faux colonial or neoclassical mansions with circular driveways that one usually associates with funeral homes. The building houses Fernwood's offices, preparation room, crematory, and the Remembrance Room, where gatherings and rituals take place. That's where we set up to record an interview with Tyler. The backdrop behind him is a solid wall of glass looking out onto a courtyard with a Frank Lloyd Wright–ish waterfall. This water feature in such a drought-prone landscape is clearly human-made but nods to the fact that nature can provide a sense of peace.

Tyler comes with a reputation. He is better known as the developer of Hollywood Forever Cemetery in Los Angeles. Despite being the resting place for the likes of Cecil B. DeMille and Jayne Mansfield, by the late twentieth century Hollywood Memorial Park (as it was then called) had become a patch of neglected marble and weeds. The city was selling it for a song in 1998. Tyler bought the cemetery and brought it back to life by reorienting the space to serve the diverse community of immigrants who now make LA their home—Thai Buddhists, Orthodox Armenians, Mexican Catholics, Russian Jews, et alia. More radically, he also transformed it into a community space and a cultural events venue for the living, hosting everything from indie rock concerts to film screenings (it *is* Hollywood).

While Hollywood Forever was an obsession, Tyler says that Fernwood was more of an epiphany. It arrived while he was swinging in a hammock one day.

I thought, people always say cemeteries are a waste of space. Hollywood Forever is not a waste of space in an urban jungle. People need it. They need trees. They need the peacocks and they need the swans—just to feel better. It is palliative and curative. It reminds people of life and death. What if cemeteries were actually to preserve space? Couldn't death then become a way to preserve natural landscapes?

Marin County was the perfect place to try this idea, *and* it had another neglected cemetery up for grabs. The area around Mill Valley consists of a patchwork of dairy farms, suburban Hispanic communities, and hippie holdout small towns. But the county is better known for harboring one of the highest concentrations of wealth in the country, while leaning liberal.[3]

Tyler is the kind of entrepreneur whose success derives from an aptitude for social observation. He can sense rising cultural tides and historical turns. He has come to think about American death care as "cyclical." In the twentieth century, he says, "We were in a very materialistic culture, and I think that the American way of death reflected that. [It] was very close to the middle-class ideal: 'I want what everyone else has.' It was a form of community status. The casket was no different than your car. Everyone wanted a nice metal casket." He notes that as a society we are becoming more secular, but also suggests that we are becoming less materialistic, which is a curious juxtaposition. Perhaps even more paradoxically, death is also becoming more biblical even as the number of Americans who identify as Christian or religiously Jewish has been on a precipitous decline since the 1980s. Among Fernwood's potential clients, Tyler sees "an embrace of the body and a sense that honoring the body is not to drain it and pump it full of chemicals and paint it. Honoring the body is returning to that from whence it came. And by doing that we're going full circle to dust to dust." The phrase "dust to dust" comes from Genesis 3:19: "By the sweat of your brow you will eat your food until you return to the ground, since from it you were taken; for dust you are and to dust you will return." When Tyler and other prospective green-cemetery operators approach city and county planning agencies, they often come up against the assumption that embalming is legally required and that therefore they are asking for something exceptional. To correct this misconception, Tyler points out that Orthodox Jewish burial is "green" in all the same material ways and that barring it would violate the First Amendment's protection of religious freedom.[4]

"This is biblical burial from the Old Testament. This is not new. It's something old. Stripping away all the things that were added that didn't work. So many people you hear [say], 'Oh, just put me in a plain pine box and throw me in the ground'—I think that's actually true. They want a return and a release." David, owner of Chicago Jewish Funerals, verified Tyler's characterization: "The Jewish funeral is a green funeral . . . very low on the carbon footprint. We come from the earth, we return to the earth." He added that the ritual of bathing and shrouding the body is a "beautiful thing" that family members are taking up again. The purification ritual (called *taharah*) shows respect to the deceased but also to the planet. As with the at-home funeral movement, some of the current changes in death are really just about a return to a preindustrial past.

Tyler's reference to Americans becoming more "secular" at the same time that they are re-embracing biblical burials at first sounds contradictory. Secularism has been a hot topic of debate in anthropology in recent decades, stimulated by the work of Talal Asad. Asad argues that secularism fails to be what many people think it is—a value system free from religious influence or notions of the sacred. Many nominally secular states like the United States actually sanctify certain types of rituals, beliefs, and ethical principles. Ironically, even a belief in "freedom of religion" requires a kind of faith and a judgment about what should be revered and protected, which is the basic definition of "the sacred." Further, secular systems often hide a prejudice, not against all religions but only against certain ones. Asad cites his experience as a Muslim living in "One Country, Under God" after the 9/11 terrorist attacks. While definitions and tenets of secularism have shifted over time and vary by cultural context, anthropologists now generally agree that "there is [no] such a thing as an absolutely secular society nor that there can be such a thing as a perfectly secular state of mind."[5] Stated another way, it is nearly impossible for human beings to wipe their minds of metaphysical and ethical habits of thought.

Green burial may attract people who self-identify as secularists, atheists, or agnostics, but it is hardly a practice without piety. As we were wrapping up our conversation, Tyler reflected,

> I think those of us who are very sensitive to climate change, to ecological degradation—we feel a sense of responsibility and a sense of guilt. And that was the beauty and inspiration of this concept for me—that this would be a way in which we could alleviate some of that with a great last act. And that the more of us that could do that, the more chance we had to harness our own deaths to reverse the death that we were causing to the planet.

The green-burial movement represents the ritual expression of an ethical worldview and a belief in redemption. People are testifying with their corpses. And healing with them. It may not be that far out to think about them as a form of ritual sacrifice.

Ω Ω Ω

Cemeteries are a natural draw for historians and archaeologists looking for clues about past societies. The literature on this particular death topic far outpaces research on embalming or mantelpiece urns. Cemeteries—those specialized neighborhoods for the dead—started to appear regularly on the landscape after humans settled down to hoe fields and live in towns—that is, during the Neolithic period, about twelve thousand years ago. It was never the only form of interment. Burying the dead under the floor of a house or in a temporary pit before moving the clean bones to a charnel house were among the most common forms of premodern disposition. Still, ground burial or entombment in a space set aside from the living is a practice found all over the world, with particularly strong traditions in Asia and Europe.

Archaeologists have tracked major transitions in US history through its cemeteries. In the 1960s, James Deetz and Edwin Dethlefsen examined the design elements of headstones in Massachusetts graveyards from 1680 to 1820. They documented thousands of examples and discovered a pattern of shifting popularity of three primary motifs: death's-heads, cherubs, and a willow-and-urn design. Their work was groundbreaking in applying techniques developed from the archaeology of ancient societies to more recent ones. They demonstrated that archaeologists can detect things that historians might miss. In terms of American studies, their study found that the evolving designs indexed fundamental shifts in ideology. Using the evidence of headstones, they developed what resembles a refined version of Philippe Ariès's phases of Western death for the American context.

According to Deetz and Dethlefsen, the early "death's-head" period (1680–1740) reflected the colony's Puritan roots, with its emphasis on humility, mortality, and judgment. They noted that epitaphs on these gravestones often made reference to dust, decay, and worms as a reminder not to be too vain about this worldly life. Then, between 1740 and 1760, a dramatic style change occurred with the appearance of grave markers featuring a cherub head with angel wings. This shift in mortuary culture followed the mass religious movement called the First

Great Awakening. The new Evangelicals focused more cheer-fully on the joys of heaven and the life-affirming power of salva-tion. In Baptist and Methodist theology, death was heralded as "good news," because the hereafter was reputed to be a nice place. The sweet angel design was an apt symbol for the spirit of the times. Soon, however, motifs of willows and urns began to make an appearance alongside them in New England grave-yards, gradually displacing the cherubs. Willows and urns had a longer run, enduring well into the Victorian era. Deetz and Dethlefsen interpret this mortuary aesthetic as a "depersonaliza-tion" and secularization of death. But there I think they might have been confusing de-Christianization with an absence of spiritual ideas. More likely, the trend reflects a Romantic obses-sion with the Greeks and Romans (remember Shelley). An al-ternative explanation is that headstones with the willow-and-urn motif expressed the idea that death is timeless, universal, and perhaps a bit of a mystery—like a Roman archaeological site.[6]

Ω Ω Ω

Social history unfolds in the layout and location of deathscapes. In colonial America, as in medieval and early modern Europe, there were, in fact, no cemeteries but instead churchyards and temple yards where the dead were crowded together under tumbling tombstones. Graves were reused, with coffins often stacked belowground, several generations deep. The profound economic changes wrought by the slow end of feudalism and the fast rise of industrialization in the 1700s led to intense ur-banization in Europe. Overcrowding extended to the Old World's graveyards, and they came to be seen as crowded slums of the dead. As historian Thomas Laqueur writes, concerns over noxious smells and sanitation problems merged with investor hunger for new urban land in the late eighteenth century to create a movement to reform death. Cemeteries (from the Greek meaning "sleeping places") started to appear on the outskirts of cities *and* outside the authority of churches. Generally nondenominational, cemeteries could be municipally or privately owned. At the same time, the aesthetics of cemeteries came to be subjects of careful planning, design, and theorizing, leading to clean and rational "grid cemeteries," like Père Lachaise Cemetery in Paris (which also harks back to Roman-style aboveground tomb cemeteries), and to the "garden cemeteries" of England and the "rural cemeteries" of the United States.[7]

Garden and rural cemeteries were intended to be places where *actual* willows would shade picnicking visitors among twisting paths, flowering vines, ferny woods, and urn-shaped planters. Mount Auburn Cemetery was the first rural cemetery in the United States, established in 1831 in Cambridge, Massachusetts. It quickly became the model for peri-urban cemetery design in a fast-growing nation with plenty of available land.[8] By location, the rural cemetery solved a perceived sanitation problem in an era plagued by cholera and yellow-fever outbreaks. The dead were to be segregated from the living. The rural cemetery movement expressed a new death culture rising out of the sentimentalism of the Romantic period in which the focus shifted from the afterlife to the ongoing memorializing and mourning activities of the living. A pan-Western movement Philippe Ariès called the period of "Thy Death," its practices and iconography emphasized a bond between the living and the dead but also shifted attention from the deceased to the mourner. This death culture matured into the full-blown Victorian "cult of the dead," with its gothic black clothing, memorial jewelry, and postmortem photography.[9] Earlier generations would have thought this indulgence of grief to be an un-Christian preoccupation. And indeed, the new rural cemetery featured a lot of pagan elements, referencing a much longer arc of human history. Laqueur aptly describes it as "a historicist jumble made of borrowed bits of different pasts: Egyptian, Roman, Greek, medieval Christian, Ottoman, Moghul, and more. It belonged nowhere in particular. . . . It was a place of sentiment loosely connected, at best, with Christian piety and intimately bound up with the emotional economics of family."[10]

What often gets overlooked in accounts of Victorian mourning culture (circa 1840–1900) is that it coincided with the florescence of American spiritualism. While spiritualism comprises a diverse set of practices and beliefs with early influences from the United Kingdom, Sweden, and Germany, the American variant has been, in terms of converts, the most successful. Historians often point to the 1840s sensation of the Fox sisters from upstate New York as its unofficial launch. Kate and Margaret Fox said that they could communicate with a dead man, a murdered peddler. He answered their questions through a series of knocks around a table. The Fox sisters became the first celebrity mediums. Others soon appeared on the scene as did other forms of communication—such as spirit possession, hypnotism, automatic writing, spirit photography. And, of course, Ouija boards. Early American spiritualism also contributed to the revival of older occult practices (magic, witchcraft, divination, and their technologies) and to the invention of Theosophy (an esoteric attempt to resolve the tension between science and religion). American spiritualist practices waned after World War I. But a revitalization blossomed in the 1960s and spiritualism has thrived ever since under the esoteric eclecticism of the New Age movement.[11]

While efforts to formally organize spiritualism into a recognized religion have been fleeting, two shared beliefs that unite all spiritualists have significant implications for how to read American deathscapes. The first item of faith is that the dead exist in an unseen, parallel world where they continue to have lifelike experiences that make them wiser than the living. The second is that, with some effort (which often requires the assistance of some kind of artifact), it is possible to open up channels of communication between the two dimensions. Deetz and Dethlefsen's chronology stopped with the antebellum period. If we extend their study to consider cemetery designs in the late nineteenth and early twentieth centuries, spiritualism starts to look like another important ideological transition in the American afterlife.

In the lush deathscapes of the pre–World War I era, families could memorialize their loved ones with unique headstones and ostentatious monuments, and publicly mourn through weekend strolls and family gatherings. Statues of angels, sleeping children, devoted mothers, and fallen heroes abounded. The rural cemetery was designed to prolong an emotional connection between the living and the dead. The dead were idealized, but they were neither unfamiliar nor far away. Cemeteries were such vital institutions in the nineteenth century that they increasingly came to resemble a microcosm of the living social landscape—or at least what those with money and power desired the social landscape to be. Patriarchs built small temples and palaces, even miniature pyramids, out of luxuriant marble to claim their place in history by anachronistically invoking it. But this is also the era of society tombs and monuments—Freemasons, firefighters, and foresters all had their own types of collective monuments and cemetery sections, as did ladies' benevolent societies and veterans. American cemeteries of the postbellum period capture social affiliations and identities like a snapshot in stone. And also the inequalities. Nineteenth- and

early twentieth-century American cemeteries were usually segregated by race, by religion, by ethnicity, and by class. Exclu-
sions might start at the cemetery gate or be inscribed in divided
sections within. The choice spots were located on hilltops or
near large trees and water features.

Historian-philosopher Michel Foucault used cemeteries as
an example of what he called a "heterotopia." He invented this
term to refer to specialized spaces that mirror society by exag-
gerating its dominant social norms in microcosm. Heterotopias
reinforce classifications of difference, deviance, and hierarchy.
The social ideal projected by the American rural cemetery was
that everyone had a different role to play in society and that
one's identity derived from belonging to a specific group. And,
most resoundingly, that there was no equality, even in death.
Perhaps this is utterly unsurprising, given that the rural cemetery arose in an era of slavery, anti-immigrant politics, dramatic
wealth disparities, and long before women gained the right to
vote. But it proves the point that cemeteries are decent indicators of what is going on among the living, if you learn how to
read them.[12]

In the twentieth century, yet another type of deathscape
came on the scene, epitomized by Forest Lawn Memorial Park
in Glendale, California. Established in 1906 as a rural cemetery,
its management and design were taken over by the Disneyesque
figure of Hubert Eaton in 1917. Eaton and Forest Lawn were the
main inspirations for Evelyn Waugh's *The Loved One*. But satire
shouldn't prevent us from a serious consideration of how Forest
Lawn both transformed and reflected American society. An as-
pirational linguistic shift (again) marked Eaton's new
approach—from "cemetery" to "memorial park." Now more
commonly called "lawn cemeteries," these tightly controlled
spaces reflected the suburban aesthetic of conformity and

manicured lawns of mid-century America. In stark contrast to the Victorian clutter of effusive monuments that characterized rural cemeteries, management of suburban lawn cemeteries dictated minimalism and uniform flat markers that could be easily mowed over, reducing maintenance costs. It was a design quickly adopted by a growing number of private, for-profit cemetery operators.

In its enforced uniformity of grave markings, the lawn cemetery appears to declare, "we are all alike, we are all middle class." While this dramatic aesthetic shift away from the rural cemetery might appear to reflect social-leveling ideals of the Progressive era and the civil rights movement, privately owned lawn cemeteries were in fact *more* likely to be segregated than older ones, unmitigated by the ethical missions of either religion or civil government. They were essentially gated communities for the dead. Corporations were free to make up their own rules. After they had decided who they would let in, they then dictated how their clients could interact with the dead. The emotional expression of love and loss allowed in the older cemeteries through flowers, holiday decorations, or the leaving of gifts and offerings on special occasions was strictly prohibited in a one-price-fits-all burial package and tightly regulated lawnscape. Although Eaton and followers renamed the cemetery a "memorial park," in truth, the form and policies of these institutions ushered in an end to memory and cemetery visitation. It was no longer decorous to prolong an emotional relationship with the dead, and it wasn't all that pleasant to visit their final resting place. As historian David Sloane says, the memorial park's streamlined, standardized approach to the deathscape "turned the cemetery into a storage space." Through their rigid design and policies, lawn cemeteries said, "Leave your loved one to us" and move on. Don't linger.[13]

Jessica Mitford was probably correct to say that Forest Lawn reflected an American obsession with sanitation. Above all else, its design shouts cleanliness and order. A cemetery didn't have to be old and haunted. But, as Evelyn Waugh detected, there is still something creepy about these hushed, intensely manicured spaces. The lawn cemetery bespoke a radical break in the relationship between the living and the dead. A growing discomfort with death (what Ariès described as the "forbidden" or "sequestered" death of the medicalized twentieth century) developed in tandem with these unwelcoming cemeteries throughout the twentieth century. The lawn cemetery arose right at the time that the dying were being banished to hospital wards and nursing homes, away from view. Esmerelda refers to them as "subterranean parking lots." And with their paved lanes rather than winding paths, they do seem to manifest car culture and a mid-century confidence in the American ability to design a space-age future. It takes some serious hubris to think you can design a better afterlife. Or is that optimism?

Ω Ω Ω

Although lawn cemeteries became ubiquitous across the United States by the mid-twentieth century, the older rural cemeteries persisted. "Rural" refers to the romantic nineteenth-century style, not the location. Those originally placed on the outskirts of large cities now reside well within their borders. Many became sad and forlorn places. Built for active strolling and the stimulation of memory and social values, by the late twentieth century, many of them had become abandoned, neglected, and vulnerable to vandalism. But now that is changing. In addition to Tyler's two California experiments, preservation efforts have cropped up in places as diverse as Indianapolis, Memphis, and

Boston to restore rural cemeteries and invite them back into urban life by encouraging five-kilometer runs, movie nights, Easter egg hunts, recycling drives, haunted history tours, and weddings. Another way they are being revived is through the creation of "new" green sections to meet a burgeoning demand, although in fact there were a good number of unembalmed souls already there.

Tyler is right, culture is cyclical. Although beliefs and practices do not return in exactly the same form, the past is a renewable resource. In archaeological time, we don't have to go back very far. Before the Civil War, nearly all American deaths were handled at home with body washing and a vigil. The unembalmed body would then be placed in the ground.

Tyler says that when he sits next to people on airplanes and explains what he does, the reaction is often, "cemeteries—what a waste of space!" I have heard that same line countless times when I ask people what they want done with their bodies and they profess a preference for cremation. While it is true that in some of the country's denser cities, real estate in the center of town can cost ungodly sums, the United States is not in any real danger of running out of cheap land in the exurbs. Even many older in-town (formerly "rural") cemeteries have plenty of space still available. "Waste of space" might be a real issue in small island nations like Japan or the United Kingdom, but in the American case, this phrase more accurately expresses a state of mind. It's a mental fact, not a material one. A cemetery plot is not a waste of space; it is a waste of *real estate*.

This is another thing that marks American death as a bit weird compared to the rest of the world, even within the West. Americans take for granted that they "own" a cemetery plot as a tiny piece of real property. No one else can occupy the space. Not even a renter. And your personal "lawn" will be mowed for eternity. In a private cemetery, part of your purchase price goes toward an endowment for "perpetual care," so that long after you—and the current groundskeeper—are gone, someone will be taking care of your property. The American dream has long been equated with home ownership, although for so many Americans the dream has been elusive, or shattered, in recent decades. Cemetery plots have deeds—they can be bought, sold, and inherited. But unlike a house, they are rarely mortgaged or repossessed. With a plot to call your own forever, it is the most secure form of real-estate ownership in the United States. This fact points to an unusual American fixation on permanence within the landscape. In other parts of the world, it is much more common to lease a cemetery plot or family mausoleum. Terms range from as little as thirteen months to as long as seventy-five years, but unless a family re-ups the lease, the cemetery has a right to reuse the space for another paying customer. When that happens, hopefully all that is left is dry bones and dust that can be swept into a corner or moved to a mass grave. This arrangement is acceptable because these evictions don't usually happen until the flesh has melted away and anonymity has been achieved. When there is no one left to pay, there is often no one left to remember, or to protest.[14]

While these lease arrangements are not unknown in the United States, most Americans who are interested in burial insist on becoming a permanent fixture on the landscape. They are attracted to a concrete kind of eternity. You leave a mark on the world by taking an eight-by-three-foot section of it out of commission. If you think about it with the eye of a stranger, it's another rather odd concept. Maybe it's a microcosmic expression of manifest destiny, or the settler's appetite for territory. Certainly it's about the sanctity of private property—doubly so. But belief in the necessity of permanent occupation is now faltering. Maybe that is what people mean by "waste of space." Buyers of conventional cemetery plots, in fact, pay to ensure that the space will never be recycled. It is the land equivalent of single-use plastics. Cremation, though, is not the only solution to the problem of wasted real estate.

Ω Ω Ω

Green burial is changing the American landscape one cemetery at a time, one person-tree at a time. But it is also creating a market for related products like "plain pine boxes" and wicker coffins, biodegradable urns made from pressed paper or salt, and natural grave markers. Some of these products are innovations not seen before, others are throwbacks to earlier, even ancient, times. Entrepreneurs are taking advantage of this cyclical turn in the history of death. The simplest of all death-care products is a shroud. To make a shroud, you can use a sheet from the deceased's bed (known as a "winding sheet"), a tablecloth, or a nice length of calico pulled from a bolt of remnant fabric. But linen and silk are the more classic choices.

Esmerelda grew up near Hollywood and worked for decades in the film and television industry as a costume designer. She has an affinity for cloth and aesthetics and loves to research different cultures and historical periods. She, too, experienced something like an epiphany that led her to establish a business. Or maybe "apotheosis" is the more accurate term. Not of her, of her mother.

On election night 2000, that of the Bush-Gore battle, Esmerelda got a call that her mother was fading fast. She quickly threw some things in a bag and got on a plane that transported her from Northern California to Southern; then she drove a rental car through the desert at night. She arrived at the convalescent home in time to see her mother, who had fallen into a kind of twilight. She sat with her. A few hours later her mother sat bolt upright in bed and let out an audible breath before slipping away in Esmerelda's arms. In a trancelike state, as she describes it, Esmerelda asked the medical staff to leave the room. She then threw away everything that had to do with sickness. She washed her mother and wrapped her in some saffron silk that she had impulsively grabbed from her costume supplies and thrown in her luggage. She lit candles and incense and meditated. Two hours later, the staff gently knocked on the door and witnessed a transformation. According to Esmerelda, "It was one of the most profoundly mystical experiences I've ever had. I shrouded my mother. I just knew to do that. You can call it past life remembrance or whatever. I just knew that's how I take care of my dead in my world."

Three years later, as the post-9/11 recession was still rocking the film industry, Esmerelda established Kinkaraco Green Funeral Products to offer shrouds to those who might want a similar experience. "Up until really recently, the only people who could be buried in a shroud were people of particular religions—the Jewish faith and the Muslim faith are both traditionally people that in the United States are able to be buried right into the ground in a shroud. Now, I thought that tree huggers should be afforded the same choice, should they want that." As her business grew, Esmerelda found another market among families with roots in East and South Asia, who follow a tradition of wrapping the body in a shroud before cremation. She likes to keep things classic, offering primarily cotton muslin and linen, but her inventory also includes bright, lavish silks and kente cloth. She recommends lining the shroud with flowers and herbs. She refers to the historical precedents of Jesus Christ, whose shroud was packed with aloeswood and myrrh, and to

an old English tradition of wrapping wildflowers in the winding sheet. Herbs and flowers help cover the olfactory signs of natural decay.

I asked Esmerelda what accounts for the rapid transition we are seeing away from the embalmed corpse. She surmised that the World War II generation really believed that the person *was* the whole body. This belief would explain the popularity of Permaseal caskets ("sealed" from elements and bugs) and efforts to make the person appear to be in comfortable slumber. She, like most critics of the mid-century American tradition, interprets these practices as evidence of extreme death denial. According to her, those days are gone, for two reasons. First, "people want authenticity. They are *craving* authenticity. When you wrap a body in a shroud, you see the outline of grandma. You *know* that grandma—or whoever you put in the ground—is going to get eaten by microbes, and you're *good* with that. You're good with moisture. You're good with the decomposition. Where for someone in denial, that's like a horror movie." The second

reason she thinks embalming is doomed is the rise of environmental ethics exhorting us to waste fewer resources and leave a
less toxic footprint: "A lot of people believe that the body is just
like the skin of the banana, and the banana has been eaten and
one needs to responsibly deal with the banana skin. And so composting that banana skin would be what is ethical."

For someone in denial, composting must be like a horror
movie.

$$\Omega \ \Omega \ \Omega$$

Katrina specializes in human banana peels, although that's not
what she calls them. A lot hinges on carefully chosen language
in this visceral business. Katrina established the nonprofit
Urban Death Project in 2014 as an outgrowth of her work on a
student architecture project in sustainable urban design. She
proposed developing a way to compost human bodies in small
urban spaces, inspired by the process used to rapidly break
down deceased livestock in industrial agriculture. She then col-
laborated with forensic anthropologists to figure out how it
might work.

The pilot project and resulting nonprofit organization gar-
nered design awards, but human composting remained more of
a concept than a workable enterprise until Katrina converted
the effort into a public-benefit corporation. Recompose is a
start-up based in Seattle, Washington, with $7 million in ven-
ture capital. Katrina has a patent pending for her process of
quickly converting humans to dirt. It involves temporarily
burying them in a special blend of soil, wood chips, and straw,
creating a perfect environment for hardworking microbes to do
their work. By controlling moisture and rotating the compost,
everything—including bones and teeth—gets reduced to soil

in as little as thirty days. According to Katrina, what gets returned to the family looks "much like the topsoil you'd buy at your local nursery." Recompose asserts that the public benefit of the process, besides providing families with an alternative form of disposition, is to sequester carbon and improve soil health.[15]

Recompose has found enough support that backers succeeded in getting a law passed in the Washington state legislature in January 2019 revising the statutes covering allowable disposition of human remains. Washington State SB 5001 states that *recomposition*, defined as "the contained, accelerated conversion of human remains to soil," as well as alkaline hydrolysis, will now be "allowable reduction methods for handling deceased persons' bodies." While Katrina's Recompose project clearly intersects with the environmental-spiritual ethics that Tyler and Esmerelda articulated, it also intersects with a utilitarian reductionism that has long buttressed American capitalism. It is an effort to convert the corpse into something *useful*—a recycling approach to human disposal. It approaches the body as a renewable resource. Katrina's project attempts to appeal simultaneously to environmental ethics and waste-disposal pragmatics.[16]

Katrina's inspiration comes from a different place than that of most of the entrepreneurs I have met. Her love of cities and her certificate in permaculture came first. Permaculture is an approach to intensive sustainable agriculture and landscape design. Its central tenet is that you work with local ecology, not against it. Permaculture principles include "catch and store energy," "produce no waste," and "integrate rather than segregate." One can see how Katrina has applied these ideas to the problem of dead bodies in urban space. Rather than continuing to segregate them to the outskirts of cities, she said in our phone interview, she seeks to "fold them back into the urban setting." Like Tyler of Fernwood, she recognizes that "there's something very special about green spaces in the city." Denser cities, especially those hemmed in by waterways, don't have a lot of options for the expansion of conventional cemeteries. Recompose proposes instead to regenerate the green spaces that already exist in a city—its public and private gardens. She asks: Why destroy the potential of all those nutrients through cremation?

Some of the people I have talked to about Recompose are fascinated; others are repulsed. Recompose directs the attention immediately to the natural processes of biological decomposition (worms, oozing, smells) that in the past many Americans found disgusting. Their minds might also leap straight to tomatoes. Eating grandma is taboo in most cultures, even if she's been broken down into unrecognizable organic bits. Katrina has found it necessary to specify that the precious dirt they produce should be used for tree plantings and ornamentals, *not* vegetable gardens. I suspect she has been compelled to say this in order to manage public perceptions, not because it would pose actual health and safety risks. She told me that questions from reporters and the public about fertilizing food crops became a "distraction." So she redirected.

Katrina says there is something intriguing about producing dirt with humans, although through the process you also "cease to be human." For her, it is not just about the material process. While she's not that interested in memorialization, she does think that embracing decomposition offers opportunities to "dive into the sacred." She's working on a ritual framework that Recompose can facilitate, and she encourages clients to create their own ceremonies with the returned dirt. She sees one of the biggest problems with direct cremation as the loss of ritual.

"It's so transactional," she says. Instead, Katrina advocates doing something transformational.

It is true that cremation can be numbingly transactional if all you do is fill out a form on a website, and a few days later the US Postal Service delivers a small cardboard box. But it can also open up the possibility for a wide range of DIY rituals. In the United States, most cremated remains are destined to be scattered in a garden or natural landscape, even if they first sit in an urn for a few years. This precedent of reintegrating human remains into gardens and natural areas helped lay the ground for the Recompose project. While cremation is not particularly sustainable, it does provide an easy means to symbolically "return to the system from which we came," as Chris of Fernwood Cemetery put it. Through natural ash scattering, the dead are turned into dirt in the broad sense of being returned to the landscape and the planet's molecular flows.

Ω Ω Ω

Rod can serve as a poster child for the new American tradition of ash scattering. In fact, he had a poster he wanted to show me and Daniel. It is a white three-by-four-foot, tri-fold poster board—the kind you might use for the presentation of a science fair project. On a picnic table in his yard in Sebastopol, California, he opens it to reveal a collection of landscape photos, labeled with names and dates. These are collaged with several other photos of heart-shaped scatters of ash. Rod calls this his storyboard. It is a record of his journey with the cremated remains of his wife, Shelley. After her tough and gradual defeat by cancer, Rod hopped in his truck and just drove. He sought out as many places in the Western landscape that he could think of that were special to her—places they had visited together, ones important to their love story, others that she had told him about. He traveled from Sonoma County up the Oregon coast, back down through California, and over to Nevada. When last we spoke, he had not yet made it to the Canadian Rockies. Once he did, his journey would be complete, and so would hers.

Clearly, Rod was doing this not only as a self-designed ritual but as a self-designed therapy. They can be the same thing. Rod was in love with Shelley for thirty-five years and still is. They had met when he was living in a tepee with a waterbed in a small wild town in Northern California. They met at a firemen's barn dance where a favorite local band was playing. They danced all night before falling into the tepee. In the morning, Shelley said she had to go home and walk her dog. Rod picked a yellow rose from a bush growing along a fence and handed it to her, telling her that was okay but she had to come right back, "because I'm no good at one-night stands." After a while, they settled in Sebastopol and built a house on a large lot with gnarled apple trees, remnants of the orchards that were once the backbone of the local economy. The property now borders a vineyard, but when they first bought it, the area was not out of reach for a school cafeteria cook and an office manager. They loved to garden and be outside, and it showed in the vibrant plant life around us as we talked under some young redwoods. Rod says Shelley was a "true nature's child." She never wore makeup or a bra. Rod has his own care-free look. In recent years, he's had a side gig as Santa Claus during the holiday season. He looks the part.

Shelley endured a long time with cancer and its complications. Rod took care of her. He makes it sound like she was the strong one. I'm not so sure, but Shelley was clearly the pragmatic one who labeled and organized things. Rod was the romantic who carved whimsical walking sticks. They did talk about the coming end and agreed that, "they wanted to be compost." (At the time that we spoke, Recompose was still two years away). If he had been able to, Rod says, he "would have wrapped her body up in an Indian blanket and buried her under a tree—so we could become plant food." They looked into burial on their land but found that the legal hoops to allow that in California were nearly insurmountable.[17]

After Rod is talked out, we all jump in the truck. He wants to show us one of the special spots, a coastal valley where Shelley grew up. We drive south along Highway 101 about an hour, passing the Paradise Drive exit before taking the turnoff for Fernwood Cemetery. But we drive on past and start winding our way up the mountain. Near the summit, Rod pulls over into a small parking lot for Mount Tamalpais State Park, and we step out into the summer heat. We follow him along a path through the dry golden grass, warm with the sound of crickets. After about a quarter mile, we arrive at a massive, spreading oak tree with a commanding view of the Pacific Ocean a few miles away. It feels like a remote, secret spot, so we are startled to see a couple of young children playing in the shade, just beyond their mom, who is sitting at the base of the tree. Rod approaches and talks with them a few minutes to explain what he would like to do and why we are there. They stand up, getting ready to leave, and he gifts the girls one of his heart-shaped rocks. They bound away, leaving him at peace with the tree (well, except for the nosy film crew).

Rod had premixed some of Shelley's ashes with those of her parents. Their ashes had been sitting around the house in urns for several years. The depositing ritual Rod has invented allows him to give them a final resting place too. The family is reunited in death, while he is, ritual step by ritual step, slowly released from responsibility for their care. It's a gradual, and thus less painful, form of social death. In a discreet spot between two

thigh-like roots, Rod spreads the ash in a heart-shaped scatter. He then stands up and pats the big tree and tells it to look after them. Despite all his practice with these rituals, he chokes up a little.

Shelley exists not only on Mount Tamalpais but at over a dozen spots scattered across the Western landscape, separated by hundreds of miles—an intensely distributed personhood. With cremation objects, some bit of the person gets captured within an inanimate object, but in natural ash scattering the person gets folded into an animate landscape. Often, it is a landscape that shaped that person in the first place. A return, as Tyler said.

The final "person on the street" interview that Daniel and I filmed happened in February 2019. Well, it wasn't a street, actually, but a nature trail. Virginia and her middle-aged son Alex were walking after a rainstorm in Eaton Canyon, a wildlife area on the edge of Pasadena, up against the San Gabriel Mountains. The valley was unusually green, and the creek in the arroyo an impassable gush of whitewater. We had come to film some trees, thinking about all those times that people had said they wanted to become one. Alex was walking with a carved stick and wearing an eye patch. He caught my eye, but Virginia was the talkative one in the quick interview they kindly indulged us with, in a steely-eyed, mother-boss kind of way. When I asked her what they would like done with their bodies, Virginia said that she had already told her children that she wanted to be cremated, because "everything is so expensive in California." That was how to beat the system. Her children could scatter her ashes in the mountains, in the ocean, or right there in Eaton Canyon—"wherever we've been." She added grumpily: "It's really a pity how we've done such bad things to nature." I don't think she entertains a notion that returning her cremated remains to nature would help heal the planet. It felt more like she was saying that it would be a suitable punishment for being a wasteful human.

After exploring other corners of the canyon, I steered Daniel toward a particularly evocative old oak tree, its strong trunk wrapped with wild vines. He took a wide angle shot from a distance and then approached for a close-up of its intricate gray bark. As he set up the tripod, I looked down at the ground and gasped, startling him. I pointed to a spot at the base of the trunk, just a couple of inches from one of the tripod feet. There was a pile of something that looked like thick, crushed eggshells and coarse beach sand—something we had become quite familiar with. If in that inevitable future Virginia's children choose Eaton Canyon, she will have good company. Somebody had found a sweet spot to deposit their loved one's ashes, under the same tree that had beckoned me.

Eaton Canyon lies just a few miles away from Hubert Eaton's Forest Lawn Memorial Park, but there's no relation to the canyon's namesake.[18] And the two parks couldn't be further apart as deathscapes. Ash scattering in natural areas has become so popular as a new American ritual that the federal government and most states have had to pass laws to control how and where it is done. You have to apply for a permit to scatter remains in one of the national parks and then follow the park service's guidelines so that ashes don't pile up in high-traffic areas or places where they might be mistaken for an ancient archaeological deposit or a crime scene. Otherwise, you need the permission of a private property owner. So long as permission is granted, you're good to go.

Unfortunately, Disney does not allow ash scattering on its properties (even if you ask politely), although there have been confirmed reports of illicit acts at the Haunted Mansion and Pirates of the Caribbean rides. A growing number of Americans appear to get a thrill from what religious scholar Stephen Prothero calls "wildcat scattering." Perhaps the adrenaline from the risk heightens emotions that make the ritual feel all that more significant. One family friend (whom I shall not incriminate here) called it her husband's final act of "civil disobedience." Such furtive rituals seem to declare, "I love you so much, I am willing to get in trouble." And perhaps there is an undercurrent of rebellion against what was almost a national policy dictating uniformity for all in the afterlife. There's also something powerful about performing a private ritual in a public place. It goes back to the quality that Craig of Memory Glass values: "no one has to know." Secret rites are to magic what liturgy is to religion. Wildcat scattering also expresses a willful determination to return the person to where they belong, to the important places that shaped them: stadiums of favorite sports teams, golf courses, historic and personal landmarks. In these cases, returning to the dirt is not so much about fertilizing the earth as

marking a beloved territory. One of the people I spoke to on
Halloween night in New Orleans said that her still-living parents had made their wishes known: they wanted their children
to drop a small bit of their remains under tables at all of their
favorite restaurants. This combination of irreverent humor and
culinary obsession is *very* New Orleans. But the impulse is similar to Rod's more sentimental one—that a place makes the person. While American practices are veering away from cemetery
real estate, they can still be about coming home.[19]

Ω Ω Ω

"The memorial of most enduring life is a tree. Tombs and
temples of ancient kings have crumbled and passed away, yet
we have living trees which were old when they were erected."[20]
So wrote Jon Plumb, superintendent of New York City's Wood-
lawn Cemetery in 1932. I don't know if Plumb was thinking
about redwoods, which don't grow anywhere near New York,

but their growth rings can be measured in rising and falling empires. I grew up surrounded by redwoods. In Armstrong State Park, a specimen that locals call "the Old Colonel" is estimated to be fourteen hundred years old. Farther east, a giant sequoia named "the President" is over thirty-two hundred years old. Thirty-two hundred years is still not eternity, but for those who want to become a tree, or memorialize someone through one, redwoods are not a bad choice.

Death entrepreneurship has been expanding so quickly that some start-ups have emerged in the short time that I have been working on this project. One of these is Better Place Forests. Sandy, the visionary founder, describes it as "America's first conservation spreading forests," a new type of landscape where cremated human remains are scattered (spread) among living trees. We met at the company's offices in the Marina district of San Francisco in early 2020, before we knew the world was going to come to a standstill due to a new virus. Sandy gave me a quick tour of the sun-filled, white-and-teal space with views of Alcatraz Island. It includes a kitchen stocked with espresso and alternative milks, comfortable couches scattered around for power naps, and glassed-in, flexible work spaces. There were lots of young employees buzzing around. Sandy and his partners started the business on paper in 2015. They now have seventy employees and start-up capital of at least $12 million. Most of the employees seem to have been plucked from Silicon Valley. This is Sandy's third start-up (he's named on an internet list of "Tech Tycoons"). After making an unspecified fortune from his last company, he decided to devote himself to a new "mission-driven" venture. We met in a small conference room with a new hire from the public relations department.

What Better Place Forests does is acquire stands of old-growth forest and develop them into a new kind of memorial park—but one based on the model of a national park rather than the suburban lawn. It began with the acquisition of some expensive acres of old-growth redwoods in Northern California and has expanded rapidly with forest properties across the country. What the company sells is "spreading rights" to bury cremated remains at the base of a "memorial tree" of your choosing. The rate depends on whether you will share the tree with strangers (a "community tree") or want to purchase rights for a single individual or a family. Prices range from $2,900 to $25,000 and up. Value is calculated based on the size and age of the tree, as well as the species and its location. Modest bronze markers are installed at the base of the tree to identify persons who have bought memorial rights. The contracts also provide family and friends exclusive membership access to a private reserve of quiet, old-growth forest, protected from the throngs of tourists who normally hit California parks in the summertime. Better Place Forests' impressive website shows a nice visitor center. I imagine it has an espresso machine.

Better Place Forests is an interesting paradox. It partakes in the general environmental ethics that are driving green burial and human composting, but its marketing does not promote the idea that the body's materials are being used to create new life-forms—the trees already exist. In fact, redwoods don't even like our ashes, which are alkaline and salty. They prefer acidic soils. In order to reduce harm to the local ecology, on-staff forestry scientists have developed a method for mixing the cremated remains into native soil with additives to dilute their harmful effects. That said, in the bigger picture, the easements and conservation certifications that Better Place Forests is working on to preserve its forest stands (now totaling nearly three hundred acres) help protect natural habitats. As part of its spreading rights package, it will also donate to programs that plant seedlings in order to expand existing forest land and create new carbon sinks. Sandy says that the concept is popular across the country: "It's not just a coastal or liberal thing. Conservative religious people like it but so do atheists. What connects them is a love of nature. Sometimes I feel that Better Place Forests is the only thing that people can agree on right now."

Sandy is a bit of a paradox, too. The painful experience of losing both parents at a young age led him to start Better Place Forests. His grief had been compounded by how their funerals went and where his parents ended up—in an urban cemetery next to a busy road in Ontario. He wanted to visit and remember them in a "better place." As we talk, Sandy interweaves narratives of this experience, and of his mother's influence as the founder of a nonprofit, with inspirational quotes of authors he cites by name—from CEO Eugene O'Kelly to psychological anthropologist Ernest Becker, and several others that I didn't catch (this was not a filmed interview). With caffeinated business acumen, Sandy is quick, inspiring, confident. He might be a good candidate for a TED Talk. And he knows how to make a pitch to potential investors. I was not in charge of the interview. So I just let him talk and took notes as fast as I could.

Using an appropriate California metaphor, Sandy said, "the entrepreneur's job is to identify a big wave coming and ride it without falling off." According to him, the death industry has not responded quickly enough to the shift toward cremation. As for green burial, he calls it a "niche market" that is not particularly cheap: "Green burial's product is not good. It is failing because there's no real difference than a potter's field." He implies that green burial lacks dignity—it means treating the privileged like the pauper. I am startled but also fascinated. This is a point of view I had not yet encountered.

Sandy clearly knows his customer base—most of it a discerning class of baby boomers. They care about environmental ethics, but he said they also care about having access to a "private space" for burial. And they want something, if not permanent, then pretty damn long-lasting, to memorialize their lives. Better Place Forests is primarily a "pre-need" company, meaning it is an option for those planning on death. When I checked in with him later, he said that business has grown during the Covid-19 pandemic, because "people are much more mindful of end of life now." They are thinking ahead, like he is.

Toward the end of our fast-moving conversation, I was just able to squeeze in my two zinger questions. Yes, he's already picked out the tree where he wants his ashes to go. It's a big beauty surrounded by rhododendrons, which his mom loved. He said he saw it and thought: "This is what forever looks like." As for what happens next? Here, again, Sandy surprises me. Of all of the death entrepreneurs I have talked to, not only was he the most forthright with his business philosophy, but he was the only one who said, after a pause, "Actually, I'm quite religious." The young woman from PR gave him a surprised look. He added that he tries to keep it quiet because it's not something that's cool to talk about in "nihilist" California. I try to get him to elaborate a little, asking if his beliefs were on the Christian spectrum. He hesitated again but then added: "Let us just say I believe in a Creator with a capital C." The devil in me thinks "Capitalism." But clearly, that's only half of Sandy's story.

Ω Ω Ω

It was only after I started combing through two-hundred-plus hours of the film footage that I realized how common it was for people to say, one way or another, that they wanted to "become a tree." Some of these expressions were from professionals like Chris, who know and understand the ecology of green-burial and conservation cemeteries. Others were notional, like the young woman in New Orleans dressed as Sally from the *Nightmare before Christmas*, who said she had heard of this "cool new thing" where your ashes are put into a container to grow a tree. She was probably referring to the Bios Urn, which made a splash on social media when it first launched a few years ago. According to the company's website, its product is "designed to turn you into a tree in the after-life." The biodegradable urn looks like a Starbucks Venti cup but comes filled with a "proprietary" soil mix. The company's motto is: "Together let's convert cemeteries into forests." Bios Urn is tapping into a desire that came up over and over again in my conversations with nonprofessionals.[21]

Trees and entrepreneurs are one part of the new story. Microbes and designers are another. Recently designers have sponsored competitions and built careers around challenging our ideas about death and disposition. In the course of our conversation, Sandy referred to the role of the "creative disruptor," a term now common in corporate speak, and I assume an apt descriptor for how he sees himself in the death-care field. Arguably, designers like Katrina of Recompose are disrupting more radically. Another designer who has successfully moved from prototype to start-up is Jae Rhim Lee, whose provocative "mushroom suit" won the internet a few years ago after her TED Talk. The Infinity Burial Suit is seeded with fungal spores that will not only decompose your corpse but do so in such a way that removes and neutralizes the toxins in our bodies. A body prepared in the mushroom suit is the total opposite of the toxin-heavy embalmed corpse. Now Lee's company, Coeio, is taking orders for spore-specked suits and shrouds. While the concept behind

Katrina's design is about the untapped environmental benefit of the corpse, the idea behind Lee's design is about the potential environmental harm of the corpse. Human remains, as ever, teeter ambiguously on the line between good and evil. Recompose and Coeio are united, however, in being start-ups that embody an ecological ethos driving major innovations in American death care in the twenty-first century. The market now offers so *many* ways to return to the dirt. And some of them virtually guarantee a verdant afterlife as another being.[22]

If we apply the premise behind Deetz and Dethlefsen's classic archaeological study of American cemeteries, in which changes in material culture index changes in dominant ideologies, then we are witnessing a revolutionary metamorphosis in American beliefs and values. Cemeteries are becoming forests. The entire country is a potential deathscape. The dead could be anywhere. And that's okay. Americans are being tilled back into the soil that nurtured them. What is starting to come into focus looks something like a disorganized form of earth worship. Its rituals involve dirt and microbes and becoming an ancestor in the form of a tree. The embodied person "returns" to dust and dirt. Recycled, they might also be reincarnated or at least replanted. Dare we think that these new death practices suggest a (re)emerging belief in the regenerative power of the universe? Entrepreneurs are betting on it.

CHAPTER 5

Spirit

We held the memorial about three months after my dad died, on a blistering dry July day. It took the form of a picnic at a park along the Russian River with invited friends and in-laws. My brother was barbecuing. My mom was the center of attention, meeting and greeting people, sharing stories. At some point, she stood up on a bench and read something she had written about Jim. It was going well—a successful celebration of life for a complicated man. But I was having trouble modulating my feelings and seemed unable to muster the relaxed good humor expected of me. I fluctuated between despair at his loss, which felt heightened by the event, and gratitude that so many people had something nice to say about him. Something in me has always resisted events and settings where social etiquette dictates what an appropriate emotional response should be. It is why I don't like weddings. I can't perform on cue. But I survived, making small talk as best I could. I remember my inner struggle during the event, but the details are a blur.

Much clearer is a scene that took place earlier that day, before the crowd gathered. Ten of us, mostly family, drove to an old, single-lane truss bridge a couple miles upriver from the park. When I was growing up in the 1970s, you could access a nudist beach by scrambling down the riverbank at this spot. The erosion of the river since that time has gobbled up the path to the beach, and nudism ain't what it used be, so there was no one down below to see what we were up to. My dad, though, would have been amused by our choice.

We parked the cars on a narrow dirt shoulder, got out, and started to walk along the bridge. I remember being nervous that we might be doing something vaguely illegal. Technically, public nudity is illegal too. In the funkier parts of Northern California, there is a "don't look, don't tell" culture about a lot of things. My dad often made me nervous with the risks he would take. In a past life, he might have been a smuggler or a poacher.

That morning I just hoped everyone would try to act natural as the occasional car passed by, although it must have looked suspicious that a group of ten people were slowly ambling along the narrow bridge. It was going well enough until our procession was suddenly interrupted when my mom's foot missed a break in the rough pavement. She stumbled and fell. My heart leapt as I tried to catch her. I couldn't lose her too. As we helped her up, she insisted cheerily that she was just fine.

About halfway along the bridge, we stopped. Peering over the railing, I could see a deep pool of calm, clear water within the sandy river directly below. The river was low and slow, in its summer phase. In the winter rainy season, it can become a beast, consuming nearby towns. Twice, my family has lost nearly everything to the floods. And with seasonal regularity, nearly every summer, there would be a drunken adult who lost their way back to the surface or misjudged the boulders below a rope swing. Us kids knew the river better. We spent most of our days in it or next to it, unsupervised. We explored its willow-covered islands and sandbars that would appear one year and be gone the next. The beginning of each summer meant getting to know it all over again, until we had formed a mental map of its invisible contours, especially the dark cold parts that seemed to have no bottom. Those were no-swim zones. For us "river rats" (as kids at my high school derisively called us), the river is something to be feared, but it is also a part of us. We don't resent it. It's like a god in some ways. Sometimes rising up with the power of destruction, other times nurturing peace and mirth.

I helped my mom pull a box out of the tote bag I was carrying. It was white, made of pressed paper dotted with dried flowers, about the size of a shoe box, only more square. Months earlier, I had been with her when she picked out the box at the funeral home the day after my dad died. He had drifted away in a hospital bed at home, unable to speak through the fluids drowning his lungs from secondary pneumonia. We had watched the kidney cancer gnaw away at his body for eight months. For much of that time, he was in denial that he would die, or at least didn't want to talk about it. Given the grim prognosis, who could blame him? A little death denial was probably what allowed him to continue to enjoy local outings and the company of his three grandchildren up until the last month, although it also meant he left a lot of things unsaid and unmended. On our trips back to California from Chicago, he played many chess games with my then seven-year-old son. They made big plans together. I was never sure about what exactly. My dad was a dreamer and a schemer. The future was always full of potential bounty, peace, and pleasure. It was a magical place. Fantasies of possibility were his solace for a traumatic past and an ever-struggling present.

The box containing what was left of his body was surprisingly heavy, like it had a couple of bricks inside. All of us lined up along the bridge so everyone could have a view of what was about to happen. Some of us said a few parting words, addressed to the box. Then my mom held it out over the handrail. She let go. I was nervous it would make a mess, but it fell straight down—like a box of bricks. Thirty feet below, it hit the water with a dignified splash that set off a ring of ripples. It quickly settled onto the river bottom, displacing a gentle plume of sand. We watched to see what would happen. We didn't know how long the paper box would take to disintegrate in the water. We had forgotten to ask—minutes? days? How would we know when to leave and walk away? Bubbles started to emanate from the box. For all of my emotional haze that day, I have a crystalline memory of what happened next. Attracted by the sound, a small school of five fat carp swam from upstream to investigate. These invasive fish eat grass, so they didn't think the box was food. They just seemed curious. They appeared to be sniffing it, checking it out. And then they started to circle the box in a perfect formation as it continued to send bubbles up to the surface. We watched, transfixed. I think I was the one who interrupted the startled silence and said, "Look! He's still talking. He's found a new audience." My dad could bend anybody's ear. And his stories tended toward the big fish variety.

That was one of the most spiritual experiences I have ever had. I don't know what else to call it.

Ω Ω Ω

I didn't spare anyone my two basic questions.

What do you want done with your body?

What happens after we die?

Not too surprisingly, most of the traditional funeral directors I talked to want to be embalmed and have a traditional casket-and-vault burial. But they also tend to prefer a lighthearted memorial to a somber religious rite. It is the material bits they are conservative about. Even the younger funeral directors, like Wilson, sided this way. We met Wilson at the National Funeral Directors Association convention back in Indianapolis. We set up to talk to him in front of a hundred-year-old hearse in the lobby, an exhibit piece that greeted visitors as they walked into the convention center. In its white and gold cheerfulness, it looked more like a fancy ice cream truck.

Wilson is in his thirties and Hollywood handsome, with curvy cheekbones and slicked-back hair. He is impeccably dressed in tailored clothes, down to the cuff links. He knows how to prepare the body. When I ask him about his own arrangements, he lights up with a smile: "I have thought about what kind of service I want to have, and what my funeral looks like. Personally, we have a family plot, a family cemetery where we want to be buried. I would like to be embalmed and viewed." He adds that he would also like some personalized component to the service, maybe his favorite U2 song.

Although a fourth-generation funeral director, in our conversation Wilson was attuned more to the present than the past. We talked about the changes the industry is experiencing. Despite his own classic and conservative style, he recognizes the trend away from formality and the growing demand for personalization and attention to the uniqueness of the individual. But Wilson worries that Americans are becoming less ritualistic in their daily lives and that we are at risk of losing something, particularly when it comes to death. He doesn't mind if the rituals change or become more humanist (i.e., not religious), but he doesn't think we should go without them.

Ethnographically, he identifies some other currents: "One thing we are seeing a great increase in is family difficulties. Families are more divided today." He says that he has to act as a mediator for a majority of his clients over one issue or another—disposition of the body, aspects of the ceremony, or simply clarifying who should legally be considered next of kin. The faster death practices change, and the more options that are available, the more potential there is for conflict. It makes sense. The trends I have followed are leading in interesting directions but not toward a consensus. At least not yet. And change rarely happens without conflict. The generalizations I offer should be taken with a grain of salt in the sense that no death option will be without its detractors. In the years over which I researched and wrote this book (2015–20), the United States was becoming the most politically divided it has been since the Civil War. Americans are having trouble finding ground for consensus about anything. Death is no different. In all social realms, wherever there are fault lines of sharp disagreement, that is a signal that tectonic plates are shifting and realigning. Big change is coming.

Wilson says that what he does is "not just a business." Funeral directors must have compassion for their clients. At other times, he sounds like an ambitious young executive with an MBA. Perhaps conscious of the industry's vulnerability that Sandy of Better Place Forests can smell, he is forthright about the declining prospects of funeral directors who resist change. Camps usually break along generational lines. The ones who want to keep doing things the way they've always done them "have their hearts in the right place. Their motives are good, [but] it is very difficult because they are not connecting with that consumer."

Wilson wanted to share a transformative experience in his career, an *aha* moment when he realized what the funeral industry could and should be. There is a luxury hotel chain that he prefers to patronize because it exceeds his expectations for service every time. On one occasion, when Wilson didn't

answer a wake-up call, the hotel manager followed up personally with a wellness check. Wilson had woken up early and gone
to the gym but forgot to cancel the scheduled call. This extra
effort stayed with him. Perhaps because he knows how real and
unexpected death can be, he especially appreciated the manager's concern. Wilson contacted the CEO of the company to
express his gratitude but also to learn something about the
chain's operation. He informed the executive that he'd love to
meet the person responsible for their staff training program
"and talk about the crossover in our industry and profession."
The executive put him in touch with the training director, who
happened to be based in Hong Kong. Despite the eleven-hour
time difference, Wilson persisted, calling her in the middle of
the night to pick her brain. "They think I'm crazy. I'm a funeral
guy. Why do you want to know about the hotel business? But
there is so much crossover in the hospitality industry and the
funeral profession—the way we treat folks, the experience
people are having, whether they are willing to pay for that service or not. I mean, value is not being low cost, it's about providing a high level of service." On short notice, he decided to fly
to Hong Kong to learn more. This focus on service and hospitality has become a mission for Wilson.

In our daily lives as general people, we look for the experience. Why do you go to Starbucks and pay five dollars for a
cup of coffee? You could get a cup of coffee at the Circle-K
or the 7–11 for 85 cents. It's the *experience*. It's that cup—the
way it feels. Maybe you like that little mermaid logo and you
connect with that vibe of the place. Maybe it's the authentic
cedar they use when they build a Starbucks—they put authentic cedar in the building so you smell this fresh, clean
scent. Maybe it's the music they play at every Starbucks in

the world. When you go in, it's a very similar environment. There's CDs you can buy so you can have the same vibe in your own place. That experience you pay for. And the same's true with death and with funerals. We hope that the public sees the value of that.

Wilson became animated as he spoke, talking quickly and with passion. He spoke of different levels of service and different vibes: "I believe that we can operate multiple brands in the same market." He pointed out that the parent company can run a Ritz-Carlton and a Courtyard Inn in the same market and everything in between.

I was fascinated by this crossover between mainstream American consumerism and a young visionary of the death-care industry. The anthropologist in me agreed that a funeral ritual should be thought of as an "experience" rather than a "product." But I was also troubled. All these changes in American death I was documenting—do they just boil down to consumer choice? Are we just entering a Starbucks phase of the afterlife, where you can get the equivalent of a no-foam extra-hot skinny vanilla latte?

"Yes" would be the answer that you will find in a lot of writing on the American way of death, from Jessica Mitford's classic rant about death salesmen to recent scholarly publications.[1] And yet. *Why* are American consumers demanding keepsakes made with bits of the corpse? *Why* are others demanding to be composted? Or scattered like birdseed? Reducing something down to "consumer choice" doesn't explain anything about the beliefs and values that influence those choices. There is no such thing as a universal economic rationality—about death or anything else. And then there's the cost issue. Mitford railed against the high cost of the embalming-vault-burial complex. It is true that monopoly power is fixing these prices more than ever in some markets.[2] But the cost of burial still varies widely by region per local land prices, overhead costs, and demand. Green burial should cost significantly less than a conventional burial. Cremation can be the cheapest option if you forgo any assistance from the funeral home beyond the "transactions" of body removal, incineration, and paperwork. And there are a lot of people going this route, citing cost and simplicity.

But it's such a strange and contradictory choice for a culture that reveres the individual. Why would the social value of the person plummet at the moment of biological death? Is it because they are no longer a productive member of society? Why is spending money on funeral arrangements considered a waste of money? As many of the funeral directors I spoke to point out, ceremonies and funerary comforts are primarily for the survivors, not the dead. This point gets lost in individualist logic, leading to a public misconception that the intended beneficiary is the person in the casket or the urn. And they may no longer care. The economic critique of elaborate funerals demeans the needs of the bereaved, or at least frowns on them using material means to work things out. People like to say that when their time comes, they "don't want a big fuss." But other rites of passage like weddings, bar mitzvahs, and quinceañeras are all about the fuss. They don't come in for nearly the same disapproval—big fusses are fun and important transitional events. They are about a change in social status and the terms of relationships. Funerary rituals are no different, at least when done well. Perhaps another factor driving the economic critique of the traditional American funeral is the reality that material goods like expensive, well-crafted caskets *are* quickly converted to waste—in other words, sacrificed to the earth's underground ecosystem. Consumers may be troubled by mortuary artifacts that mess with the line between durable and disposable goods. They are big and will last a pretty long time but are disposed of within days of purchase. Of course, all consumer goods, and many carcasses, will eventually end up in a landfill or incinerated, just maybe not so quickly. The use-life of a casket is a perplexing question.

It is also true that some people want to become postmortem objects that look an awful lot like commodities. And entrepreneurial creativity around death is frenetic right now. Becoming a plant or a tree may represent a less materialistic kind of afterlife but, as we have seen, there are lots of people nevertheless trying to profit off this newborn desire. It may not be possible to separate capitalism from spiritualism, especially in the American case. But perhaps the temptation to separate the worldly from the heavenly was a wrongheaded way to think about it in the first place. Or at least unrealistic.

Ω Ω Ω

Another caveat. Not everyone wants to become something after death—a beautiful corpse, a glass tchotchke, a tree. Some just want to dissolve, dissipate, disappear. Ash scattering on water is a popular option and preferred by Buddhists and Hindus. There is a humility to it—an admission that the body-person lacks permanence. Maybe those who select the most ephemeral of dispositions are more at peace with a vast unknown. They are okay leaving no object, no marker, no visible trace of their life. It would be hard to say that water scattering is about commodification. You don't have to pay anyone to do it. After a relatively inexpensive direct cremation, you can do like we did with my dad, pick a section of a river and DIY it (although be sure to check state laws on freshwater scattering—we were a bit clueless).

You can also go big. The Environmental Protection Agency allows ash scattering at sea so long as it takes place three nautical miles offshore and doesn't involve any additional nonbiodegradable materials. If you don't have a boat, you can employ one sponsored by the well-named Neptune Society and let them do it. Either way, water currents carry off the remains, so there will be no place to visit. They are *gone.* Burial at sea of the whole body, the choice of sailors, is more heavily regulated. US law now dictates use of a biodegradable coffin or shroud in this case so as not to add to the pollution of the oceans. It is a logistically challenging option and increasingly rare.

The ritual expression of water burial and water scattering aligns with green burial's ethos about returning to the planet—it's just a different part of the planet. But there's also an important distinction. With water scattering and water burial, there is no place-marking involved, no territory to stake a claim on. Are you a water person or an earth person? Perhaps there is something to the four elements and what draws people to different kinds of disposition, religious doctrine permitting. Glass, ceramics, and diamonds could be considered fire elements, since their forging requires intense heat and a secondary firing. Then there's the air element. Not everyone who wants to disappear does so quietly. You can go out (a second time) in a puff of smoke.

Ω Ω Ω

Gonzo journalist Hunter S. Thompson famously requested that his ashes be fired out of a cannon. Perhaps he was the inspiration for the affordable Loved One Launcher that Stan in Vermont offers in his catalog (the same guy who once promoted the 3D-printed urn of Obama's head). You can fill the air gun,

basically a backyard toy, with cremated remains and confetti.
OUT WITH A BANG, says the product page. The copy promises:
"The sight of blasting the ashes into the sky will bring to mind
feelings of celebration, happiness, and companionship." It will
also launch the dead person over seventy feet into the air and
disperse their remains over a wide area. The Loved One
Launcher materializes the swing toward celebration taking over
American death rituals. There is a spirit these days about making death fun—putting the "fun" in funerals, as they like to say.
Even in the case of tragic and untimely deaths, many people I
have encountered express a sense that focusing on the positive
aspects of the person and their life story is a better way to honor
them than to focus on the melancholia of survivors.

It turns out there are many ways to launch your loved one. I
spoke to Jason, a young vice president of a family funeral business based in Springfield, Missouri. Despite being lodged in the
middle of the conservative Bible Belt, his company has succeeded in taking personalization to a new level. All the staff at
Green Lawn Funeral Home get trained to be "celebrants," a
term that nationally may replace "funeral director" before too
long. Green Lawn focuses on individualized celebration rather
than traditional rituals. The staff tries to learn as much as they
can about the deceased, or soon-to-be-deceased, in their client
interviews. They encourage families to be playful and creative
as they consider options for personalizing the event. They
might bring in slot machines for someone who liked gambling,
or a Harley-Davidson motorcycle for a biker. Green Lawn's celebrants have also been finding small ways to surprise the family
with a special added touch. Following the lead of wedding plan-
ners, staff suggest personality-appropriate favors for guests to
bring home from the event. Jason's own uncle loved Jimmy Buf-
fet, so at his reception the staff surprised the family by playing

"Cheeseburger in Paradise" and unveiling a table catered by a local restaurant—filled with cheeseburgers. Maybe this is the kind of experience and exceptional hospitality that Wilson was talking about.

Green Lawn is passionate about personalization. But what drew me to take the long drive to Springfield was a special service that the company has cornered the market on. For an extra fee, it will work with a local pyrotechnics expert to load cremated remains into firework rockets. Green Lawn also owns a cemetery, which provides a venue it can control to safely and legally set up a ten-minute finale. The first firework funeral took place for a man who loved the Fourth of July, but it has been a popular offering ever since. Celebrations are usually held in the summer months, when the skies are clear and it is comfortable to be outside. For memorials like these, it is not as important to have an immediate ritual as it is to have a fitting one. Often there's a picnic in the late afternoon, transitioning into nighttime for the fireworks show. Families have come from as far away as North Carolina to be able to send their person off by launching them into the sky like flamboyant stardust.

At first, Green Lawn did get some flak from the local community for its peculiar pyrotechnics. It had to wrangle with county officials over some concerns that "Dad would end up in the potato salad" or that attendees would end up looking like the victims of Pompeii. But that's all cleared up now. At the time we spoke in 2017, Green Lawn had performed fifteen of these services—all for male decedents. Air seems to be a particularly masculine element, at least among the dead.

This impression was reinforced by another, quite unique death-care product start-up called Holy Smoke that I came across on the internet. One day I made another long drive from New Orleans, this time to meet cofounder Thad at the

Stagecoach Restaurant in Stockton, Alabama, to learn about his specialty business.

Thad and his partner, Clem, met as fish and wildlife officers. They shared a military background and a dedication to nature conservation. One of their motivations for opening their business in 2011 was to leave a smaller ecological footprint in death. Small-town Alabama is a long ways away from Mill Valley, California, both in miles and culture, but a similar drive lies behind an entirely different option for a nature-friendly death.

In their day jobs, Thad and Clem issued permits and tickets to people with guns, and they regularly wore guns as law enforcers. In their off-hours, they were hunters themselves. They are now semiretired, and their clients are like them—fellow veterans, hunters, law enforcers, and gun handlers. What Holy Smoke does is take your remains (there's a lot of preplanning among its particular clientele) and hand-load them into an ammunition cartridge of your choice. Thad explained that it is not an uncommon practice among gun hobbyists to craft their own bullets or shells. It is often necessary to outfit antique guns. Other motivations are to reuse spent cartridges, to improve accuracy (and lethality), or—for extreme preppers—to have the know-how in case the government outlaws guns and ammo. In the case of Holy Smoke, though, the purpose of hand-loading is to put a little something extra in the round. Thad and Clem can also add red, white, and blue powder to the mix to emit a special smoke upon firing, in a value-added product they call the Patriotic Salute. They underscore that the powder is made with organic pigments.

Thad readily acknowledges that their product is not for everyone. Not only do you need to know how to handle a gun, but this sort of celebration needs to match the spirit of the person. They've got to get a kick out of it. There's a lot of winking going on.

Thad's partner, Clem, got the idea for the business while talking to a friend and fellow hunter after the death of a relative. He
and his friend were musing about what they wanted for their
own arrangements. Clem shared that he had some waste-of-
space and ecological issues with burial. His friend said: "You
know, I've thought about this for some time and I want to be
cremated. Then I want my ashes put into some turkey-load
shotgun shells and have someone that knows how to turkey
hunt use those turkey load shotgun shells with my ashes to kill
a turkey. That way I will rest in peace knowing that the last thing
that one more turkey will see is me, screaming at him at about
1,000 feet per second."[3]

There is something triumphant about this. If your death
causes the death of another creature, does that mean that you
somehow win? That you remain undefeated? Holy Smoke offers the dead an opportunity to be animate and agentive. The
will of the hunter continues after biological death, having an
effect in the world. As if to say, "I'm still here." There can be a
dark last-laugh quality to this ending. But not everyone takes
Holy Smoke lightly. For those who select their services for a
funeral with military honors, it's a serious form of patriotism.
You can give your death for your country, even if you didn't give
your life. And there is another possible use for these human
bullets, which is mentioned on Holy Smoke's website but did
not come up in our conversation. Perhaps because it is so
eyebrow-raising, and Thad wasn't sure what a probably left-
leaning academic would make of it. In addition to hunting rifles,
Holy Smoke can customize ammunition for small arms and
automatic rifles, so "you can have the peace of mind that you
can continue to protect your family and home even after you
are gone." The will to live on means, for some of Thad and
Clem's clients, a will to kill. There is no misreading the meaning

here. Hunting and protecting are life-affirming activities for some Americans. If not an afterlife exactly, Holy Smoke offers a kind of life extension and a postmortem capacity to cause death to others. A pretty literal cycle of life and death.

Here is more proof that it is not quite right to say that Americans are death-denying. In a society where lethal means are defended as a fundamental right, and violence is ubiquitous in headlines and entertainment, death doesn't seem to be denied at all. From another point of view, the United States looks like a death-*loving* society. At the very least, conflicted about it. Perhaps this is why so many Americans were ready to accept a high death toll from Covid-19 and insisted on the right to go about their normal lives without the restrictions of masks and shutdowns. When a reporter asked President Trump about the high death toll in the United States compared to other countries, he responded: "It is what it is." That sounds like a kind of death acceptance, not a denial.[4]

Ω Ω Ω

If air guns, fireworks, and bullets don't scatter your remains far enough, there is always space. Celestis Memorial Flights got a precocious start in death innovation. It started in Houston in 1994 with an option to take a loved one's remains for a ride in earth's orbit. Its first celebrity client was *Star Trek* creator Gene Roddenberry (or rather his wife, who made the arrangements). Now Celestis can launch your ashes—or just your DNA—to the moon or, like the Voyager spacecraft, to an unknown destination beyond the solar system to spin into eternity, à la Carl Sagan's stardust. The company's advertisements make it clear that what it offers is a fulfillment of the dream of space travel. Few people alive have ever, or will ever, experience space travel, but some essential *part* of the person can. This is distributed personhood taken to an extreme. Your family might or might not be able to watch the rocket launch while a part of you is loaded up with a bunch of other dead person parts and maybe a satellite. There will be no entertaining display through fireworks, colorful smoke, or confetti. But parallel to these other options, it is the *ritual* of launching the loved one that seems to fit the spirit of the person. They won't see you, but they'll know you're out there.

While Celestis is a relatively expensive option with a small customer base, a start-up in California called Elysium Space is betting that options like these will become more popular in the years to come. It offers competitive pricing, starting at $2,500, and has partnered with Elon Musk's SpaceX to propel cremated remains into orbit around the earth. After two years, "in a last poetic moment, the spacecraft will harmlessly re-enter the Earth's atmosphere, blazing as a shooting star," in the words of Elysium's CEO. What is interesting about these astral afterlives is that they are spatially approximating the realm of heaven—some airy world floating above the earth. Elysium is well named. This version of paradise, according to Greek mythology, was an exclusive place reserved for heroes and half-gods. Like Silicon Valley CEOs.[5]

The American afterlife has rarely been about equality.

Ω Ω Ω

During the world-ending days after Katrina, I found myself visiting Holt Cemetery more than once. I first went to evaluate the damage as part of my job to document the disaster's impact on the historic landscape. But I kept going back, perhaps a bit counterintuitively, to remind myself of pre-storm *life*. And to

get in touch with my feelings below the numbness of shock and trauma. It was easy to become an emotional zombie against that apocalyptic landscape.

Holt Cemetery sits fenced and mostly unnoticed next to the parking lot for a local community college. Inside, with grand old oaks draped with Spanish moss and tombstones leaning this way and that, it looks the part of a Southern gothic grave-yard. As you walk, you start to notice odd details. Large, rough drainage ditches cut across the plots. Human bone, bits of cloth, and artifacts jut out from the dirt. The ground is bumpy with fresh mounds and sunken grave shafts. On a warm day, the aroma of death is undeniable. Maybe one-half of the visible graves have markers, or at least remnants of them. Some are a simple, professional type prepared by a stonemason, like those provided for war veterans. But what stands out are the hand-made markers: wooden planks with hand-painted or hand-carved text and more durable DIY cement forms with scratched text. Many of the narrow plots are outlined by hand-built frames to make them easier to find in the jumble and to make sure they don't disappear too quickly into the ever-churning rubble of an overactive cemetery. The frames are made out of wood, garden fencing, paving bricks, PVC plumbing pipe—whatever the makers could get their hands on. Inside the frames, the grave surface is sometimes covered with materials to keep the weeds down—ornamental rocks and artificial turf are the most popular. And the place is *full* of artifacts. Visitors have left all kinds of objects on the graves, from the predictable vases with plastic flowers to children's toys, pottery, lawn ornaments, bottles, and photos. Some are faded by sun and rain; others are fresh and colorful.

New Orleans is known for its observance of All Saints' Day on November 1, when families visit cemeteries, as they do throughout Catholic Latin America and the Mediterranean, to clean graves, leave flowers and offerings, light candles, and maybe have a picnic. But at Holt, these practices happen year-round and appear to be nondenominational. Judging by the timing and the type of artifacts left, people come to observe birthdays, death days, Mardi Gras, and Christmas. Cards, balloons, beads, and little artificial trees are easy-to-read signs of a continuing relationship between the living and the dead.

If you have the money, you will probably be buried somewhere else. Holt has long been the last stop for many of New Orleans's poor. This city-owned cemetery charges no plot fee, but families are granted usufruct rights only for as long as they "use" the plot. Frequent visiting and maintenance—personal care rather than perpetual care—is how they maintain those rights. If a grave goes unmarked for 101 days, it can be recycled by city workers. Most of the plots at Holt have been reused three times or more.

Holt is beyond full, so the city has also contracted with a bleakly modest private cemetery called Resthaven Memorial

Park. This cemetery, which sells the cheapest real estate in the city, sits in the sprawling suburban fringe neighborhood known as New Orleans East. Resthaven is squeezed on three sides by the city dump, a junkyard, and industrial ruins. The fourth side is swamp. Most of the graves have regulation flat bronze or stone markers, on the model of Forest Lawn, consistent with the neighborhood's mid-century origin. Beyond them, in the direction of the swamp, lies a large grassy field surrounded by a chain-link fence. It is here that the city morgue buries the cremated remains of the unclaimed dead in mass graves— hundreds per year. I have wondered what archaeologists of the future will make of this site. It might be interpreted as a killing field, or at the very least as an index of extreme social inequality reflected in the cavalier disposal of certain kinds of people. It would not be unreasonable for them to assume that the culture responsible for it was one at perpetual war, or swept by pandemics, or that practiced a form of slavery.

Most of the individuals buried in these graves are not Jane and John Does. The deceased have names and Social Security numbers. They just didn't have anyone willing, or able, to pick up their remains, much less figure out something special to do with them. Sometimes this is due to family estrangement, but more often it is just about money. If you sign a form to take responsibility for a person's remains, you will have to pay fees for the death certificate, transport, and storage, not to mention cremation or preparation for burial. Even with the cheapest of cremation options selected, the minimum estimated cost at the time of this writing is $700. If the deceased was on Social Security, the feds will pay a $255 benefit toward that. If they were under sixty-two when they died, there is nothing. In the United States, the safety net for the living is frayed, but it is almost nonexistent for the dead. Counties and cities, and kindly funeral directors, take care of the unclaimed and indigent dead on their own dime as best they can. There was an epidemic of the unclaimed dead in the United States long before the Covid-19 pandemic. It was, and is, happening all over, from New Orleans to Chicago, Los Angeles to New York.[6] The mass disposal of the indigent dead is a big, ugly exception to the dreamy idea that you can "have your own version of death," as Nick of Memory Glass put it.

It is a long drive out to the dump and Resthaven. A lot of families still prefer Holt Cemetery, despite the overcrowding.

Not all the grave-tenders at Holt are family members. Some people adopt graves, especially those of musicians and children. Other graves just seem to have a life of their own. Before Katrina, it was hard to miss the one that locals called "the homeless grave." It hosted a dense tangle of lawn chairs, a colorful plastic tarp, and an assemblage of useful items for the dead like food, dishes, clothes and shoes, and blankets. I never figured out whether the homeless grave was called this because someone had seen a homeless person tending it, or if it just looked like a homeless encampment. This dead person, though, was being cared for with more personal attention than most living homeless people. Someone came by regularly and replenished the plot, making sure it was well "used" and protected from recycling. Some people want to be recycled after death. Some do not. Privilege resides in the ability to choose.

In the catastrophic flooding that followed the levee breaks, Holt was inundated with four to six feet of water, and many grave markers and votive artifacts were swept away. But people trickled back. Including me. When I saw fresh graves with fresh artifacts it perversely made me glad—it meant some connection between the past and the future was still possible. On one visit, at the back of the cemetery among some leaning oaks, I found a chicken carcass hanging from a limb, and wine and rum bottles stuck in the nooks and crannies of the trunk. Used candles were scattered around on the ground. Someone had been practicing some form of magic—voodoo, pseudo-voodoo, or New Ageism. All New Orleans cemeteries attract this sort of activity, but the loose, fresh graves of Holt are especially vulnerable to grave robbing for human skulls and bones used for magical practice. Or that fetch a nice price on eBay. These two outcomes are not contraindicated. The dead are a perennial source of magic, both good and bad. And magic can be profitable.

Holt Cemetery was established as an indigent cemetery in the wake of the city's nineteenth-century population explosion, evolving from the site of a mass grave needed for the victims of a yellow-fever outbreak. At first, poverty was the only common denominator of the interred, but by World War I—the peak of Jim Crow—the population served by the cemetery had become almost exclusively African American and Afro-Creole. Buddy Bolden, the mythic founder of jazz, lies somewhere in an unmarked grave, or at least he used to. His bones are likely now blended and scattered with dozens of others.

While the votive activity and DIY markers at Holt exist in part because of poverty and the need to maintain usufruct rights, they are also artifact assemblages of great beauty and meaning. This type of grave-tending has been documented as a long-standing tradition across the South, especially in African American cemeteries. There are few conventions that dictate how to relate to your loved one. In fact, uniqueness and creativity are signs of love. At Holt, I've seen dolls, mosaics made with found objects, and whirligigs. These grave-decorating practices were a form of "personalization" long before it became a buzzword in death-care marketing.[7]

This is another reason that the desire for personalized expression in death cannot be reduced to crass consumer choice.

Sure, today mass media nudges us to "brand" ourselves through objects, as if each person were a corporation. But not all forms of material expression are market-driven or the result of cynical manipulation. The kind of visitation and low-cost creative votive activity that has long been a feature at Holt is now spreading all over the country. Votive artifacts are dense at Guerneville, but I have also recorded them at cemeteries in Chicago, Indianapolis, and New York. This is not to say that the practice is simply diffusing from African American tradition. Cultural influences are multidirectional and nearly impossible to trace. In Mexico, family visits to the cemetery to tend graves and leave offerings are not limited to Día de Muertos. On the Chinese holiday of Qingming, families leave food and burn incense and fake money on the grave so that the dead can buy what they need in the afterlife. Immigrants have imported these traditions into the United States, as they always have. But devotional activities are clearly no longer obeying ethnic divides, if they ever did. And cemeteries are no longer fussing over the "messes" left behind like they once did. Commemorative grave visits and artifact offerings have become so common that even uptight Forest Lawn Memorial Park has been forced to adapt. In a newer section of the Glendale cemetery that slopes down to the neighborhood below, out of sight of the older manicured lawns, families are now allowed to decorate their family's graves according to tradition and personal inclination. In a dramatic overturning of its signature strictness, Forest Lawn now permits lawn ornaments. And there, too, food and lawn chairs appear. On a Friday afternoon when I visited in 2019, living people were sitting in the lawn chairs, eating food, hanging out with their loved ones, and playing music from their phones. It was a busy day for picnicking with the spirits.

Ω Ω Ω

In 1905, the great German sociologist Max Weber argued in *The Protestant Ethic and the Spirit of Capitalism* that the religious beliefs of Puritans created a set of values that helped drive the development of capitalism as we know it. Puritanism lauded frugality and hard work and held that inequality in the world was a sign of God's judgment. Work and trade must be done, but God had already decided who was destined to be wealthy and who was going to heaven. Death was a sign of God's judgment but that fate, at least, fell equally on all sinners. The skulls on New England Puritans' gravestones reminded early Americans of their grim God. Weber recognized that these religious foundations shifted as early Protestantism splintered into Calvinism, Methodism, Baptist movements, and so on. Some of these new forms of Christianity allowed pleasure, even joy, back into worldly life. But the ideas of the Puritans didn't evaporate. Instead, they morphed into a secular ideology. Principles of self-interest, efficiency, labor productivity, competition, conspicuous consumption, and tolerance for social inequalities are a cultural legacy of what Weber called the Protestant ethic. He worried that capitalism was causing a "disenchantment of the world." He saw mysticism, magical thinking, and the arts falling by the wayside of human history, victims of a global takeover of our minds by economic rationality.

Weber was only half right. Scholars since have pointed out that there is a great deal of the market that, in fact, *succeeds* due to magical thinking. Consumer items and services attract us because they offer to heal us, transform us, make us beautiful, get us a job, make us wealthy, find us a mate. These are the same reasons people around the world have forever sought out witches, healers, shamans, voodoo priestesses, and other, less obvious, purveyors of magic, like embalmers.[8]

Ω Ω Ω

What is happening to the American death ritual?

For many years, critics interpreted the American tradition of the embalmed corpse as a "disenchantment"—a form of medical sanitation and a retreat from sacred considerations of the afterlife. What this reading misses is that the embalmed corpse is understood by its faithful to have mystical healing properties. It is not a religious object but a magical one. American funeral directors are not worried that we are "losing our religion"—that has been happening for some time—but that we are losing our ritual. They sound like Weber. They are worried about a changing world. And they, too, are only half right. We are losing *our* ritual—a shared national ritual that most Americans once understood as giving dignity to the dead and comfort to the living. But we—as individuals—are not losing our ability to process death through ritual. In fact, ritual practices around death are prospering.

From the most radical entrepreneurs to family members who take matters into their own hands, ritual is everywhere. Everyone seems to agree that a "good death" requires a ritual. But it is no longer solely in the hands of the ritual specialists we call embalmers and funeral directors. In fact, the more improvised and individual the ritual, the more efficacious it may be for the bereaved. DIY enchantment is booming.

The face of American death is shape-shifting before our eyes. The proliferation of new practices looks like a tree growing at the speed of kudzu. So many branches, so many directions, so much variety. There is an openness, a state of play, toward death and its rituals in the early twenty-first century. The influence of different religious and ethnic traditions is creating a cross-fertilization of practices, or "cultural hybridization" as David Sloane calls it. But there has always been significant ethnic and religious diversity in the United States. What is different now is the abandonment of a national ritual that once overrode these differences. There is an openness to new ideas for death rituals, wherever they might come from. There is a yen to borrow, experiment, improvise, and invent ritual.[9]

If anything, the new American death demonstrates a hunger for ritual meaning and a remarkable creativity in satisfying it. The study of ritual behavior has been an enduring topic for anthropology, to the point that it holds some fuddy-duddy ideas about what makes for a proper ritual. Some anthropologists would not consider contemporary American death practices as ritual at all, because they would define it as the revered Victor Turner once did: "a *prescribed formal* behavior for occasions not given over to technological routine, having reference to beliefs in mystical beings or powers."[10] The descriptors "prescribed" and "formal" do not fit well with the act of dropping my dad's ashes into the Russian River or with the lively embalming of Ms. Mae. These acts, however, are intensely meaningful interruptions of daily routines that seem to serve no practical purpose. The dead, for those who talk to them and do things for them, are mysterious entities whose supernatural status and powers are unknown. Anthropologists have also historically defined ritual as a shared *social* custom. By the standard definition, ritual involves a community that agrees on the rules and proper elements of a ritual—its timing, participants, uttered words or texts, objects, bodily movements, location, and performed steps. Within this classic view, what Americans are now doing with their improvised DIY activities involving human remains is by definition *not* ritual. It not only lacks the involvement of specialists such as priests or shamans but there is no "community of practice" to which such acts are readable, much less that could evaluate whether they have been performed "correctly."

If the community of practice that once defined the death ritual was broadly national in the United States, that community has now disintegrated into tiny bits. Even within the small family unit, as Wilson and Jeffrey attested, there are often disagreements about arrangements, and funeral directors can find themselves mediating fierce squabbles. Legally, decisions come down to the wishes of "next of kin"—a spouse, child, or parent. *Unless* the matter has already been settled by someone else— the deceased person who planned ahead. The point on which Americans seem to be converging is that the death ritual is best controlled not by the group but by the individual. This means taking the last *will* (and testament) very seriously. For those who want a heavy-metal playlist and Chicago deep-dish pizza for their last event, with their remains in a Cubs urn serving as a centerpiece, their final act, to *choose*, is nearly sacred in the American system of values. Consumer choice has become something more than taste. It is an act of self-determination that carries over into their afterlife.

I offer a dissenting anthropological opinion. The new American death practices that I have described in this book absolutely count as rituals. And the more idiosyncratic and inventive they are, the more potent the magic. Anthropologists for the past forty years have become comfortable with the thesis that traditions can be "invented"—that they don't necessarily evolve slowly over generations but can arise through pivotal events and the proactive actions of artists, entrepreneurs, gurus, and politicians.[11] Ash scattering in natural areas in the United States is a ritual tradition that started somewhere, with someone, in the late twentieth century. It is now a widespread and unremarkable practice. Facebook memorials and Zoom funerals had more recent moments of invention.

Even if ritual acts do not become shared traditions, that does not mean they are not *intended*, by their creators and practitioners, *as* rituals. Rod, who decided to visit different places in the Western landscape that were important to his wife, Shelley, scattered her and her parents' remains in a heart-shaped pattern out of a small, handcrafted box, then placed a heart-shaped stone in the center, said a few words, and took a photo. Later, he pasted a copy of this photo onto his storyboard. He understood what he was doing as a ritual, although no one taught him to do this, and no text laid out the "proper" way to do it.

In recent years, psychologists have picked up ritual as a tool in therapeutic practice, influenced by the efficacy of some alternative medical practices. Meanwhile, anthropologists have become interested in the psychotherapeutic effects of traditional shamanism as well as the cultural practice of "neo-shamanism" and other New Ageisms. According to anthropologist Jane Atkinson, these esoteric practices present "a spiritual alternative for Westerners estranged from major Western religious traditions. Particularly appealing for its 'democratic' qualities that bypass institutionalized religious hierarchies, the new shamanism is compatible with contemporary emphases on self-help." Or, in the words of advocates for ritual in psychotherapy, "at the core of New Age spirituality is a focus on the importance of finding one's own path and trusting one's experience." It is a kind of spiritual practice wholly compatible with a faith in individualism and self-reliance. We can view DIY death rituals as part of a broader movement toward spiritual self-help.[12]

As highly variable as they are, DIY death rituals refer—like all other rituals—to an underlying belief system. In fact, it is precisely their tailor-made uniqueness that gives loyal expression to a core belief system that Americans broadly share—individualism. *What we are witnessing is the cult of the individual overtaking the cult of the nation.* These two fealties have long been in tension in the United States, as noted by Alexis de Tocqueville's 1831 proto-ethnography. He worried that the pervasive dynamics of self-interest and self-reliance he observed among American pioneers would eventually handicap them from working for the common good. Significantly, he bundled together his worries about a neglect for ancestors with the potentially destructive effects of individualism: "Not only does democracy make every man forget his ancestors, but also clouds their view of their descendants and isolates them from their contemporaries. Each man is forever thrown back on himself alone, and there is a danger that he may be shut up in the solitude of his own heart."[13] But as Rod's fashioned hearts suggest, perhaps there are also ways in which these new death rituals, while honoring individualism as a core value, are at the same time overcoming this "forgetting" of ancestors and descendants. While he may be isolated from a living ritual community, Rod's ritual creates new imaginative connections across generations. It is striking to me how many of the new death options Americans are selecting are designed to connect the dead not only to the living but also to the not-yet-born. The turn toward heirloom diamonds and carbon-capturing redwood trees suggests an expansion in how we think about the connections between individuals across long spans of time.

Ω Ω Ω

What is happening to the American afterlife?
Increasingly, the afterlife exists in the here and the now, all around us. Or, better said, *afterlives*—the shades of the dead are

tangible, sitting on our mantelpiece, worn on our finger, imprinted in the bark of a tree. I find it difficult to separate the spirit of capitalism and the spirit of the new American dead. Some entrepreneurs are taking advantage of the expanding baby boomer market, and some designers are creating new markets through innovations that educate our desires. Americans are increasingly turning the biological remains of their loved ones into what look like commodities. Commodification is facilitating a transformation that allows the dead to persist as social beings in our lives. Jessica Mitford scolded Americans for allowing the professional funeral industry to commercialize the funeral ritual. I imagine she would also sneer at the colorful bazaar that is today's death market. But her error would be in thinking that this material customization of death is devoid of spirituality or antithetical to the types of rituals that cultures around the world have practiced in order to slow down social death after the body stops pulsing. The emerging new death practices I have documented in the United States are emphatically material and aimed to facilitate a relationship between the living and the dead. The best term for it might be "material spiritualism."

When Daniel and I started doing impromptu "person on the street" questions that Halloween night in 2015, I was winging it. Maybe I added "what do you think happens to us after we die?" because we were surrounded by ghosts and ghouls. The answer to this question is much harder to answer than the disposition question, both for myself and for the majority of the people I interviewed. But I have become quite convinced that the answers to both, even if still "under construction," are deeply connected. Perhaps more so than they ever have been. What Americans want done with their bodies reflects contemporary beliefs and values but also their speculations about the afterlife.

In asking the afterlife question, I was often forcing people to articulate ideas about it for the first time. I was interfering in their lives, messing with their heads. In that regard, I was not conducting ethnography of a found object; rather, the investigation itself was producing a new object—a narrative about personal metaphysical beliefs. In other words, it was a dialogue. Some interlocutors seemed to surprise themselves with their own answers. Beliefs about the afterlife are emerging and evolving. They sit in some slippery state that the French anthropologist Pierre Bourdieu called "heterodoxy," as opposed to "orthodoxy." In a state of heterodoxy, experimental ideas and competing ideologies rise up to question the status quo. Bourdieu argued that heterodoxy often precedes a major cultural shift or paradigm change.[14]

Looking over my field notes, I found that almost no one offered a classic version of heaven or paradise as a different *place* to go. There were really only two people who leaned this way, both of whom we encountered on the street after the San Francisco Marathon in 2016. Sophia had just finished the race. She believes in heaven and laughingly said that what happens to her body doesn't matter, it is just going to be eaten by worms. Jed, a disabled veteran panhandling on a nearby street corner, also believes in Christian heaven. He expects he'll be buried at Arlington National Cemetery, which he thinks everyone should visit to appreciate the sacrifices made for this country. "That's integrity you don't see nowadays," he said, choking up. He is still sacrificing.

We ran into Henry a couple blocks away, taking a break from moving barricades off the street in his duties as a security guard for the marathon. Henry was raised Christian in Louisiana, but he said he had lived in California for so long that now he believes "I might come back as a fly." He sounded open to it.

None of these three Californians were native to the state (their accents gave them away). It is damn difficult to make regional generalizations about such a mobile society. My samples are biased toward where I had connections—California, Louisiana, Illinois—although I did seek out entrepreneurs elsewhere. I make no claims for statistical significance. It was not that kind of project. What I can offer is a survey of musings on the afterlife that my interlocutors shared. While I did not intentionally avoid talking to religious traditionalists in interviews, they just weren't that common. But avowed atheists were just as rare. Only one person said, "You just disappear." The most common response from death-care professionals was a version of "it's the great mystery," an unassailable answer that will offend no one. Some offered a version of the law of thermodynamics—that our spiritual energy and bio-matter will become something else. They can't just cease into nothing. As Dean at LifeGem said, these days, scientific and religious thought seem to be merging when it comes to the afterlife. Other ideas that people shared with me suggested the realm of the occult, where science and religion have long been compatible.

At one point, I thought the question for this book was going to be, "what does a secular afterlife look like?" but now I know that that was the wrong question. It is not that Americans are becoming more secular (a troublesome category in any case), it is that they are becoming more spiritual. The Pew Research Center recorded an 8 percent jump in Americans identifying as "spiritual but not religious" in the five-year span between 2012 and 2016. These polls also found that the 27 percent of Americans who now identify this way do not skew toward any particular demographic: "[The shift] has occurred among men and women; whites, blacks, and Hispanics; people of many different ages and education levels; and among Republicans and

Democrats."[15] The death entrepreneurs I sought out know this.
Their customer base is broad, diverse, and growing. These are
not people who believe in "nothing." But what they *do* believe
is all over the map—eclectic, syncretic, speculative, woo-woo,
and whackadoo. This is not to discount these beliefs as inau-
thentic or erroneous. People believe what they believe. It is the
anthropologist's job to record what she sees and hears, not to
judge. If I were an alien ethnographer writing a report on US
society for my home planet based on the interviews I conducted for this project, I would have to include a whole bunch
of caveats about what a diverse society it is, shaped by invasion,
migration, and revolution. But knowing my readers would be
hungry for some sort of helpful generalization, I would start the
entry under "The Afterlife" as follows: *American cosmology is
shaped by beliefs in ghosts, reincarnation, and stardust.*

One of the traditional funeral directors and embalmers I interviewed said he talks to the people he's working on all the
time. "I have this kind of spooky, spiritual thing—that I think

they're still around for a little bit watching over us. So I talk to them: 'So, this tie look good? You want to change ties? Come on, cooperate, sit up!'" He laughs. I ask him about his spooky theories. He doesn't want to be recorded on film (so I am not identifying him here). "I think that it's bad luck if you don't treat people how you want to be treated, even when they're dead. And I think you should; that's kinda my theory." Rod said that he felt his wife Shelley's presence on an almost weekly basis in the year after she passed away. When we talked, this feeling was gradually becoming less frequent. You could say she was passing away very slowly. But as we chatted at his picnic table under the trees, he said, "I'm getting goose bumps right now." On cue, a breeze moved through and all the wind chimes around us started chattering. "Wow!" we laughed together. Nick's story about the glass globe that kept breaking was also a goose-bump story. The experience was unnerving and had forced him to open up his mind to possibilities he had once dismissed.

Jerrigrace said that she often sees animals appearing around the body, whether it is while the caregivers are doing preparations, at the burial, or on the way back from the crematory. In addition to the dragonfly that she thought was communicating for her friend Carolyn, she's seen butterflies, hummingbirds, and wild turkeys acting suspiciously in the proximity of a corpse or the grieving. "It's one of the greatest mysteries in the world. One thing I know for sure is that our spirit goes on. I've seen too much over the last twenty years not to believe that. Where it goes is different for different people, but I know it connects a lot with the people left behind—that's for sure." Jerrigrace, like so many professionals, demurred when it came to expressing her own beliefs, striving to remain open to everyone's ideas. Heterodoxy is her ethic. I was struck by how lively the world must appear to her if any animal could be a messenger from the dead or might even *be* them. And then I thought about Holy Smoke and how, if that's the case, turkey shooting could really backfire.

Eric, the young man we talked to at the Guerneville cemetery, was startlingly well prepared for my questions. He wants a Viking cremation. He would like his friends to construct a boat and burn it. I imagine it floating down the Russian River, where my dad swims with the fishes. Eric articulated a belief in reincarnation as self-improvement—that we keep coming back until we get things right, and only then do we get to "become one with the universe." Nancy, one of the attendees at the Final Passages training, said that she was influenced by her Mexican heritage and the recent revival of Day of the Dead practices, but when it came to the afterlife, her mind did not go to a place like Mictlān, the Aztec underworld. Rather, she believes in reincarnation. "I believe you get to come back and work on your lessons." These ideas clearly resonate with Hinduism, Buddhism, and several other eastern philosophies in the New Age mix. The influence of Asian culture, through both immigration of people and migration of ideas, is not to be discounted, particularly on the West Coast. However, in this Americanized folk form of reincarnation, believers often assume that one is reincarnated as a *human*, which is not necessarily the case in these other belief systems. In other words, American reincarnation sounds like a hyperextended version of individualism and self-improvement psychology.

Only a handful of people I spoke to formally identify as Hindu or Buddhist. We encountered a group of South Asian tech professionals who had run the San Francisco Marathon together who were matter-of-fact about cremation and reincarnation. Esmerelda, the shroud designer, is a devout Buddhist who follows a Tibetan teacher. She has been studying and practicing for many years, though she jokes about being a "bad Buddhist" who loses her patience too often. She says that getting to be a human being for a turn on earth is an extraordinarily rare thing—one in billions (of insects, frogs, birds). She also believes in multiple dimensions. "I believe that all life—past, present, and future—is happening simultaneously, so [that explains] the shrouding of my mother—when there was no reason why I should even know about shrouds or do that. I'm sure that many of us that I've met in the death-care field have been involved in that in other lifetimes—in Egypt, for example. Or just in that position—shamanism, all that sort of thing." Esmerelda then hesitated and seemed to be editing her thoughts before deciding to let down her guard: "I've taken a lot of LSD, and so I have a lot of multidimensional remembrance, shall we say, of things." Her smile positively glows as she says this, eyes twinkling at me, cheeks rosy. Her expression seemed to say, "you're going to think I'm silly." But at the same time, she doesn't care *what* I think because she "just knows." This is who she is and what she believes. That is faith.

Maureen, who runs the gallery of artist-designed urns, believes we become "stardust" but that we also endure in the archaeological traces we leave behind. Sometimes I think about archaeological sites as a kind of scientific séance where the living try to read the ambiguous signs of the dead. "I believe that after we die, we become stardust again, that mass and matter doesn't disappear, it just transforms into a different entity." Tyler at Fernwood was one of the most articulate people Daniel and I interviewed. But on the afterlife question, he was at first stumped. "I think that when we die . . . uh . . . oh, that's a big question." He paused, rocking a little on his feet while he thought it over and then rebooted. "My personal belief is that something survives. I don't know if it is that twenty-one grams or whatever—the weight difference when we die." Whatever it is, he says, it returns to the "vastness." A number of people acknowledged that while they didn't know, what is important is what we *want* to believe. Amanda, one of the participants at the Final Passages home-funeral training, offered: "Maybe the afterlife is whatever *you* want it to be, so that it is different for everyone." Another participant at Final Passages, who may have been the youngest trainee, shook her bohemian pigtails as she expressed amazement at all she was learning that day. In an unfeigned Valley girl accent (the last word of every phrase should be delivered in a singsong up-tone), she said, "Death—it's just so *com*plicated! Who knew? I mean, it's just so COMplicated." I feel her.

I suspect that popular culture, television in particular, has as much influence on American ideas about the afterlife these days as organized religion. I can't prove this. But neither can you prove the existence or nonexistence of ghosts. According to polls taken in recent years, 45 percent of Americans believe in ghosts. That is only a little less than the 50 percent who still identify with an organized religion.[16] The same polls show that church attendance and belief in heaven have been in a steady decline for the past twenty years. This is interesting, but correlation is not causation. The twentieth-century American funeral rite with embalming-casket-vault was never theologically driven. Protestants, Catholics, Reform Jews, and atheists all had nearly identical death rituals with embalming, fancy caskets, and a gravestone. And now many adherents of these same faiths embrace cremation. What one does with the dead has been of surprisingly little religious concern in the United States. In *Celebrations of Death: The Anthropology of Mortuary Ritual*, Peter Metcalf and Richard Huntington observed that religion as we conventionally conceive it could not account for "the uniformity of American death rites." Nor does it account for today's growing diversity. What the United States had in the twentieth century was a *national* ritual that united across religions. The national ritual complex is now breaking down, but it's not because death is being reclaimed by temples, mosques, and churches.[17]

Ω Ω Ω

What does an archaeologist make of all this?

Archaeologists use the term "horizon" to refer to the sudden but geographically widespread appearance of something new within material culture—a new style of pottery, a sudden change in iconography, or a break in the soil stratigraphy indicating a mass event like abandonment or disaster. I visualize it as the light from the morning sun appearing on the horizon and quickly fanning out across the landscape—a new dawn. These sorts of markers can be useful for periodizing major shifts such as the fall of an empire, the fast spread of a new religion, or the social effects of a technological innovation.

When archaeologists James Deetz and Edwin Dethlefsen tracked changes in iconographic styles on New England tombstones and correlated them with shifts in dominant American ideology, they were mapping horizons, from Puritanism to the Great Awakening on to the Enlightenment. They worked up from the gravestones to the ideas and values they seemed to illustrate. Their study tested the proposition that material death practices change in sync with other social movements. Cultural historian Philippe Ariès did the opposite operation, building a multiphase history of Western European ideas about death through textual evidence of *mentalité* (mindset), then looking for confirmation in tomb reliefs and death masks.[18]

We can do something similar for the past two hundred years in the United States, picking up where Deetz and Dethlefsen left off, but instead of zeroing in on gravestones, I suggest we follow the corpse. Throughout most of the nineteenth century, the American death ritual focused on the home wake, with the body surrounded by family members who orchestrated and performed most of the rituals. Death was intimate, and the living witnessed the body through its transformation from an immediate material world to a presumed afterworld where loved ones would be waiting. Family relations were highly valued and presumed to last for an eternity. Priests and ministers assisted as Charons who guided the dead across the divide. Healing was enacted through rote religious rites and through social gathering. We could call this the period of "Homegoing," a term still current in the African American community.

Then, in the late nineteenth century, along came embalming and professionalization, gradually reversing the importance of the family, as ritual specialists (embalmers and funeral directors) took over. Mortuary practices went from focusing on the family to focusing on the deceased. By the mid-twentieth century, corpse treatment and the material accessories of death had become remarkably uniform across the United States, suggesting high cultural conformity, respect for expertise, and a strong imagined community. The body of the individual became a kind of sacred object around which the ritual centered, with purification steps and a focus on healing and the manipulation of time. Each body was subject to a uniform treatment that focused less on individual personhood and more on community standards. Religious elements were present, but denominational differences were muted by a nationalized ritual. The corpse was held to have magical healing properties for mourners, while embalming and restoration appeared to cure the dead of death itself, or at least its sunken face. As Esmerelda said, in this era, "the body *was* the person." But the differences among these bodies were downplayed. I think of this long period as the time of the "Nation-Body."

Then, at the turn of the twenty-first century, the corpse started to lose its sacred importance in the national death ritual, and mourners lost faith in the healing properties of embalming and visitation. More and more people came to see the dead body as nothing more than a "hollow shell"—a waste of space, or inert matter best disposed of through incineration. The dominance of funeral directors as ritual specialists and funeral homes as ritual spaces began to slip, along with a decline in religious conformity. Hyper-individualization, questioning authority, and bucking convention are cultural inclinations of this phase, which continues to the present day. Taking cremated remains home without a plan, Americans have tried to approach death with self-reliance, at some risk of being "shut up in the solitude of [one's] own heart" as Tocqueville put it. Rugged individualism meets existentialism. It is a period about questioning traditions that are no longer serving us. Autonomy and deferral have meant isolation and confusion in grief but also that Americans now hold the dead closer than they did in the era of the Nation-Body. Individualism has also gotten metaphysical. Americans are pushing harder to get what they want from the death-care industry. What most of them want are services and products (rituals and artifacts) that affirm the individuality of the person, or what the business calls personalization. Let's call this horizon "Rugged Grief."

While we are still in the midst of this phase, with plenty of overlaps and revivals of previous ones to complicate these simple heuristics, I believe that today Americans are at the dawn of a fourth cultural horizon. Or, if we add Deetz and Dethlefsen's periodization of the earlier Puritan, Evangelical, and Enlightenment periods, it would be the seventh since

English dissenters invaded the eastern coast of North America. Rather than perceiving the corpse as dead matter, a growing number of Americans see it as containing an essence of the person *and* as a resource for spiritual and ecological regeneration. In DIY rituals invented by self-made shamans, we see hints that hyper-individualism may be slowly giving way to a sense of connection and continuity—across generations and with other species. What should we call this new era?

If we apply the archaeological conceit I started with, that mortuary practices can be read as symptoms of deeper social currents, then what does this sudden new horizon in American death practices point to? The breakdown of a unifying national ritual into a fragmented mosaic of "have it your way" death practices could suggest that the United States is falling apart as a cultural unity. In other words, that its internal cultural diversity and the cult of the individual are shouting down any shared beliefs about what it means to be an American, much less a patriot. But we already knew that. Political scientist Benedict Anderson argued that nations are "imagined communities," meaning that members of these large societies imagine themselves united in a shared identity through common narratives, values, and traditions. Anderson accounted for the rise of the modern nation-state in the nineteenth century (giving much credit to newspapers), but he didn't say what it takes to undo one. What seems to be emerging now is a new kind of imagined community that Anderson didn't anticipate—a planetary one based on shared ecological values.[19]

Ω Ω Ω

The moment I began writing this book, it started to become history. All ethnographies are snapshots of a culture or a community at a moment of time. The inherent limitations of trying to understand a slice of time that you are still living doesn't trouble me nearly as much as the expectation that the anthropologist be a kind of palm reader, able to project trend lines from the present into the future. Human societies are far too complex, with too many factors and contingencies entering their ebb and flow, for anyone to accurately forecast what happens next. I prefer archaeology's long view—that cultural change is itself an expression of the cycle of life. When one tradition dies, another will rise up.

Ernest Becker seems to have felt this same humility when confronted with the question of the future—all the more keenly when it came to the uncertain future of what happens after we die. He ended his book, *The Denial of Death*, with these words:

Who knows what form the forward momentum of life will take in the time ahead or what use it will make of our anguished searching. The most that any one of us can seem to do is to fashion something—an object or ourselves—and drop it into the confusion, make an offering of it, so to speak, to the life force.[20]

I have been thinking about what the present moment will look like archaeologically in a few hundred years. My hope is that this new horizon will deserve a name like the Grand Awakening. And that my future colleagues will find lots of confused offerings to the life force.

Epilogue

She paused to wipe the sweat from her forehead. Salty beads of moisture trickled from the back of her hand. She took a swig of water from her flask and then knelt down to dig again, slowly scraping with her trowel. Every so often she paused to gather up the loose dirt and dump it into buckets that her excavation partner took to the screen to shake and sort. After she had broken through the dry, tough sod of native oat grass at the surface, the soil had been boring and uniform. She kept scanning for telltale color changes. There was no sign of the burial they thought might lie nearby. She and her work partner had set their one-by-two-meter unit just below a distinctive flat boulder with a carved symbol resembling a dragonfly wing. This marker, and others scattered around this patch of oak prairie, had led the research team to believe that the area might have once been a twenty-first-century cemetery.

Finally, she saw something new emerge below the loosened dirt. At first it looked like a network of hairlike roots, lacy and delicate. She switched to a soft-bristled brush to gently wipe the dirt away. The "roots" turned into thready tendrils of faded cloth that was disintegrating into the soil. She hesitated for a moment. It felt sacrilegious to interfere in the natural process, but this was her job. The grave was going to be destroyed by a new high-speed train tunnel. Her team's assignment was to respectfully excavate, remove, identify, and reinter any burials in a safer spot, unless the decomposition process was so advanced that entity transformation had been macroscopically completed. Her dig partner stood above, digitally recording her careful unwrapping of the shroud. Within, she found clean but fragmented bones, roughly in their original prone position, although a gopher tunnel had churned through the torso and carried off some vertebrae. This body had apparently not been dressed. There was no second layer of cloth. It had been wrapped like a newborn baby. That was a little different, but so was the rusted metal trowel lying next to the skeleton's right hand and a dark brown, rectangular object lying next to the left one. She recorded the position of the trowel with her handheld photo-GPS unit and then carefully loosened the trowel from the dirt and placed it in a reusable specimen box. Then she turned to the other side and gently worked around the edges of the crumbling brown artifact, cutting a block of protective dirt around it. After an hour of meticulous work, she was able to get under it with her trowel and gingerly lift it out of its resting place. She transferred it to an acid-free box that her colleague had already labeled. She hoped that back at the lab they would be able to use radiography to help them read this old, decaying analog book. The pages appeared to be fused together by time and pressure. Perhaps it would yield a clue about who this person once was.

Ω Ω Ω

NOTES

Chapter 1. The Hole

1. See Preface for an explanation of research protocols, and my approach to interview transcription.

2. Mitford, *The American Way of Death Revisited*; Waugh, *The Loved One: An Anglo-American Tragedy*.

3. Lynch, *The Undertaking: Life Studies from the Dismal Trade*, 84.

4. Cremation Association of North America, *Annual CANA Statistics Report*; National Funeral Directors Association, "The Future of Funerals: COVID-19 Restrictions Force Funeral Directors to Adapt, Propelling the Profession Forward."

5. Hayasaki, "Death Is Having a Moment."

6. I am not suggesting that mortuary practices provide a mirror to society, a problematic assumption corrected long ago in the archaeology of death. A sample of recent and seminal works: Arnold and Jeske, "The Archaeology of Death"; Stutz and Tarlow, *The Oxford Handbook of the Archaeology of Death and Burial*; Tarlow, *Bereavement and Commemoration: An Archaeology of Mortality*; Pearson, *The Archaeology of Death and Burial*; Ucko, "Ethnography and Archaeological Interpretation of Funerary Remains"; McGuire, "Dialogues with the Dead: Ideology and Cemetery"; Chapman and Randsborg, "Approaches to the Archaeology of Death."

7. See, for example, Arnold et al., *Death and Digital Media*; Kneese, "QR Codes for the Dead"; Moreman and Lewis, *Digital Death*.

8. Becker, *The Denial of Death*; Heidegger, *Being and Time*.

9. Kübler-Ross, *On Death and Dying*.

10. Ariès, "The Hour of Our Death," 41.

11. Ibid., 45–46.

12. Ibid., 47.

13. Doughty also cites the influence of Ernest Becker, although his was a universalist argument that never singled out Americans. Doughty, *Smoke Gets in Your Eyes*; Doughty, *From Here to Eternity*.

14. Though based in the United Kingdom, Tony Walter offers one of the best assessments of the philosophy and effects of the hospice movement. Walter, *The Revival of Death*.

15. Metcalf and Huntington, *Celebrations of Death: The Anthropology of Mortuary Ritual*.

16. In the four short years between the time I talked to Juju and the writing of this book, cremation tattoos have soared, not only in popularity but in acceptance. Donnelly, "Memorial Tattoos: Ashes in the Ink!!!"; Neptune Society, "What Can I Do with Cremation Ashes?"

17. Save My Ink Forever.

18. Hertz, "A Contribution to the Study of the Collective Representation of Death."

19. Tschumi, *Buried Treasures of the Ga: Coffin Art in Ghana*.

Chapter 2. Flesh

1. For orientations to the home-funeral movement, see: National Home Funeral Alliance; Hagerty, "Speak Softly to the Dead"; Olson, "Domesticating Deathcare: The Women of the U.S. Natural Deathcare Movement."

2. Hertz, *Death and the Right Hand*, 80. Many scholars do not realize how much Arnold van Gennep, the more famous anthropologist of rituals, was indebted to Hertz. Gennep, *The Rites of Passage*. Still, Hertz's legacy remains influential within death studies; see: Metcalf and Huntington, *Celebrations of Death*; Engelke, "The Anthropology of Death Revisited"; Robben, "Death and Anthropology: An Introduction"; Fabian, "How Others Die: Reflections on the Anthropology of Death"; Malinowski and Redfield, "Death and the Reintegration of the Group."

3. Hertz, *Death and the Right Hand*, 81–82.

4. For a contemporary hospital experience that echoes this, see Horsley, "'How Dead Dead the Dead Are'"; Horsley, "Death Dwells in Spaces."

5. In Haitian vodou, Christ is understood to be a zombie. McAlister, "Slaves, Cannibals, and Infected Hyper-Whites: The Race and Religion of Zombies"; Dawdy, "Zombies and a Decaying American Ontology."

6. Many countries actually outlaw embalming. It became legal in the Netherlands only in 2010. David Sloane says that the "taboo" is now dying and the United States is currently enjoying a "death revival." Sloane, *Is the Cemetery Dead?*, 1, 67.

7. Trafton, *Egypt Land*; Dawdy, "The Embalmer's Magic."

8. Laderman, *The Sacred Remains: American Attitudes toward Death, 1799–1883*; Laderman, *Rest in Peace: A Cultural History of Death and the Funeral Home in Twentieth-Century America*; Ruby, *Secure the Shadow: Death and Photography in America*; Schwartz, *Dead Matter: The Meaning of Iconic Corpses*.

9. Schantz, *Awaiting the Heavenly Country: The Civil War and America's Culture of Death*, 62.

10. Bondeson, *Buried Alive: The Terrifying History of Our Most Primal Fear*; Roach, *Stiff: The Curious Lives of Human Cadavers*.

11. On Covid-19 and regulations, see National Funeral Directors Association, "Embalming and Covid-19." For the argument regarding "civil religion," I am indebted to the suggestions made in Metcalf and Huntington, *Celebrations of Death*, 211–14.

12. Chiappelli and Chiappelli, "Drinking Grandma: The Problem of Embalming"; Bryant and Peck, *Encyclopedia of Death and the Human Experience*, 404–6.

13. World Health Organization, "Management of Dead Bodies: Frequently Asked Questions."

14. Douglas, *Purity and Danger: An Analysis of Concepts of Pollution and Taboo*.

15. Holloway, *Passed On: African American Mourning Stories*, 25. Black death studies is a fast-growing field, due in no small part to the Black Lives Matter movement and heightened awareness of continuing disparities in experiences of trauma, violence, and health outcomes. For example, see McIvor, *Mourning in America: Race and the Politics of Loss*; Howie, "Loss in/of the Business of Black Funerals"; Carter, *Prayers for the People: Homicide and Humanity in the Crescent City*. On Latinx and Southern funerals, see Cann, "Contemporary Death Practices in the Catholic Latina/o Community"; Wilson, "The Southern Funeral Director: Managing Death in the New South."

16. In a jazz funeral, a brass band with drums leads the procession of mourners and pallbearers, playing a dirge as the mourners enter the cemetery. After the burial, the band plays an upbeat, danceable "second-line" tune on the way out and into the streets, celebrating the departed's arrival in heaven.

17. Kessler, "How Extreme Embalming Works: Cost, Process and Appeal"; Vanacore, "Socialite Easterling Goes out as She Wanted—with a Party."

18. Spera, "'Uncle' Lionel Batiste Gets Sendoff as Unique as the Man Himself."

19. Donaghey, "Family Poses Slain Teen's Body with PlayStation and Doritos at His Funeral."

Chapter 3. Bones

1. Stephen Prothero, in his history of cremation in the United States, claims that crushing bones was done to make the remains more palatable for families interested in scattering the remains, but funeral directors also resisted (and continue to resist) ash scattering, because it eliminates the market for urns, columbaria (wall niches), urn burial plots in cemeteries, and other memorials. Prothero, *Purified by Fire: A*

History of Cremation in America, 149–50. Several funeral directors I spoke to, including Adam, worry that families will regret ash scattering because there will be no permanent marker to remember the dead.

2. "A single cremation, which lasts between two and three hours and during which the crematory is heated to 1,600 degrees, releases roughly 540 pounds of carbon dioxide into the atmosphere. With over 1.1 million Americans cremated annually, the amount of CO_2 released is startling: roughly 594 million pounds (269,434 tons), or the equivalent of 287.5 million pounds of coal." Sloane, *Is the Cemetery Dead?*, 57. Public health experts and environmental agencies have become increasingly concerned about crematory emissions, although the US EPA has taken significant action only with regard to mercury from dental fillings. Along with centralization and cost-cutting measures, public health risks are an additional reason modern crematories are quietly being moved out of residential areas into industrial zones. O'Keeffe, "Crematoria Emissions and Air Quality Impacts."

3. Prothero, *Purified by Fire: A History of Cremation in America*; Laqueur, *The Work of the Dead: A Cultural History of Mortal Remains*; Arnold, "Burning Issues: Cremation and Incineration in Modern India." Throughout Asia, both burial and cremation are practiced with a great deal of regional, ethnic, and religious variation, but cremation in the twentieth century has come to dominate, not without controversy. Cremulation, however, has not been as widely adopted; in Japan and Taiwan, devout Buddhists still prefer to handle whole bones as part of the funeral ritual. Bernstein, "Fire and Earth: The Forging of Modern Cremation in Meiji Japan."

4. Olley et al., "Single-Grain Optical Dating of Grave-Infill Associated with Human Burials at Lake Mungo, Australia"; Cerezo-Román, Wessman, and Williams, *Cremation and the Archaeology of Death*; Kuijt, Quinn, and Cooney, *Transformation by Fire: The Archaeology of Cremation in Cultural Context*; Laqueur, *The Work of the Dead*.

5. Informed Final Choices: Crestone End of Life Project. With Crestone, for the second time in the course of this project, I was prevented from conducting a formal interview due to an exclusive contract with a television production, another indicator of current interest in death alternatives. McKinley, "Missouri's 'Jedi Disposal Act' Goes up in Flames with Gov. Mike Parson's Veto."

6. Olson, "Flush and Bone: Funeralizing Alkaline Hydrolysis in U.S. Deathcare Markets"; Promessa.

7. Prothero, *Purified by Fire: A History of Cremation in America*, chap. 3.

8. Cremation Association of North America, "Industry Statistical Information."

9. Solon, "Ashes to Pottery: How a Designer Makes Dinnerware from the Dead"; Parting Stone.

10. Huberman, "Forever a Fan: Reflections on the Branding of Death and the Production of Value"; Cann, *Virtual Afterlives: Grieving the Dead in the Twenty-First Century*; Dobscha, *Death in a Consumer Society*.

11. That said, there is a growing minority of "transhumanists," who believe that the body can be transcended through life-extending biological manipulation and/ or brain uploads. Cryogenic freezing is the preferred form of disposition for these faithful, preserving their body-minds until technology improves enough that they can be revived. For a perceptive account of this movement, see Farman, *On Not Dying: Secular Immortality in the Age of Technoscience.*

12. To complicate things, a legal "person" need not be human. The Supreme Court's 2014 decision in *McCutcheon v. FEC* determined that corporations are persons. Many Americans have objected to this ruling precisely because they conflate personhood and the individual. As a result of legal actions by indigenous peoples in New Zealand, India, and Colombia, several rivers have been declared legal persons in those countries. In Bolivia, Mother Earth herself (*Pachamama*) was recognized in legislation passed in 2010. One way that popular culture works through the problematic ambiguities of personhood is through science fiction. From *2001: A Space Odyssey* to *Battlestar Galactica*, screenwriters have speculated about what will happen when artificial intelligence reaches the point of appearing to have consciousness and a unique personality. Will it/they count as *persons*, legally and ethically? Pietrzykowski, *Personhood beyond Humanism: Animals, Chimeras, Autonomous Agents and the Law.*

13. Strathern, *The Gender of the Gift: Problems with Women and Problems with Society in Melanesia*; Smith, "From Dividual and Individual Selves to Porous Subjects," 53; Gell, *Art and Agency: An Anthropological Theory.*

14. Cremation Association of North America, "Cremation Process"; Madoff, *Immortality and the Law: The Rising Power of the American Dead.*

15. Every one of the death practices I describe in this book is also available for pets. The pet-human crossover in funeral practices would be a fruitful avenue for more research. It is too often dismissed as comedic, which can foreclose what it might say about contemporary American spirituality and ideas of personhood. On a visit to Hinsdale Animal Cemetery in suburban Chicago, Daniel and I noticed that artifacts and holiday decorations were more common there than at any human cemetery we had visited in the area. It was at once touching (animal love) and sad (human neglect). In the sales office for the attached crematory, we saw cases full of designer mini-coffins, urns, and jewelry. Just before we left, a young man in his twenties came in to choose something for a dearly departed guinea pig. The staff spoke in gentle tones; the mood was somber.

Chapter 4. Dirt

1. Fernwood is a National Wildlife Federation Certified Habitat.

2. For context in the United States, see Green Burial Council; in the United Kingdom, the Natural Death Centre. Hockey et al., "Landscapes of the Dead? Natural Burial and the Materialization of Absence."

3. Per the 2010 census, Marin County had the fifth-highest median income in the United States.

4. The courts have often been called upon to determine what might be a reasonable limit on religious freedom in the name of public health, an ongoing fight with new skirmishes amid the Covid-19 pandemic. Unembalmed corpses pose very little threat to safety if properly buried away from sources of drinking water, even when death has resulted from a highly infectious disease. Anthrax is one of the only disease-causing agents that can survive in the dirt for longer than a few days, but it is exceedingly rare. World Health Organization, "Management of Dead Bodies: Frequently Asked Questions."

5. Asad, *Formations of the Secular: Christianity, Islam, Modernity*; Cannell, "The Anthropology of Secularism," 86.

6. Dethlefsen and Deetz, "Death's Heads, Cherubs, and Willow Trees: Experimental Archaeology in Colonial Cemeteries." For updates to this general approach to reading ideology in cemeteries and the material culture of death, see McGuire, "Dialogues with the Dead: Ideology and Cemetery"; Hallam and Hockey, *Death, Memory, and Material Culture*; Sørensen, "The Presence of the Dead: Cemeteries, Cremation and the Staging of Non-Place."

7. Laqueur, *The Work of the Dead*, chap. 5.

8. I am speaking here of planned cemeteries in towns and cities. Outside of urban centers, there were—and are—other types of burial grounds: family plots on farms and homesteads, plantation graveyards (for both owners and the enslaved), raised tomb cemeteries like those of New Orleans, and western frontier graveyards (often ad hoc and open to all comers).

9. Sweeney, "The Cemetery's Cemetery"; Cothran and Danylchak, "The Rural Cemetery Movement"; Curl, *The Victorian Celebration of Death*.

10. Sloane, *Is the Cemetery Dead?*; Laqueur, *The Work of the Dead*, 212.

11. Moreman, *The Spiritualist Movement: Speaking with the Dead in America and around the World*; Morrisson, "The Periodical Culture of the Occult Revival: Esoteric Wisdom, Modernity and Counter-Public Spheres."

12. Foucault, "Of Other Spaces, Heterotopias."

13. Sloane, *Is the Cemetery Dead?*, 185.

14. Goody and Poppi, "Flowers and Bones: Approaches to the Dead in Anglo-American and Italian Cemeteries."

15. I suspect the Recompose system deploys insects and larvae as well, given the speed of the process, but neither Katrina nor the Recompose website elaborated on the biological agents used. Quirk, "The Urban Death Project: Bringing Death Back into the Urban Realm"; Recompose.

16. This same logic undergirds Eternal Reefs, a successful nonprofit in the business of creative death. It offers an aquatic alternative to Recompose, though with a

larger carbon footprint: mixing cremated remains into concrete balls to form artificial reefs. They aren't pretty, but they do help regenerate coral ecosystems. I am not sure that the typical six to eight pounds of cremation ash that an adult body produces contributes all that significantly to reef restoration (we'd have to dispose of *a lot* of bodies to make a difference). But that just underscores that Eternal Reef's mission is a symbolic one—don't waste a good death. Eternal Reefs, "Welcome to Eternal Reefs."

17. In California, Washington, and Indiana, burials at a home property are banned except through a special, and arduous, permitting process. In the rest of the states, home burial is technically legal, but in reality most applicants won't make it past their local zoning board. The big exception is if there is an already existing cemetery on the land, which is actually quite common in the South and not unheard of in older farming and ranching communities elsewhere, where family plots were maintained far from churchyards. With changes in ownership and land use, these cemeteries are often forgotten and covered over, especially if there were few stone markers or no boundary fence. Archaeologists are frequently called in to locate unmarked cemeteries or have to inform inconvenienced developers that they will have to move their project. In most states, it is illegal to disturb graves, even when the identities of the interred are unknown or direct descendants cannot be found.

18. The canyon was named after Benjamin S. Eaton, a pioneer rancher and judge.

19. Yoshino, "Woman Seen Scattering Ashes at Disneyland"; Prothero, *Purified by Fire: A History of Cremation in America*, 198.

20. Cited in Sloane, *Is the Cemetery Dead?*, 45.

21. Bios, "Bios Urn."

22. Dennis White was Lee's first volunteer for a fitted mushroom suit. The story of his life and coming death were documented in the film *Suiting Dennis*, which helped make the burial suit more than a novelty. Coeio, "The Infinity Burial Suit"; Lee, *Suiting Dennis: A Family Story of Green Funeral*. For examples of other designers challenging how we think about death, see Designboom, "Design for Death"; Auger and Loizeau, "Afterlife"; Charlesworth, "The MeMo Organisation."

Chapter 5. Spirit

1. Mitford, *The American Way of Death Revisited*; Walter, "Ritualising Death in a Consumer Society"; Dobscha, *Death in a Consumer Society*. The more I have worked on this project, the more I have come to realize that the leading critics of the American funeral complex have been British, going all the way back to the 1780s. It has made me think that perhaps *they* are the ones out of step with the rest of the world. As one Brit said to me, "we don't like to make a messy show" at funerals.

2. I am referring here to the ominous-sounding Service Corporation International, which now controls about 20 percent of the US funeral market and has been

subject to a string of lawsuits for price-fixing and deceptive sales tactics. SCI is a publicly traded company that has gradually gobbled up other conglomerates, though not without some intervention from the Federal Trade Commission. Covert, "The Visible Hand: How Monopolies Have Taken over Our Everyday Lives."

3. Thad related this origin story to me, but it also appears on the Holy Smoke website.

4. Cummings, "More than 176,000 in US Have Died of COVID-19; 57% of Republicans Polled Say That Is 'Acceptable'"; Swan, "President Trump Exclusive Interview."

5. Celestis: Memorial Spaceflights; Kharpal, "You Can Send Your Loved One's Ashes into Space on Elon Musk's SpaceX Rocket for $2,500." As Abou Farman's ethnographic work elucidates, a significant subculture of "transhumanists" with deep ties to Silicon Valley seeks to deny death in more literal terms, by extending life indefinitely. Farman, *On Not Dying: Secular Immortality in the Age of Technoscience.*

6. Rosen, "How Covid-19 Has Forced Us to Look at the Unthinkable."

7. Gray, "A Comprehensive Survey and Digital Home for Holt Cemetery, New Orleans"; Vlach, *By the Work of Their Hands: Studies in Afro-American Folklife*; Rainville, "Protecting Our Shared Heritage in African-American Cemeteries."

8. Weber, *The Protestant Ethic and the Spirit of Capitalism*; Weber, *The Vocation Lectures*; Saler, "Modernity and Enchantment: A Historiographical Review"; Moeran and de Waal Malefyt, *Magical Capitalism: Enchantment, Spells, and Occult Practices in Contemporary Economies.*

9. Sloane, *Is the Cemetery Dead?*

10. Turner, *Forest of Symbols: Aspects of Ndembu Ritual*, 19.

11. Hobsbawm and Ranger, *The Invention of Tradition.*

12. Atkinson, "Shamanisms Today," 322; Poulin and West, "Holistic Healing, Paradigm Shift, and the New Age," 258.

13. Tocqueville, *Democracy in America*, 1:509.

14. Bourdieu, *Outline of a Theory of Practice.*

15. Lipka and Gecewicz, "More Americans Now Say They're Spiritual but Not Religious." For more on this trend, see Brown, *The Channeling Zone: American Spirituality in an Anxious Age*; Fuller, *Spiritual, but Not Religious: Understanding Unchurched America.*

16. Newport, "Five Key Findings on Religion in the U.S."; Ballard, "45% of Americans Believe That Ghosts and Demons Exist"; Lipka and Gecewicz, "More Americans Now Say They're Spiritual but Not Religious."

17. Metcalf and Huntington posited that it had something to do with a crypto "civil religion"—a patriotic, state-centered ritual in which life and death are controlled by the government. It is a fascinating argument, but I have not found

much evidence to support their political theory. Metcalf and Huntington, *Celebrations of Death*, 213; Dawdy, "The Embalmer's Magic."

18. Dethlefsen and Deetz, "Death's Heads, Cherubs, and Willow Trees"; Ariès, *The Hour of Our Death: The Classic History of Western Attitudes toward Death over the Last One Thousand Years.*

19. Anderson, *Imagined Communities: Reflections on the Origin and Spread of Nationalism.*

20. Becker, *The Denial of Death*, 285.

REFERENCES

Anderson, Benedict R. O'G. *Imagined Communities: Reflections on the Origin and Spread of Nationalism*. Rev. ed. London and New York: Verso, 2006.

Ariès, Philippe. "The Hour of Our Death." In *Death, Mourning, and Burial: A Cross-Cultural Reader*, edited by Antonius C. G. M. Robben, 40–48. Malden, MA: Blackwell Pub., 2004.

———. *The Hour of Our Death: The Classic History of Western Attitudes toward Death over the Last One Thousand Years*. Translated by Helen Weaver. 1st American ed. New York: Knopf, 1981.

Arnold, Bettina, and Robert J. Jeske. "The Archaeology of Death: Mortuary Archaeology in the United States and Europe 1990–2013." *Annual Review of Anthropology* 43 (2014): 325–46.

Arnold, David. "Burning Issues: Cremation and Incineration in Modern India." *NTM Journal of the History of Science, Technology and Medicine* 24, no. 2 (2017): 393–419.

Arnold, Michael, Martin Gibbs, Tamara Kohn, James Meese, and Bjorn Nansen. *Death and Digital Media*. London: Routledge, Taylor & Francis Group, 2018.

Asad, Talal. *Formations of the Secular: Christianity, Islam, Modernity*. Stanford, CA: Stanford University Press, 2003.

Atkinson, Jane Monnig. "Shamanisms Today." *Annual Review of Anthropology* 21 (1992): 307–30.

Auger, James, and Jimmy Loizeau. "Afterlife," 2009. Auger-Loizeau.com. http://www.auger-loizeau.com/projects/afterlife.

Ballard, Jamie. "45% of Americans Believe That Ghosts and Demons Exist." YouGov, October 21, 2019. https://today.yougov.com/topics/lifestyle/articles-reports/2019/10/21/paranormal-beliefs-ghosts-demons-poll.

Becker, Ernest. *The Denial of Death*. New York: Free Press, 1973.

Bernstein, Andrew. "Fire and Earth: The Forging of Modern Cremation in Meiji Japan." *Japanese Journal of Religious Studies* 27, no. 3/4 (2000): 297–334.

Bios. "Bios Urn." Accessed May 26, 2020. https://urnabios.com/.

Bondeson, Jan. *Buried Alive: The Terrifying History of Our Most Primal Fear*. New York: W. W. Norton & Co., 2001.

Bourdieu, Pierre. *Outline of a Theory of Practice*. Cambridge Studies in Social Anthropology, 16. Cambridge and New York: Cambridge University Press, 1977.

Brown, Michael F. *The Channeling Zone: American Spirituality in an Anxious Age*. Cambridge, MA: Harvard University Press, 1997.

Bryant, Clifton D., and Dennis L. Peck. *Encyclopedia of Death and the Human Experience*. Gale Virtual Reference Library. Thousand Oaks, CA: SAGE Publications, 2009.

Cann, Candi K. "Contemporary Death Practices in the Catholic Latina/o Community." *Thanatos* 5, no. 1 (2016): 63–74.

———. *Virtual Afterlives: Grieving the Dead in the Twenty-First Century*. Lexington: University Press of Kentucky, 2014.

Cannell, Fenella. "The Anthropology of Secularism." *Annual Review of Anthropology* 39 (2010): 85–100.

Carter, Rebecca Louise. *Prayers for the People: Homicide and Humanity in the Crescent City*. Chicago, IL: University of Chicago Press, 2019.

Celestis: Memorial Spaceflights. "Celestis: Memorial Spaceflights—Send Ashes into Space." Accessed May 26, 2020. https://www.celestis.com/.

Cerezo-Román, Jessica, Anna Wessman, and Howard Williams. *Cremation and the Archaeology of Death*. 1st ed. Oxford: Oxford University Press, 2017.

Chapman, Robert, and Klavs Randsborg. "Approaches to the Archaeology of Death." In *The Archaeology of Death*, edited by Robert Chapman, Ian Kinnes, and Klavs Randsborg, 1–24. Cambridge: Cambridge University Press, 1981.

Charlesworth, Jessica. "The MeMo Organisation." MeMo. Accessed May 26, 2020. http://www.me-mo.co/.

Chiappelli, Jeremiah, and Ted Chiappelli. "Drinking Grandma: The Problem of Embalming." *Journal of Environmental Health* 71, no. 5 (2008): 24–28.

Coeio. "The Infinity Burial Suit." Accessed May 26, 2020. https://coeio.com/.

Cothran, James R., and Erica Danylchak. "The Rural Cemetery Movement." In *Grave Landscapes: The Nineteenth-Century Rural Cemetery Movement*, 33–128. Columbia: University of South Carolina Press, 2018.

Covert, Bryce. "The Visible Hand: How Monopolies Have Taken over Our Everyday Lives." *Nation*, November 28, 2020.

Cremation Association of North America. *CANA Annual Statistics Report*, 2019. https://cdn.ymaws.com/www.cremationassociation.org/resource/resmgr/statistics/2019statssummary-web.pdf.

———. "Cremation Process." https://www.cremationassociation.org/page/CremationProcess.

———. "Industry Statistical Information." Accessed May 26, 2020. https://www.cremationassociation.org/page/IndustryStatistics.

Cummings, William. "More than 176,000 in US Have Died of COVID-19; 57% of Republicans Polled Say That Is 'Acceptable.'" *USA Today*, August 23, 2020.

Curl, James Stevens. *The Victorian Celebration of Death*. Stroud, UK: Sutton, 2000.

Dawdy, Shannon Lee. "The Embalmer's Magic." In *The New Death: Mortality and Death Care in the Twenty-First Century*, edited by Shannon Lee Dawdy and Tamara Kneese. School of Advanced Research. Albuquerque: University of New Mexico Press, forthcoming.

———. "Zombies and a Decaying American Ontology." *Journal of Historical Sociology* 32, no. 1 (2019): 17–25.

Designboom. "Design for Death." Accessed May 26, 2020. https://www.designboom.com/competition/design-for-death/.

Dethlefsen, Edwin, and James Deetz. "Death's Heads, Cherubs, and Willow Trees: Experimental Archaeology in Colonial Cemeteries." *American Antiquity* 31, no. 4 (1966): 502–10.

Dobscha, Susan. *Death in a Consumer Society*. New York: Routledge, 2016.

Donaghey, River. "Family Poses Slain Teen's Body with PlayStation and Doritos at His Funeral." *Vice*, July 10, 2018. https://www.vice.com/en_us/article/a3qza5/new-orleans-teen-body-posed-video-games-doritos-funeral-vgtrn.

Donnelly, Jennifer R. "Memorial Tattoos: Ashes in the Ink!!!" *Tattoodo*. Accessed May 26, 2020. https://www.tattoodo.com/a/memorial-tattoos-ashes-in-the-ink-4522.

Doughty, Caitlin. *From Here to Eternity: Traveling the World to Find the Good Death*. 1st ed. New York: W. W. Norton & Co., 2017.

———. *Smoke Gets in Your Eyes and Other Lessons from the Crematory*. New York: W. W. Norton & Co., 2015.

Douglas, Mary. *Purity and Danger: An Analysis of Concepts of Pollution and Taboo*. London and New York: Routledge Classics, 2002.

Engelke, Matthew. "The Anthropology of Death Revisited." *Annual Review of Anthropology* 48 (October 2019): 29–44.

Eternal Reefs. "Welcome to Eternal Reefs." Accessed May 26, 2020. https://www.eternalreefs.com/.

Fabian, Johannes. "How Others Die: Reflections on the Anthropology of Death." In *Death, Mourning, and Burial: A Cross-Cultural Reader*, edited by Antonius C. G. M. Robben, 49–61. Malden, MA: Blackwell Pub., 2004.

Farman, Abou. *On Not Dying: Secular Immortality in the Age of Technoscience*. Minneapolis: University of Minnesota Press, 2020.

Foucault, Michel. "Of Other Spaces, Heterotopias." *Architecture, Mouvement, Continuité* 5 (1984).

Fuller, Robert C. *Spiritual, but Not Religious: Understanding Unchurched America*. Oxford: Oxford University Press, 2001.

Gell, Alfred. *Art and Agency: An Anthropological Theory.* Oxford, UK: Clarendon Press, 1998.

Gennep, Arnold van. *The Rites of Passage.* Translated by Monika B. Vizedom and Gabrielle L. Caffee. Chicago, IL: University of Chicago Press, 1960.

Goody, Jack, and Cesare Poppi. "Flowers and Bones: Approaches to the Dead in Anglo-American and Italian Cemeteries." *Comparative Studies in Society and History* 36, no. 1 (1994): 146–75.

Gray, D. Ryan. "A Comprehensive Survey and Digital Home for Holt Cemetery, New Orleans." Unpublished report on file, University of New Orleans, 2014.

Green Burial Council. Accessed May 26, 2020. https://www.greenburialcouncil.org /recommended_reading.html.

Hagerty, Alexa. "Speak Softly to the Dead: The Uses of Enchantment in American Home Funerals." *Social Anthropology* 22, no. 4 (January 1, 2014): 428–42.

Hallam, Elizabeth, and Jenny Hockey. *Death, Memory, and Material Culture.* Oxford, UK: Berg, 2001.

Hayasaki, Erika. "Death Is Having a Moment." *Atlantic*, October 25, 2013. https://www .theatlantic.com/health/archive/2013/10/death-is-having-a-moment/280777/.

Heidegger, Martin. *Being and Time.* Translated by J. Macquarrie and E. Robinson. Oxford, UK: Basil Blackwell, 1962.

Hertz, Robert. "A Contribution to the Study of the Collective Representation of Death." In *Death and the Right Hand*, translated by Rodney Needham and Claudia Needham. Glencoe, IL: Free Press, 1960.

———. *Death and the Right Hand.* Translated by Rodney Needham and Claudia Needham. Glencoe, IL: Free Press, 1960.

Hobsbawm, Eric J., and Terence O. Ranger. *The Invention of Tradition.* Cambridge and New York: Cambridge University Press, 1983.

Hockey, J., T. Green, A. Clayden, and M. Powell. "Landscapes of the Dead? Natural Burial and the Materialization of Absence." *Journal of Material Culture* 17, no. 2 (2012): 115–32.

Holloway, Karla F. C. *Passed On: African American Mourning Stories; A Memorial.* Durham, NC: Duke University Press, 2002.

Holy Smoke LLC. Accessed May 26, 2020. http://myholysmoke.com/home.html.

Horsley, Philomena. "'How Dead Dead the Dead Are': Sensing the Science of Death." *Qualitative Research* 12, no. 5 (October 5, 2012): 540–53.

———. "Death Dwells in Spaces: Bodies in the Hospital Mortuary." *Anthropology & Medicine* 15, no. 2 (August 2008): 133–46.

Howie, LaShaya. "Loss in/of the Business of Black Funerals." In *The New Death: Mortality and Death Care in the Twenty-First Century*, edited by Shannon Lee Dawdy and Tamara Kneese. School of American Research. Albuquerque: University of New Mexico Press, forthcoming.

Huberman, Jenny. "Forever a Fan: Reflections on the Branding of Death and the Production of Value." *Anthropological Theory* 12, no. 4 (December 2012): 467–85.

Informed Final Choices: Crestone End of Life Project. Accessed May 26, 2020. http://informedfinalchoices.org/crestone/.

Kessler, Sarah. "How Extreme Embalming Works: Cost, Process and Appeal." *Cake* (blog), November 18, 2019. https://www.joincake.com/blog/extreme-embalming/.

Kharpal, Arjun. "You Can Send Your Loved One's Ashes into Space on Elon Musk's SpaceX Rocket for $2,500." CNBC, May 17, 2017. https://www.cnbc.com/2017/05/17/elysium-space-spacex-rocket-funerla-ashes-orbit.html.

Kneese, Tamara. "QR Codes for the Dead." *Atlantic*, May 21, 2014. https://www.theatlantic.com/technology/archive/2014/05/qr-codes-for-the-dead/370901/.

Kübler-Ross, Elisabeth. *On Death and Dying.* 1st Macmillan Paperbacks ed. New York: Macmillan, 1970.

Kuijt, Ian, Colin P. Quinn, and Gabriel Cooney. *Transformation by Fire: The Archaeology of Cremation in Cultural Context.* Amerind Studies in Anthropology. Tucson: University of Arizona Press, 2014.

Laderman, Gary. *Rest in Peace: A Cultural History of Death and the Funeral Home in Twentieth-Century America.* New York: Oxford University Press, 2003.

———. *The Sacred Remains: American Attitudes toward Death, 1799–1883.* New Haven, CT: Yale University Press, 1996.

Laqueur, Thomas Walter. *The Work of the Dead: A Cultural History of Mortal Remains.* Princeton, NJ: Princeton University Press, 2015.

Lee, Grace (dir.). *Suiting Dennis: A Family Story of Green Funeral.* Coeio, 2015.

Lipka, Michael, and Claire Gecewicz. "More Americans Now Say They're Spiritual but Not Religious." Pew Research Center, September 6, 2017. https://www.pewresearch.org/fact-tank/2017/09/06/more-americans-now-say-theyre-spiritual-but-not-religious/.

Lynch, Thomas. *The Undertaking: Life Studies from the Dismal Trade.* New York: W. W. Norton & Co., 1997.

Madoff, Ray D. *Immortality and the Law: The Rising Power of the American Dead.* New Haven, CT: Yale University Press, 2010.

Malinowski, Bronislaw, and Robert Redfield. "Death and the Reintegration of the Group." In *Magic, Science and Religion, and Other Essays,* 29–34. Boston: Beacon Press, 1948.

McAlister, Elizabeth. "Slaves, Cannibals, and Infected Hyper-Whites: The Race and Religion of Zombies." *Anthropological Quarterly* 82, no. 2 (2012): 457–86.

McGuire, R. H. "Dialogues with the Dead: Ideology and Cemetery." In *The Recovery of Meaning: Historical Archaeology in the Eastern United States,* edited by Mark P. Leone and Parker B. Potter, 435–80. Washington, DC: Smithsonian Institution Press, 1988.

McIvor, David Wallace. *Mourning in America: Race and the Politics of Loss*. Ithaca, NY: Cornell University Press, 2016.

McKinley, Edward. "Missouri's 'Jedi Disposal Act' Goes up in Flames with Gov. Mike Parson's Veto." *Kansas City Star*, July 14, 2019.

Metcalf, Peter, and Richard Huntington. *Celebrations of Death: The Anthropology of Mortuary Ritual*. 2nd ed. Cambridge: Cambridge University Press, 1991.

Mitford, Jessica. *The American Way of Death Revisited*. New York: Random House, 2000.

Moeran, Brian, and Timothy de Waal Malefyt, eds. *Magical Capitalism: Enchantment, Spells, and Occult Practices in Contemporary Economies*. Cham, Switzerland: Palgrave Macmillan, 2018.

Moreman, Christopher M., ed. *The Spiritualist Movement: Speaking with the Dead in America and around the World*. 3 vols. Santa Barbara, CA: Praeger, 2013.

Moreman, Christopher M., and A. David Lewis. *Digital Death: Mortality and beyond in the Online Age*. Santa Barbara, CA: Praeger, 2014.

Morrisson, Mark S. "The Periodical Culture of the Occult Revival: Esoteric Wisdom, Modernity and Counter-Public Spheres." *Journal of Modern Literature* 31, no. 2 (Winter 2008): 1–22.

National Funeral Directors Association. "Embalming and Covid-19." NFDA News, April 1, 2020. https://www.nfda.org/news/in-the-news/nfda-news/id/4974/embalming-covid-19.

———. "The Future of Funerals: COVID-19 Restrictions Force Funeral Directors to Adapt, Propelling the Profession Forward." NFDA News Releases, July 7, 2020. https://nfda.org/news/media-center/nfda-news-releases/id/5230/the-future-of-funerals-covid-19-restrictions-force-funeral-directors-to-adapt-propelling-the-profession-forward.

National Home Funeral Alliance. Accessed May 26, 2020. https://www.homefuneralalliance.org/.

The Natural Death Centre. Accessed May 26, 2020. http://www.naturaldeath.org.uk/index.php?page=find-a-natural-burial-site.

Neptune Society, "What Can I Do with Cremation Ashes?" May 31, 2017. https://www.neptunesociety.com/resources/what-can-i-do-with-cremation-ashes.

Newport, Frank. "Five Key Findings on Religion in the U.S." Gallup, December 23, 2016. https://news.gallup.com/poll/200186/five-key-findings-religion.aspx.

O'Keeffe, Juliette. "Crematoria Emissions and Air Quality Impacts." National Collaborating Centre for Environmental Health (Canada), March 24, 2020. https://ncceh.ca/documents/field-inquiry/crematoria-emissions-and-air-quality-impacts.

Olley, Jon M., Richard G. Roberts, Hiroyuki Yoshida, and James M. Bowler. "Single-Grain Optical Dating of Grave-Infill Associated with Human Burials at Lake Mungo, Australia." In "Dating the Quaternary: Progress in Luminescence Dating of Sediments," special issue, *Quaternary Science Reviews* 25, no. 19 (October 1, 2006): 2469–74.

Olson, Philip R. "Domesticating Deathcare: The Women of the U.S. Natural Death-care Movement." *Journal of Medical Humanities* 39, no. 2 (2016): 195–215.

———. "Flush and Bone: Funeralizing Alkaline Hydrolysis in U.S. Deathcare Mar-kets." *Science, Technology, and Human Values* 39, no. 5 (2014): 666–93.

Parting Stone. Accessed May 26, 2020. https://partingstone.com/.

Pearson, Mike Parker. *The Archaeology of Death and Burial*. College Station: Texas A&M University Press, 1999.

Pietrzykowski, Tomasz. *Personhood beyond Humanism: Animals, Chimeras, Autonomous Agents and the Law*. Springer Briefs in Law. Cham, Switzerland: Springer, 2018.

Poulin, Patricia A., and William West. "Holistic Healing, Paradigm Shift, and the New Age." In *Integrating Traditional Healing Practices into Counseling and Psycho-therapy*, edited by Roy Moodley and William West, 257–69. Thousand Oaks, CA: Sage Books, 2005. https://doi.org/10.4135/9781452231648.n22.

Promessa. Accessed May 26, 2020. http://www.promessa.se/.

Prothero, Stephen. *Purified by Fire: A History of Cremation in America*. Berkeley, CA: University of California Press, 2001.

Quirk, Vanessa. "The Urban Death Project: Bringing Death Back into the Urban Realm." *Metropolis*, February 24, 2017. https://www.metropolismag.com/cities/the-urban-death-project-bringing-death-back-into-the-urban-realm/.

Rainville, Lynn. "Protecting Our Shared Heritage in African-American Cemeteries." *Journal of Field Archaeology* 34, no. 2 (2009): 196–206.

Recompose. Accessed May 26, 2020. https://www.recompose.life/.

Roach, Mary. *Stiff: The Curious Lives of Human Cadavers*. 1st ed. New York: W. W. Norton, 2003.

Robben, Antonius C. G. M. "Death and Anthropology: An Introduction." In *Death, Mourning, and Burial: A Cross-Cultural Reader*, edited by Antonius C. G. M. Rob-ben. Malden, MA: Blackwell Pub., 2004.

Rosen, Jody. "How Covid-19 Has Forced Us to Look at the Unthinkable." *New York Times Magazine*, April 29, 2020.

Ruby, Jay. *Secure the Shadow: Death and Photography in America*. Cambridge, MA: MIT Press, 1995.

Saler, Michael. "Modernity and Enchantment: A Historiographical Review." *American Historical Review* 111, no. 3 (2006): 692–716.

Save My Ink Forever. Accessed May 26, 2020. https://savemyink.tattoo/.

Schantz, Mark S. *Awaiting the Heavenly Country: The Civil War and America's Culture of Death*. Ithaca, NY: Cornell University Press, 2008.

Schwartz, Margaret. *Dead Matter: The Meaning of Iconic Corpses*. Minneapolis: Uni-versity of Minnesota Press, 2015.

Sloane, David Charles. *Is the Cemetery Dead?* Chicago, IL: University of Chicago Press, 2018.

Smith, Karl. "From Dividual and Individual Selves to Porous Subjects." *Australian Journal of Anthropology* 23, no. 1 (2012): 50–64.

Solon, Olivia. "Ashes to Pottery: How a Designer Makes Dinnerware from the Dead." *Guardian*, October 24, 2016. https://www.theguardian.com/artanddesign/2016/oct/24/pottery-cremation-dinnerware-ceremic-glaze-art-justin-crowe.

Sørensen, Tim Flohr. "The Presence of the Dead: Cemeteries, Cremation and the Staging of Non-Place." *Journal of Social Archaeology* 9, no. 1 (February 1, 2009): 110–35.

Spera, Keith. "'Uncle' Lionel Batiste Gets Sendoff as Unique as the Man Himself." *Times-Picayune*, July 20, 2012. https://www.nola.com/entertainment_life/music/article_78f7b478-e4e6-5490-ac61-1cd8da6cdc76.html.

Strathern, Marilyn. *The Gender of the Gift: Problems with Women and Problems with Society in Melanesia.* Studies in Melanesian Anthropology 6. Berkeley: University of California Press, 1988.

Stutz, Liv Nilsson, and Sarah Tarlow, eds. *The Oxford Handbook of the Archaeology of Death and Burial.* Oxford: Oxford University Press, 2013.

Swan, Jonathan. "President Trump Exclusive Interview." *AXIOS on HBO*, July 28, 2020. https://www.axios.com/full-axios-hbo-interview-donald-trump-cd5a67e1-6ba1-46c8-bb3d-8717ab9f3cc5.html.

Sweeney, Kate. "The Cemetery's Cemetery." In *American Afterlife: Encounters in the Customs of Mourning*, 37–56. Athens: University of Georgia Press, 2014.

Tarlow, Sarah. *Bereavement and Commemoration: An Archaeology of Mortality.* Oxford, UK: Blackwell Publishers, 1999.

Tocqueville, Alexis de. *Democracy in America.* Translated by George Lawrence. Vol. 1. Garden City, NY: Doubleday, 1969.

Trafton, Scott. *Egypt Land: Race and Nineteenth-Century American Egyptomania.* New Americanists. Durham, NC: Duke University Press, 2004.

Tschumi, Regula. *Buried Treasures of the Ga: Coffin Art in Ghana.* Salenstein, Switzerland: Benteli, 2008.

Turner, Victor. *Forest of Symbols: Aspects of Ndembu Ritual.* Ithaca, NY: Cornell University Press, 1970.

Ucko, Peter J. "Ethnography and Archaeological Interpretation of Funerary Remains." *World Archaeology* 1, no. 2 (October 1969): 262–80.

Vanacore, Andrew. "Socialite Easterling Goes out as She Wanted—with a Party." *New Orleans Advocate*, April 26, 2014. https://www.nola.com/news/article_8a880b1c-5e52-54b8-a067-30d8b08256a2.html.

Vlach, John Michael. *By the Work of Their Hands: Studies in Afro-American Folklife.* Charlottesville: University Press of Virginia, 1991.

Walter, Tony. *The Revival of Death.* New York: Routledge, 1994.

———. "Ritualising Death in a Consumer Society." *RSA Journal* 144, no. 5468 (1996): 32–40.

Waugh, Evelyn. *The Loved One: An Anglo-American Tragedy.* 1st ed. Boston: Little, Brown and Co., 1948.

Weber, Max. *The Protestant Ethic and the Spirit of Capitalism.* Translated by Peter Baehr and Gordon C. Wells. New York: Penguin Books, 2002.

———. *The Vocation Lectures.* Translated by Rodney Livingstone. Indianapolis, IN: Hackett Publishers, 2004.

Wilson, Charles R. "The Southern Funeral Director: Managing Death in the New South." *Georgia Historical Quarterly* 67, no. 1 (1983): 49–69.

World Health Organization. "Management of Dead Bodies: Frequently Asked Questions." Humanitarian Health Action, November 2, 2016. https://www.who.int /hac/techguidance/management-of-dead-bodies-qanda/en/.

Yoshino, Kimi. "Woman Seen Scattering Ashes at Disneyland." *Los Angeles Times,* Travel, April 7, 2019.

INDEX

Printed in the USA
CPSIA information can be obtained
at www.ICGtesting.com
JSHW080536211023
50487JS00002B/3

9 780691 254708